ZEW Economic Studies

Publication Series of the Centre for
European Economic Research (ZEW),
Mannheim, Germany

ZEW Economic Studies

Vol. 1: O. Hohmeyer, K. Rennings (Eds.)
Man-Made Climate Change
Economic Aspects and Policy Options
1999. VIII, 401 pp. ISBN 3-7908-1146-7

Vol. 2: Th. Büttner
Agglomeration, Growth, and Adjustment
A Theoretical and Empirical Study
of Regional Labor Markets in Germany
1999. XI, 206 pp. ISBN 3-7908-1160-2

Vol. 3: P. Capros et al.
Climate Technology Strategies 1
Controlling Greenhouse Gases.
Policy and Technology Options
1999. XVIII, 365 pp. ISBN 3-7908-1229-3

Vol. 4: P. Capros et al.
Climate Technology Strategies 2
The Macro-Economic Cost and Benefit
of Reducing Greenhouse Gas Emissions
in the European Union
1999. XIII, 224 pp. ISBN 3-7908-1230-7

Vol. 5: P.A. Puhani
Evaluating Active Labour Market Policies
Empirical Evidence for Poland During
Transition
1999. XVI, 239 pp. ISBN 3-7908-1234-X

Vol. 6: B. Fitzenberger
Wages and Employment Across Skill Groups
An Analysis for West Germany
1999. XII, 251 pp. ISBN 3-7908-1235-8

Vol. 7: K. Rennings et al. (Eds.)
Social Costs and Sustainable Mobility
Strategies and Experiences in Europe
and the United States
1999. VI, 212 pp. ISBN 3-7908-1260-9

Vol. 8: H. Legler et al.
Germany's Technological Performance
2000. X, 191 pp. ISBN 3-7908-1281-1

Vol. 9: O. Bürgel
The Internationalization of British Start-up Companies in High-Technology Industries
2000. XIV, 230 pp. ISBN 3-7908-1292-7

Vol. 10: J. Hemmelskamp et al. (Eds.)
Innovation-Oriented Environmental Regulation
Theoretical Approaches and Empirical
Analysis
2000. VI, 348 pp. ISBN 3-7908-1313-3

Vol. 11: K.L. Brockmann, M. Stronzik (Eds.)
Flexible Mechanisms
for an Efficient Climate Policy
Cost Saving Policies and Business
Opportunities
2000. VIII, 130 pp. ISBN 3-7908-1314-1

Vol. 12: W. Smolny
Endogenous Innovations
and Knowledge Spillovers
A Theoretical and Empirical Analysis
2000. VIII, 277 pp. ISBN 3-7908-1320-6

Vol. 13: M. Lechner, F. Pfeiffer (Eds.)
Econometric Evaluation
of Labour Market Policies
2001. X, 242 pp. ISBN 3-7908-1372-9

Vol. 14: M. Beise
Lead Markets
Country-Specific Success Factors of the
Global Diffusion of Innovations
2001. XVI, 305 pp. ISBN 3-7908-1430-X

Vol. 15: O.H. Jacobs, C. Spengel
Effective Tax Burden in Europe
Current Situation, Past Developments and
Simulations of Reforms
2002. X, 131 pp. ISBN 3-7908-1470-9

Vol. 16: U. Kaiser
Innovation, Employment, and Firm Performance in the German Service Sector
2002. X, 164 pp. ISBN 3-7908-1481-4

Vol. 17: J. Köke
Corporate Governance in Germany
An Empirical Investigation
2002. VIII, 184 pp. ISBN 3-7908-1511-X

Vol. 18: E. Wolf
What Hampers Part-Time Work?
An Empirical Analysis of Wages, Hours
Restrictions and Employment from a
Dutch-German Perspective
2003. X, 174 pp. ISBN 3-7908-0006-6

Paolo Cecchini · Friedrich Heinemann · Mathias Jopp
(Eds.)

The Incomplete European Market for Financial Services

With 54 Figures
and 52 Tables

Physica-Verlag
A Springer-Verlag Company

ZEW
Zentrum für Europäische
Wirtschaftsforschung GmbH
Centre for European
Economic Research

Series Editor
Prof. Dr. Wolfgang Franz

Editors

Prof. Dr. Paolo Cecchini
Avenue de l'Yser 8
1040 Brussels, Belgium

Dr. Friedrich Heinemann
ZEW
L7, 1
68161 Mannheim, Germany

Dr. Mathias Jopp
Institut für Europäische Politik
Bundesallee 22
10717 Berlin, Germany

ISBN 3-7908-0013-9 Physica-Verlag Heidelberg New York

Cataloging-in-Publication Data applied for
Bibliographic information published by Die Deutsche Bibliothek
Die Deutsche Bibliothek lists this publication in the Deutsche Nationalbibliografie; detailed bibliographic data is available in the Internet at <http://dnb.ddb.de>.

Physica-Verlag Heidelberg New York
a member of BertelsmannSpringer Science+Business Media GmbH

Printed in Germany

Cover design: Erich Dichiser, ZEW, Mannheim

SPIN 10903360 88/3130-5 4 3 2 1 0 – Printed on acid-free paper

Preface

Looking back over the last decade it can be said with some justification that significant progress has been achieved on the way towards fully integrated financial markets in Europe. The 1993 Internal Market initiative and the Euro introduction in 1999/2002 constitute important milestones. The integration process has further been intensified by market developments like the surge in mergers and acquisitions and by technological innovations like internet based distribution. As a result, some market segments today do no longer have a national character.

Nevertheless, this success should not obscure the fact that integration of financial services markets is still a long way from the level of integration that exists within national markets. Particularly for retail financial services national borders still constitute a considerable de facto barrier. The absence of frequent direct cross-border links between financial service providers and retail consumers holds true despite the fact that the Euro has made product comparisons easier and that the internet has reduced information costs to a considerable extent.

This situation poses challenging questions with high relevance to national and European legislators:

- How powerful is the integrating effect of ongoing market trends like the establishment of the internet as a distribution channel or the increasing number of cross-border mergers and acquisitions from the consumer's point of view?
- Which micro and macro benefits could be realised if a higher level of financial services integration could be achieved?
- What are the obstacles to cross-border activities in retail financial services?

The academic literature so far is remarkably silent regarding these questions. Although an abundant literature on financial market integration exists it is dealing predominantly with wholesale financial markets and thus neglecting the retail perspective.

Against this background the European Financial Services Roundtable (EFR) initiated a study to deal with these open questions. The EFR is a group of leading European banks and insurers chaired by Pehr G. Gyllenhammar (CGNU, London). The study has been carried out by an independent research team coordinated by the Centre for European Economic Research (ZEW, Mannheim) and the Institut für Europäische Politik (IEP, Berlin). The design of the study, the choice of methods, the ongoing work and the results were constantly discussed with an international advisory board consisting of well reputed academics from various European universities and experts from leading European banks and insurers.

This volume contains ten contributions documenting in full the research carried out under this project. The papers analyse the guiding questions with the help of a variety of methods and with a focus on a number of different markets.

Insurance

The first contribution by *Rainer Beckmann, Carsten Eppendorfer* and *Markus Neimke* (Ruhr-University, Bochum) analyses the extent of integration of the EU market for life and non-life insurance. The main integration indicator used is the market share (premium based) of foreign companies in domestic markets. For the calculation of this indicator, three different kinds of foreign presence are taken into account: foreign presence through merger and acquisitions, through branches and agencies and direct cross-border sales without physical presence. Whereas the static view reveals a high degree of national fragmentation the dynamic view indicates advancing integration. The results also show that integration is even less advanced for life than for non-life insurance and that mergers and acquisitions are the dominant strategy to access a foreign market. Besides summarising the liberalisation history of the European insurance sector and discussing consumer benefits from further integration, the study contributes to a better understanding of obstacles to insurance market integration. Among the obstacles tax discrimination and extensive consumer protection preventing cross-border activities are highly relevant.

Banking

Two further papers are focused on the banking sector. *Claudia Buch* and *Ralph Heinrich* (Kiel Institute of World Economics) analyse the degree of market integration for European banking and also look into the impact of integration on banking sector performance. The descriptive analysis reveals that national markets in Europe are characterised by low market shares of foreign banks compared to other industrialised countries. The authors complement the available empirical evidence on the impact of integration on efficiency by using panel data on OECD banking industries for the period 1979-1999. In contrast to some prior research, a larger foreign presence in a domestic banking market does not appear to lead to improvements in industry-wide efficiency in the sample. This is consistent with earlier findings that foreign banks are often less efficient than their domestic counterparts in developed countries, but it also suggests that in OECD countries, the – fairly low – levels of foreign entry observed so far have not significantly increased competitive pressure. With respect to the regulatory environment, EU membership, if anything, appears to be associated with higher profit levels, suggesting that competitive pressures have been below average in the EU.

Carsten Eppendorfer, *Rainer Beckmann* and *Markus Neimke* apply a case study approach to learn more about imperfect integration in banking markets from the company's perspective. The paper analyses market access strategies of European banks. The analysis is based both on aggregate sectoral data and on four company case studies (*BSCH*, *Nordea Group*, *BNP Paribas* and *HSBC*). It is explored to which extent different market access strategies contribute to the integration of the European retail markets. A clear result is that mergers and acquisition as well as co-operations and strategic alliances form the most important market access strategies. Direct cross-border sales and the establishment of branches and subsidiaries are of minor importance. All strategies are complicated by considerable natural and politically induced barriers to market access. In particular, such politically induced barriers are different national supervision of banks, different tax legislation, as well as national accounting and take-over principles. Here, further harmonisation is suited to accelerate the integration of European retail markets and thus to increase consumer benefits by lower prices and a higher product variety for financial services.

Investment funds

The analysis by *Friedrich Heinemann* (ZEW, Mannheim) reveals that the fast growing EU market for investment funds is still characterised by a continuing relevance of national borders. The papers assesses this market's degree of integration, the potential benefits from more integration and the obstacles to cross-border sales of funds. The analysis shows that markets of small member countries are particularly isolated since for suppliers of funds the market potential is too small to compensate for the fixed costs of market entry. But also in the big markets foreign funds lack market success. A better integrated European market for investment funds would provide three kinds of benefits: It increases choice of products, it allows to realise economies of scale and it intensifies competition for the benefit of private investors. It is argued that the present characteristics of fund distribution channels are mainly responsible for fragmentation today besides regulatory and tax issues.

Credit and deposit markets

The two joint contributions by *Friedrich Heinemann* and *Martin Schüler* (ZEW, Mannheim) aim at exploiting the ECB data base on retail interest rates in European credit and deposit markets.

The first paper deals with the link between market and retail interest rates. This paper argues that national differences in the speed of this pass-through process can be regarded as a retail-oriented indicator of financial integration. The basic idea is that full integration should lead to an equalisation of this pass-through speed at a high level. With standard econometric tools the speed of interest rate adjustments for different markets and countries is measured – showing a considerable fragmentation of markets. The estimated pass-through equations allow simulations showing how much consumers in some countries could gain from a convergence of adjustment speed on the fastest levels.

The second paper based on the ECB data base starts by giving a systematisation of the literature on measuring financial market integration with a focus on the distinction between wholesale and retail financial markets. In a second step, bivariate and multivariate cointegration techniques are used to assess the degree of integration in four loans and two deposit markets in the European Union. The assumption is that integration should at least establish a long-run link between retail interest rates among national markets which should show up in form of cointegrated interest rate series. It turns out that the degree of integration differs widely between financial products. Integration is relatively high for enterprise credits and deposits while it is relatively low for consumer and mortgage loans.

E-finance

The end of the internet euphoria at the stock market has led to a much more realistic assessment of this technique's consequences. The analysis by *Martin Schüler* fits well into this changing view since it shows that also in regard to E-finance the internet has only a limited capability to overcome national borders. Although, in theory, the internet should allow consumers to shop around at foreign companies, this does not actually happen in European financial markets. The analysis focuses on the most developed segment of E-finance which is the market for online brokerage. The results are disappointing from an integration point of view: Prices paid for online brokerage differ substantially across European countries. Furthermore, almost no direct cross-border activities take place, i.e. online purchases of stocks are almost always done using a domestic direct broker.

Integration Benefit

Two further papers are dealing with different aspects of benefits that would be associated with increasing integration in financial services markets.

Michael Schröder (ZEW Mannheim) looks at possible integration benefits for investors resulting from a better international diversification of private portfolios. He argues that capital market integration and diversification are connected in several ways and that the correlation between them should be positive. He then shows that European investors would indeed improve the performance of their portfolios substantially if the home bias could be reduced. A particularly interesting result is the following: Often a European diversification is already sufficient to reap the major part of the performance increase that would be possible on a global scale.

In a further contribution, the authors *Markus Neimke, Rainer Beckmann* and *Carsten Eppendorfer* explore the long-run macroeconomic effects of European financial integration. In their growth model they show that enhanced foreign financial market penetration should increase the overall growth rate unambiguously. The empirical analysis includes a wide set of indicators, each of them capturing different aspects of financial development and financial market integration. On the basis of the estimations a weak growth impact of foreign market penetration can be identified. Hence, deeper financial integration generates a growth bonus. The empirical results also indicate that the growth bonus can be transformed into an employment bonus but not without considering substantial country-specific differences.

Supervision

Finally, *Karel Lannoo* (CEPS, Brussels) deals with the reform debate in regard to financial market supervision. The national approach in European supervision is often regarded as one of the major integration obstacles. Nevertheless, Lannoo takes a very cautious stance. He does not regard a single European financial supervisory authority as an appropriate solution. Instead, he recommends to redesign the system upon the basis of the objectives of supervision, and to examine where more centralisation is needed. The biggest issue in his view is the standardisation of the supervisory practices in the EU, where work still has to begin.

We hope that this collection of papers finds interested readers not only in the academic world but also among experts in the national and European administration. A number of helpful lessons can be drawn for policymakers who take the vision of a single European market seriously: A strategy based on an attitude of "wait and see" is not justified because ongoing market trends indicate that integration is unlikely to be completed without adjustments to the regulatory framework. The substantial potential benefits for consumers and economic growth clearly show that it is worthwhile to push hard for more integration of retail financial markets. Any integration strategy should aim to simplify direct cross-border contact between suppliers and consumers. This contact would speed up convergence of prices and promote a wider product choice everywhere in the EU. The need for political action also comes from the delicate fact that the "costs of non-Europe" are higher in smaller and poorer member countries than in the bigger and richer ones.

Finally, on behalf of the whole research team we would like to thank all those who have accompanied this research project. First of all we would like to mention the EFR and its chairman Pehr G. Gyllenhammar. It should be emphasised that the Roundtable's support was by far not restricted to the material dimension. The members of EFR supported the project progress also through many valuable hints and the provision of data and insiders' experience and information. Furthermore, we would like to thank all members of the advisory board (see list below) who invested their precious time and brains to help the research team in sorting out many problems regarding methods and approaches.

September 2002,

Paolo Cecchini, Brussels
Friedrich Heinemann, Mannheim
Mathias Jopp, Berlin

Advisory Board

Chairman

Paolo Cecchini, Director General, ret., European Commission, Brussels

Members

David Ball, CGNU, London

Prof. Dr. Iain Begg, The Business School, South Bank University, London

Dr. Graham Bishop, Advisor, European Financial Affairs, Battle, UK

Prof. Dr. Franco Bruni, Istituto di Economia Politica, Università Bocconi, Milano

Julien Carmona, BNP Paribas, Paris

Prof. Dr. Karl-Olof Hammarkvist, Senior Advisor, Nordea AB, Stockholm

Dr. Karsten Kaempf, Director, Dresdner Bank AG, Brussels

Prof. Dr. Wim Kösters, Institut für Europäische Wirtschaft, Ruhr-Universität, Bochum

Prof. Dr. Hans-Eckart Scharrer, Vice President, HWWA-Institut für Wirtschaftsforschung, Hamburg

Dr. Johannes Schmoeckel, Representative of the Board of Management of Allianz AG, Brussels

Prof. Dr. Rudi Vander Vennet, Ghent University

Table of Contents

Financial Integration Within the European Union: Towards a Single Market for Insurance

Rainer Beckmann, Carsten Eppendorfer and Markus Neimke*

Ruhr-University Bochum, Germany

"Evidence of a growth in cross-border trade in insurance is mixed – possibly due to an acute scarcity of data." (OECD, 2000)

1 Introduction

There is overwhelming agreement among market observers that the European insurance industry has made a ground-breaking step towards a single insurance market by the implementation of the Life and Non-Life Third Insurance Directives on 1 July 1994. Among the EU countries since then legal barriers to cross-border insurance business have been minimised.

Conducting insurance business in a unified European market offers advantages to both market sides compared to a situation of national fragmentation. Suppliers benefit from improved regional diversification of insured risks, the realisation of economies of scale and a wider area for investing assets. Consumers benefit from a larger choice among insurance companies and products and a higher degree of competition. Provided that antitrust policy is effectively safeguarding a competitive situation policyholders should therefore get a better ratio of "insurance value for premium".

But also the EU economy as a whole should benefit from insurance market integration given the increasing weight of insurance services for growth and employment. Some data in Figure 1 point to this increasing weight.

---

* Acknowledgement: We have benefited from comments of Prof. Wim Kösters, Friedrich Heinemann, and other seminar participants at the ZEW, Mannheim and Prof. Dieter Farny. We would also like to thank Inka Schöwe for technical assistance.

Figure 1: EU-15 life and non-life premiums and life insurance share 1991-1999

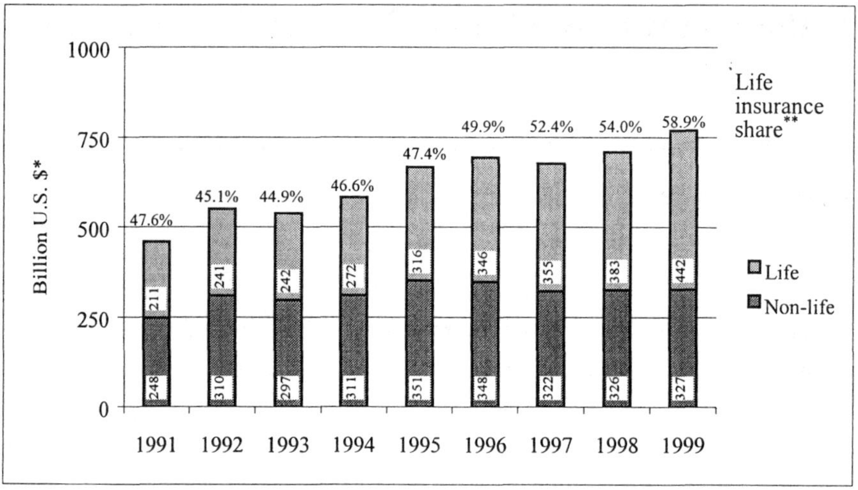

Source: OECD Insurance Statistics Yearbook (2001) and own calculations, *converted from national currencies into US dollar (average exchange rates for the reference year); ** Life insurance share is defined as the share of life insurance premiums with respect to the whole insurance market premiums.

Taken together, life and non-life business in the EU-15 countries account for a total premium income – serving as the major indicator – of 769.2 billion US $ in 1999 indicating a 8.2% share of EU-15 GDP. In 1990 this share amounted to merely 5.8%.[1] This enormous increase has been unevenly distributed among life and non-life business. While the share of non-life premiums to GDP increased from 3.0% to 3.2% the correspondent life insurance share underwent a boom almost doubling the share from 2.8% in 1990 to 5.0%. Consequently, the share of life insurance with respect to the whole insurance market (life insurance share) surpassed 50% for the first time in 1997 resulting in 59.0% in 1999. Non-life business has been almost stagnant partly due to the massive competition in a saturated market while life volumes benefited mainly from their increasingly important role in private pension schemes (see Swiss Re, 2000c).

Further general information on the EU-15 insurance market is given in Figure 2 in terms of national market shares for the life and non-life market segments.

1 Most figures that are comparable between countries are on a US $ basis since the main data pool, OECD's Insurance Statistics Yearbook, employs this standardisation, too. Furthermore, life and non-life business is categorised in accordance with usual EU and OECD conventions; that means accident and health insurance are classified as non-life business.

Figure 2: EU-15 insurance market shares in 1999

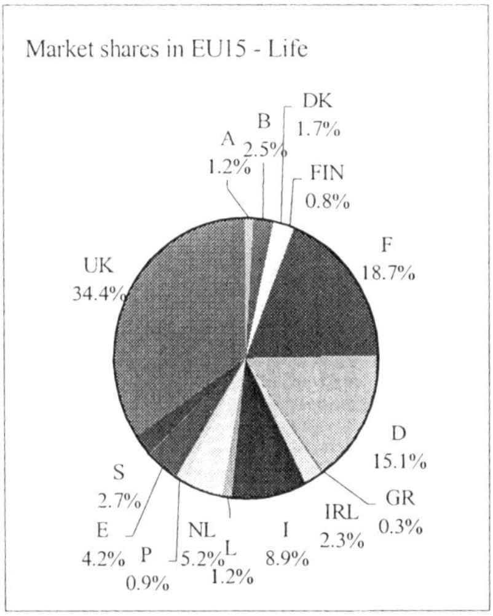

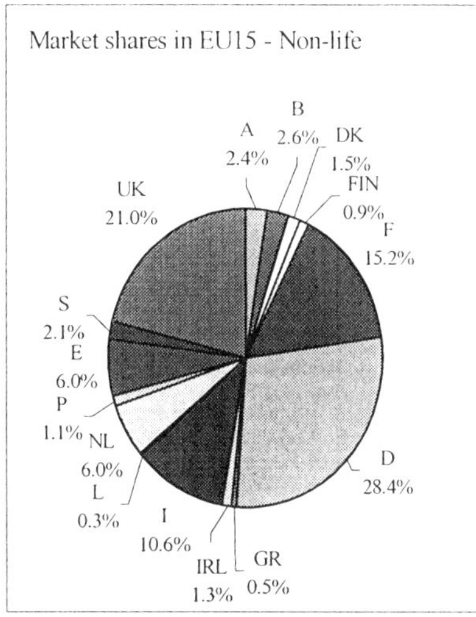

Source: OECD Insurance Statistics Yearbook (2001), own calculations.

However, these data on market size and structure do not provide much insight into the degree of market integration. More than seven years after the Third Insurance Directive and three years after the introduction of the Euro the reality of European insurance is still far away from representing a highly integrated market. The cases that consumers from EU countries shop around and choose the best insurance contracts based on a pan-European comparison still are extremely rare. Volumes of direct cross-border business are still low – even in the internet age. While integration is undoubtedly high on reinsurance markets and the market for industrial risks, the same does not hold for retail insurance markets. With this background this study tries to contribute to a better understanding of the present degree of and the remaining obstacles to integration.

After reporting on main provisions of the EU regulatory framework for cross-border business (Section 2) the second step of the analysis places emphasis on openness as a possible indicator for measuring integration (Section 3). It is shown that M&A activity has indeed led to stronger cross-border ties in the insurance sector judging from foreign controlled market shares. In contrast to that, business through office branches and direct cross-border insurance business is still marginal, though not declining. In a third step (Section 4) those policy induced and natural obstacles are discussed that are particularly relevant for the European insurance market. Here, taxation and regulation issues on the supply side and consumer confidence on the demand side are at a prominent place. Section 5 concludes and briefly refers to possible effects of e-commerce on insurance market integration.

2 Building up the Internal Market for Insurance

In general, the single market for financial services is founded on the fulfilment of the three indispensable basic freedoms provided by the Treaty of Rome (1957): the freedom of establishment, the free movement of goods and services and the free movement of capital. With respect to insurance, three generations of insurance directives have been issued between 1973 and 1992 (Figure 3) to enforce these principles (see Swiss Re, 1996 and Swiss Re, 2000a).[2]

In the first stage (1973-79) the freedom of establishment was realised. Insurance companies were allowed to open up subsidiaries, branch offices or agencies in every EU member state. Though, the national authority of the host country was held responsible for prudential supervision (host country control).[3] During the second stage (1983-90) the freedom of services was set up. Since then it was possible to do insurance business without having a fixed branch or subsidiary. The host country control, however, was abolished only for certain industrial risks (e.g. industrial fire) while for private business most EU member nations made use of their option to leave the host country control unchanged; exceptions to this rule were the Netherlands and the United Kingdom. One benevolent explanation for this may be found in the authorities' attempt to maximise the protection of the private policyholder. But also protectionist motivations most likely played a role for sticking to host country control. This regulatory regime left the domestic insurance industry being in the more comfortable situation not to operate in a contestable international market environment.

The third generation of insurance directives (1992) was thought to unfold the desired quantum leap for wholly liberalising the retail business, too. It consisted of the subsequent key elements:

- abolition of price and product regulations,
- restriction of host country supervision to solvency control,[4]
- establishment of the principle of minimum harmonisation,
- introduction of a single EU licence (+ mutual recognition) and
- home country control for all insurance classes.

---

2 In this study no special focus is being laid on the reinsurance business that already has been liberalised in 1964, including the freedom of services principle. Like MAT insurance (Marine, Aviation and Transport) this segment is in general a widely internationalised business.

3 According to a market participant that answered our questionnaire (see box in Section 4) the seventies marked the first of three phases by the setting up of branches.

4 The first two elements apply only to those countries where such systems still existed, e.g. Germany and Italy.

The most important step was the establishment of the home country control principle since market observers held the opinion that foreign suppliers were reluctant to establish a branch office under the control of the host country. Since then, companies only need a licence from their home country supervisory authority to conduct insurance business all over the EU, either under the rule of freedom of establishment or under the rule of freedom to provide services. However, the business of subsidiaries remains regulated by the host country. Additionally, the competent home authority of their head office country has to be notified of their intended business scheme. Documents indicating the member country in which the branch is to be established, the name and address of the agent or branch and a scheme of operations have to be submitted. With respect to the provisions on the freedom of services it is simply required that the competent home authority is being informed about the member country in which they intend to carry on business and about the risks they intend to cover. The respective home country authorities pay attention to the exchange of information between the supervisory authorities.

These efforts for liberalisation and deregulation led market observers to expect a strengthening of European cross-border competition and market consolidation. Yet, the ideal of a single insurance market by far has not been achieved during the time thereafter. Insurance enterprises now have to cope with both newly emerged and well known obstacles. Many uncertainties have arisen from the exact scope of the freedom to provide services and from the extent to which the *general good* principle can be invoked by national authorities. The latter principle has been developed by case law. It enables national authorities even now to set individual national rules that possibly deny market access to foreign companies if certain public interests are claimed to be violated. This claim can be based on consumer protection, prevention of fraud or worker protection, for example. The Commissions' communication on "Freedom to Provide Services and the General Good in the Insurance Sector" – announced to be published in 1997, but indeed issued only three years later – should clarify its view of the freedom to provide services and the general good principle. However, since the general good principle is being evolved by case law legal doubts persist and hinder insurance companies to approach foreign EU markets without frictions.[5]

---

5 A more detailed overview about relevant obstacles is given in Section 4.

Figure 3: Important EU Insurance Directives

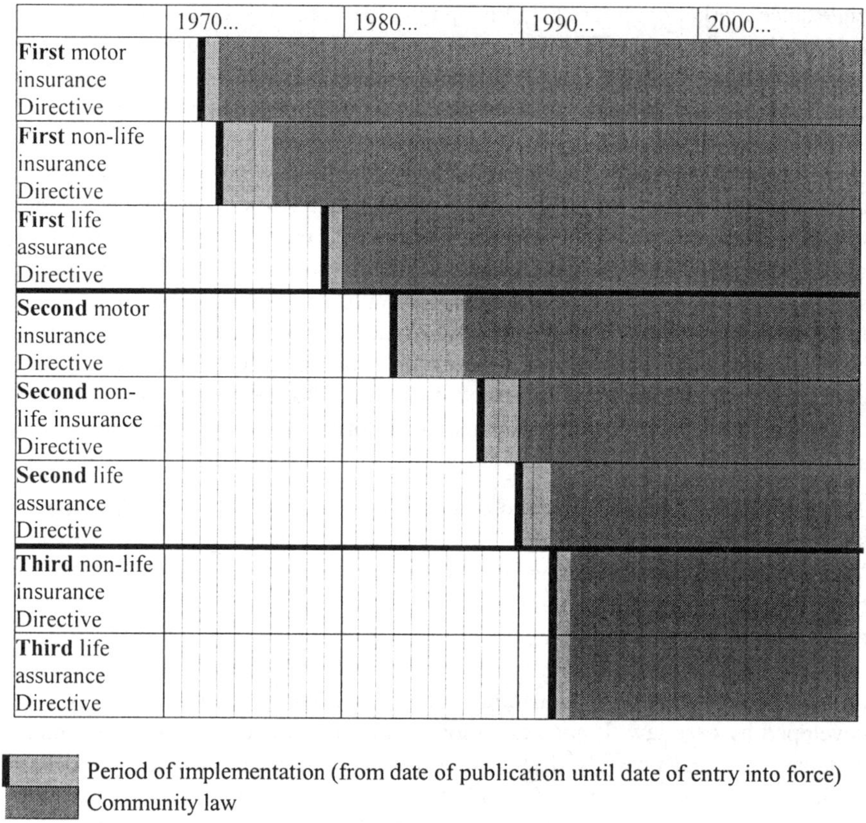

3 An Evaluation of the Present Degree of Integration

3.1 Method and Data

Two main problems arise in the assessment of the degree of EU insurance market integration. First, very different indicators are conceivable and partly may lead to contradicting results. Second, the data base is small and incomplete and does not allow to draw a detailed picture of cross-border activities in the EU insurance industry.

Important indicators to assess market integration are:

(a) The degree of openness based on an import view and measured as the foreign companies' market share in the domestic market, i.e. premiums written in the home country by host insurers.

(b) The magnitude of the home country bias in the asset structure of insurance companies.

(c) The convergence of product prices, product types and market indicators (i.e. life insurance shares, premiums/GDP, companies' efficiency and concentration).

(d) The size of the reinsurance share: a higher share indicates lower integration (i.e. the small diversification of insured risks results in a stronger shifting of risks to reinsurers).

The convergence in the design and the pricing of insurance products would best qualify to derive implications for the final customer. Unfortunately, these figures are not available. This analysis rather focuses on the first indicator, the openness of EU/EEA countries. If prudently considered the level and the dynamics of the degree of openness provide a measure for the contestability of a national market: The higher the share of foreign companies acting on a national market the better is the choice of products and companies for the final consumer.

For both the life and non-life sector market shares of foreign companies in total domestic business are described. Three basic categories are applied for foreign companies holding shares in the domestic market:

- market shares of foreign controlled undertakings,
- market shares of branches and agencies of foreign undertakings, and
- market shares of direct cross-border insurance business without a permanent physical presence.

Unfortunately, these data are only partly available. If possible, the foreign companies' market share is subdivided in EU/EEA and non EU/EEA participation.[6] We forego analysing strategic alliances and co-operations as yet another type of penetrating a foreign market since quantifying this issue is hardly possible.

The main data source is the OECD Insurance Statistics Yearbook 2001 that contains data for the period 1992-1999. This yearly updated OECD publication is an extensive pool of insurance data covering major market indicators, obtained from the governments of the OECD members. A significant effort has been made to

---

6 Some analysis includes Norway as an EEA country since the same EU rules for insurance business are applied in EEA countries.

achieve comparability among OECD countries; definitions, classifications, calculation methods and units have been standardised as far as possible.[7] The OECD data set is partly augmented by information of national and European insurance federations and by research data of Swiss Re.

Some caveats have to be taken into consideration. First, concerning the dynamics of integration an increase in cross-border operations may also be an indicator of heterogeneous tax, regulatory and supervisory structures. For example, motivated by tax avoidance strategies, insurers set up business in "tax havens" such as Ireland or Luxembourg. Second, with regard to cross-section comparisons, small countries ceteris paribus possess a higher degree of openness if activities are related to their size. This objection is mitigated by executing the relevant scatter plots. Third, if assessments are made with respect to the impact of the EU Third Insurance Directives one has to take into account that certain markets like UK, Netherlands, Ireland and France already prior to 1994 have been subject to a less regulated market.[8]

3.2 Non-Life Insurance

The structure of the analysis corresponds to the main options available for entering a foreign market: 1. merger & acquisitions and 2. establishment of branches and agencies. In a third step the combined shares of 1. and 2. are computed and analysed adding further information to the degree of openness.

Foreign Controlled Companies

As a starting point (OECD, 2001a: 42f.) data on market shares of foreign companies in the markets of OECD member countries is employed. Yet, the raw data have to be treated with caution due to a structural break. As a consequence of the regulatory changes introduced through the Third Insurance Directives, since 1995 data of EU/EEA countries do not include data on branches and agencies of foreign companies whose head offices are situated in other EU/EEA countries. Therefore, Table 1 presents corrected data of the pure market share of foreign controlled undertakings in total domestic business.[9] For reasons of data availability and comparability we compute only a sample of nine EU/EEA countries. Thereby in 1999 still 67% of the overall EU/EEA market in non-life insurance are covered.

---

7 For further methodological information, see OECD (2001a: 255ff.).

8 See Swiss Re (1996).

9 The definition of foreign controlled companies is specific to the countries' individual arrangements. Though, most countries apply the standard measure: "foreign majority interests over 50%". For exact definitions and further notes by country, see OECD Insurance Statistics Yearbook (2001: 259ff.).

At first sight a very heterogeneous picture emerges. Market shares of foreign controlled companies differ widely both in the cross-section but also with respect to national trends. While Portugal, for instance, shows an almost continuous rise starting from the lowest level of 5.1% in 1993 to 26.7% in 1999, Austria displays a very high but constant share of about 49%. Foreign companies in Spain and Luxembourg in contrast even lost ground. Also regarding the differentiation between big and small countries no clear-cut picture arises. In Germany the presupposed small share for a big country applies whereas in the UK as yet another big country the share of foreign controlled companies in 1999 was more than 20 percentage points higher than in Germany; this could be due to the fact that in the UK already prior to 1994 regulation has not been so intense. Also the Netherlands and Luxembourg both representing small countries differ by 20 percentage points with the latter showing a relative small share of 13.9%.

Table 1: Non-life insurance, foreign controlled companies in total domestic business (gross premium basis) in %

Host country	1993	1994	1995	1996	1997	1998	1999
Austria	47.9	49.1	47.4	49.2	49.0	50.7	48.7
Denmark	30.5	18.7	30.4	29.1	26.9	28.4	42.0
Germany	14.1	6.3	6.2	12.4	12.0	11.5	12.9
Luxembourg	N.A.[2]	N.A.	N.A.	20.3	16.8	13.2	13.9
Netherlands	20.1	18.4	19.2	18.4	34.1	34.3	33.7
Norway	15.2	N.A.	N.A.	17.5	18.2	20.1	18.3
Portugal	5.1	5.5	14.7	14.2	14.3	25.7	26.7
Spain	35.0	25.4	29.3	26.1	23.9	26.6	25.1
UK	N.A.	N.A.	N.A.	N.A.	29.9	29.0	34.5
Average share[1]	19.6	12.9	13.6	17.4	22.2	22.3	24.7

Source: OECD Insurance Statistics Yearbook (2001), own calculations by subtracting the numbers of OECD's Table IX.2.2 from the numbers of Table IX.2.1. [1]weighted by the resp. market share. [2]N.A.=Not Available.

Despite these ambiguous result for each singular country it can clearly be stated that on average the involvement of insurance companies from abroad has risen noticeably from 19.6% in 1993 to 24.7% in 1999. The slump to 12.9% in 1994 – mainly explained by the high weight of Germany where the share declined sharply to 6.3% – does not invalidate this conclusion. These increasing foreign linkages in the European insurance industry result from the merger & acquisition dynamics of the nineties. The rise in cross-border mergers is rather a bit surprising since M&A

activities predominantly have been executed on a national scale.[10] Although the OECD data base does not make a distinction between "European" and "non-European" market shares one has to assume that most part of those shares indeed are domiciled in the EU/EEA.

EU/EEA Branches and Agencies

The second step of the analysis broadens the picture of foreign companies' market share. Import data of European cross-border activities on a branches and agencies basis is calculated. Since the OECD was aware of cross-border data shortcomings they installed a Working Group that together with Eurostat tries to improve the data base (OECD, 2001a: 259). As a result of this work, since 1997 the OECD provides numbers for direct gross premiums earned by EU/EEA insurers through branches and agencies abroad. An import-export matrix measured in the respective local currencies of each exporting home country is presented by the OECD for the life and the non-life business. This matrix, though, has to be standardised on a US $ basis in order to extract import values and import quotas. Table 2 displays the resulting absolute values and shares of non-life premiums that have been written by EU/EEA insurers through branches and agencies in 16 EU/EEA countries for 1997-99.

Again, cross-country patterns are not homogeneous ranging in 1998, for example, from 0.29% in Germany to 7.44% in Luxembourg. The shares of business written through foreign EU/EEA branches and agencies tend to be higher in smaller countries such as Denmark, Greece, Luxembourg, Portugal. On the whole, it stands out that on average (see the last row of Table 2) only a small share of slightly above 1% of total EU/EEA non-life insurance business is conducted by foreign EU/EEA branches and agencies. Comparing Table 1 and Table 2, as a first result it emerges that the strategy of foreign companies to overtake domestic companies or to acquire majority stakes is obviously dominant in spite of the relaxation of host country control. Table 2 as well indicates, however, that the share of branches and agencies grows, too. Contrary to the generally stagnant non-life market (Figure 1) the business through EU/EEA branches and agencies increased by 12% per year on average (1997-1999).

---

10 This point all the more applies to the banking industry where cross-border mergers so far are more seldom. See Group of Ten (2001) and Eppendorfer, Beckmann and Neimke (2002).

Table 2: Non-life insurance, business written through foreign EU/EEA branches/agencies in EU/EEA countries

	1997		1998		1999	
Host country	$ value of imports (million)	import share[1]	$ value of imports (million)	import share[1]	$ value of imports (million)	import share[1]
Austria	47.61	0.56	51.78	0.63	49.07	0.61
Belgium	208.74	2.74	180.45	2.39	186.52	2.46
Denmark	101.63	2.14	142.29	2.68	295.75	5.88
Finland	7.90	0.32	10.07	0.38	14.37	0.56
France	452.17	0.94	551.41	1.14	537.80	1.13
Germany	295.01	0.30	318.31	0.29	293.87	0.27
Greece	37.17	5.38	42.92	3.81	50.45	4.11
Ireland	56.59	1.75	68.56	1.88	76.21	1.76
Italy	228.54	0.80	284.38	0.94	315.86	1.02
Luxembourg[2]	29.31	6.33	56.11	7.44	63.92	8.43
Netherlands	205.29	1.39	185.01	1.15	193.61	9.60
Norway	56.48	1.54	52.08	1.41	857.16	21.95
Portugal	141.93	5.15	118.53	3.96	106.74	3.52
Spain	318.61	2.07	268.90	1.68	183.86	1.08
Sweden	83.86	1.37	95.86	1.70	102.39	1.52
UK	1569.15	2.44	1360.73	2.01	1400.45	2.09
Total EU15/EEA	3839.98	1.18[3]	3787.40 (-1.4%)[4]	1.15[3]	4728.04 (+24.8%)[4]	1.43[3]

Source: OECD Insurance Statistics Yearbook (2001), own calculations. [1]Import share is measured in % as the computed absolute $ value of imports to total gross non-life premiums written in the respective countries. [2]Exports of Luxembourg are not available. [3]Ratio of total EU15/EEA import value to total EU15/EEA premiums written. [4]Year-on-year growth rate.

Total Foreign Presence

The third step regards total foreign presence. For that purpose, the sum of three components is calculated: the market shares of foreign controlled companies, EU/EEA branches and agencies and non-EU/EEA branches and agencies. Results for 1997 and 1999 are presented in Table 3.

Table 3: Non-life insurance, overview of total foreign presence (in % of total domestic business)

Host country	1997				1999			
	Foreign countries	Branches and agencies		Sum of col. 2-4	Foreign countries	Branches and agencies		Sum of col. 6-8
		EU/ EEA	Non-EU/ EEA			EU/ EEA	Non-EU/ EEA	
Austria	48.99	0.56	5.00	54.55	48.67	0.61	6.41	55.69
Denmark	26.91	2.14	1.73	30.78	41.99	5.88	1.62	49.49
Germany	12.04	0.30	0.66	13.00	12.93	0.27	0.67	13.87
Luxembourg	16.80	6.33	14.94	38.07	13.93	8.43	10.01	32.37
Netherlands	34.13	1.39	2.50	38.02	33.69	9.60	2.12	45.41
Norway	18.18	1.54	2.84	22.56	18.25	21.95	2.82	43.02
Portugal	14.29	5.15	0.74	20.18	26.66	3.52	0.05	30.23
Spain	23.91	2.07	3.38	29.36	25.12	1.08	0.06	26.26
UK	29.94	2.44	7.40	39.78	34.52	2.09	9.93	46.54
Avrg. share[1]	22.18	1.35	3.36	26.88	24.74	2.41	3.90	31.04

Source: OECD Insurance Statistics Yearbook, 2001, own calculations. [1]weighted by the resp. market shares.

The numbers in the fourth and eighth column of Table 3 show market shares of branches/agencies of non-EU/EEA undertakings in domestic business that have not been mentioned above. They add information on international openness in general.

In contrast to the pure growth figures of the non-life sector (Figure 1) it should be stressed that in no way a stagnancy with respect to integration dynamics is reported. Judging on basis of country averages (last row of Table 3) foreign companies market share climbed from 26.9% in 1997 to 31% in 1999. This relatively high share has to be interpreted even as a lower limit since OECD data do not contain direct cross-border transactions without having a physical presence. Through other sources it is reported, though, that direct cross-border business remains marginal representing a 1.9% share of non-life business in 1999 (see SwissRe, 2000c).

To complete the descriptive analysis of non-life insurance in the EU/EEA area it is shown in Figure 4 that countries coming up with a greater market size – measured in premiums written – tend to be less open to foreign companies. Beyond this expected finding it is interesting to observe that countries like the Netherlands or UK that already prior to the 1992 Third Insurance Directives abstained from controlling insurance policy terms, premiums and tariffs illustrate a relatively higher degree of openness. On the other hand, Germany representing a country with formerly strong control with respect to the so-called material supervision has a rather low share of foreign companies acting within its borders even though considering its size.[11]

Figure 4: Scatter plot of market size vs. total foreign presence (non-life)

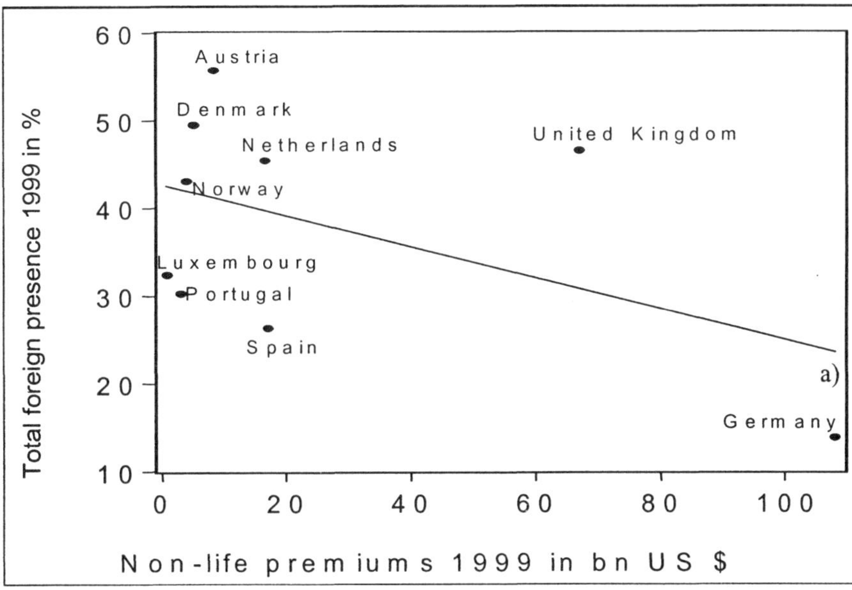

Source: OECD (2001a), own calculations; a) computed linear regression line.

3.3 Life Insurance

Turning to the prospering European life insurance industry the analysis (Tables 4-6) runs analogously to that presented above for the non-life sector.

Foreign Controlled Companies

Also for life insurance there is no uniform pattern across the 9 EU/EEA countries referred to. While Spain, Portugal and Austria point to a decline of foreign controlled companies in total domestic business the Netherlands, Denmark, UK and Germany move towards the opposite direction. Furthermore, massive particular shifts are remarkable: The share of foreign controlled companies increases for

11 See Vollbrecht (2001) for details concerning the differing history of supervision in EU countries.

example in Denmark from 5.9% in 1998 to 17.6% in 1999 while decreasing in Portugal from 23.5% in 1994 to 9.9% in 1995. It is reasonable, though, not to place too much emphasis on the partially volatile national figures since they can easily be provoked by singular merger & acquisition transactions and thus partly offsetting each other. To get an overall EU picture rather the average (last row of Table 4) should be taken into consideration. While in 1993 11.7% of total gross life insurance premiums – for data available – have been written by foreign controlled insurance companies this share decidedly increased to 20.8% in 1999.

If life and non-life figures are compared similarities as well as important differences are striking. Interestingly, for an individual country e.g. Portugal, the change in the life segment did not appear related to the change in the non-life segment. With respect to non-life insurance the share of foreign controlled companies in Portugal rises gradually (Table 1) but in the life insurance sector it shrinks on average. If instead the focus is on the group as a whole the direction and the speed of foreign companies participation in domestic EU/EEA countries on average is similar to the non-life sector. The major difference is that it runs on a significantly lower level.

Table 4: Life insurance, foreign controlled companies in total domestic business (gross premium basis) in %

Host country	1993	1994	1995	1996	1997	1998	1999
Austria	33.30	37.44	34.62	34.36	35.03	32.49	30.28
Denmark	5.95	7.99	6.96	7.00	6.48	5.92	17.61
Germany	8.33	7.15	7.05	6.38	6.48	5.50	15.07
Luxembourg	N.A.[2]	N.A.	N.A.	89.42	80.14	80.38	63.14
Netherlands	16.34	16.68	16.58	15.27	29.09	30.04	27.31
Norway	1.77	N.A.	2.48	2.78	2.81	3.43	3.55
Portugal	15.87	23.46	9.93	10.18	10.83	12.99	10.37
Spain	21.62	12.32	23.02	17.62	16.78	27.78	15.00
UK	N.A.	N.A.	N.A.	18.44	17.43	21.50	22.01
Average share[1]	11.7	10.8	11.4	14.0	16.4	19.1	20.8

Source: OECD Insurance Statistics Yearbook (2001), own calculations. [1]weighted by the resp. market share; in 1999 64% of the EU/EEA market is covered. [2]N.A.=Not Available.

EU/EEA Branches and Agencies

An important distinction has to be made with respect to the life insurance business that is written through EU/EEA branches and agencies (Tables 5 and 2). On average only 0.18% (1997) resp. 0.22% (1999) of total premiums are written through EU/EEA branches and agencies. This means less than the sixth part compared to the non-life sector (1.18% in 1997 vs. 1.43% in 1999. see Table 2). Significant shares of business through established entities only come about in Luxembourg (2.51%). Portugal (3.16) and Sweden (3.8%) for the year 1999.

Table 5: Life insurance. Business written through foreign EU/EEA branches/agencies in EU/EEA countries

	1997		1998		1999	
Host country	$ value of imports (million)	import share[1]	$ value of imports (million)	import share[1]	$ value of imports (million)	import share[1]
Austria	4.620	0.110	8.760	0.190	35.460	0.690
Belgium	0.510	0.010	0.000	0.000	1.140	0.010
Denmark	0.000	0.000	6.260	0.820	9.270	0.130
Finland	0.150	0.010	0.000	0.000	15.140	0.450
France	2.370	0.003	26.740	0.040	31.780	0.040
Germany	57.950	0.090	9.070	0.020	49.910	0.070
Greece	3.110	0.040	3.310	0.230	0.000	0.000
Ireland	0.030	0.001	1.540	0.020	1.350	0.010
Italy	48.890	0.210	57.540	0.180	2.430	0.010
Luxembourg[2]	20.490	0.470	25.740	0.540	127.610	2.510
Netherlands	1.370	0.010	7.680	0.040	20.250	0.090
Norway	3.540	0.100	12.800	0.360	23.590	0.700
Portugal	294.730	2.750	289.040	9.620	123.280	3.160
Spain	98.040	0.750	35.670	0.260	4.720	0.030
Sweden	0.000	0.000	140.310	1.480	439.130	3.800
UK	92.590	0.090	115.720	0.090	86.550	0.060
Total EU15/EEA	628.38	0.18[4]	740.19 (+17.8%)[4]	0.19[4]	971.60 (+31.3%)[4]	0.22[4]

Source: OECD Insurance Statistics Yearbook (2001), own calculations. [1]Import share is measured in % as the computed absolute $ value of imports to total gross non-life premiums written in the respective countries. [2]Exports of Luxembourg are not available. [3]Ratio of total EU15/EEA import value to total EU15/EEA premiums written. [4]Year-on-year growth rate.

Total Foreign Presence

The same tendency evolves from business through non-EU/EEA branches and agencies (Table 6, columns 4 and 8). Though on average it is significantly higher than the EU/EEA counterpart (2.53% in 1997 and 3.27% in 1999) it is lower than the corresponding non-life values (3.36% in 1997 and 3.90% in 1999). Also the fraction that is not directly covered through this analysis due to missing data, i.e. direct cross-border transactions without a physical presence, indicates much lower shares of life insurance (0.6%) compared to non-life insurance (1.9%) in 1999 (see SwissRe, 2000c). Concentrating the entire information available into Table 6, the "lower limit" of a 19.1% (1997) and a 24.2% (1999) stake in foreign participation in the domestic EU/EEA countries materialises. The respective figures for the non-life sector (Table 3) are 26.9% (1997) and 31.0% (1999).

Table 6: Life insurance, overview of total foreign presence (in % of total domestic business)

Host country	1997				1999			
	Foreign control	Branches and agencies		Sum of col. 2-4	Foreign control	Branches and agencies		Sum of col. 6-8
		EU/ EEA	Non-EU/ EEA			EU/ EEA	Non-EU/ EEA	
Austria	35.03	0.11	0.00	35.14	30.28	0.69	0.00	30.97
Denmark	6.48	0.00	0.40	6.88	17.61	0.13	0.31	18.05
Germany	6.48	0.09	2.10	8.67	15.07	0.07	2.14	17.28
Luxembourg	80.14	0.47	2.28	83.43	63.14	2.51	7.83	73.48
Netherlands	29.09	0.01	5.14	34.24	27.31	0.09	4.77	32.17
Norway	2.81	0.10	0.01	2.92	3.55	0.70	0.45	4.70
Portugal	10.83	2.75	2.33	15.91	10.37	3.16	1.66	15.19
Spain	16.78	0.75	3.63	21.16	15.00	0.03	0.75	15.78
UK	17.43	0.09	2.51	20.03	22.01	0.06	4.05	26.12
Avrg. share[1]	16.40	0.16	2.53	19.07	20.75	0.17	3.27	24.19

Source: OECD Insurance Statistics Yearbook, 2001, own calculations. [1]weighted by the resp. market share.

The country specific degree of openness derived in Table 6 is slightly negatively correlated to the size of the corresponding markets as revealed in Figure 5. This negative correlation is not as clear-cut as in the non-life sector presented above (Figure 4).

Figure 5: Scatter plot of market size vs. total foreign presence (life)

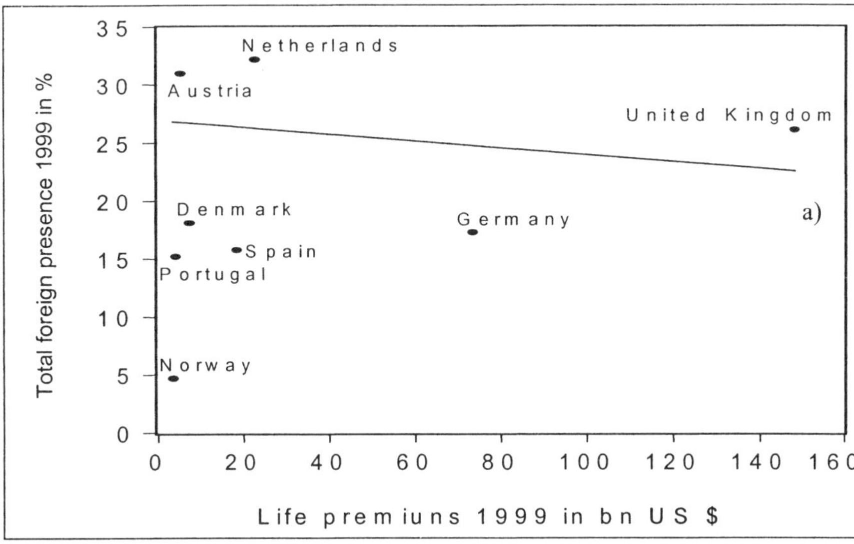

Source: OECD (2001a), own calculations; a) computed linear regression line.

But again, countries that already prior to 1992 had less severe regulations with respect to product and price control (UK and the Netherlands) prove to have a relatively high presence of foreign companies business within their borders.

3.4 Conclusions from Descriptive Analysis

The main results emerging from the descriptive analysis are condensed in Figure 6:

- The involvement of foreign insurers in national EU/EEA markets runs mainly through cross-border mergers and acquisitions.
- Branches and agencies play only a minor part as an entry strategy.
- The share of foreign controlled companies has risen significantly in the nineties, especially in the last three years.[12]
- The share of non-EU/EEA branches is even higher than for EU/EEA branches.
- The non-life sector generally is more open for all types of market entries analysed.

12 In a similar study focusing on Germany Farny (2002) elaborates an even higher market share of foreign insurers for 1999 while using firm specific micro data instead of aggregated OECD data.

- The relative difference of the non-life compared to the life sector concerning different entry strategies is highest for EU/EEA branches and agencies.

Figure 6: Non-life and life insurance, foreign companies market share 1997 and 1999 in %

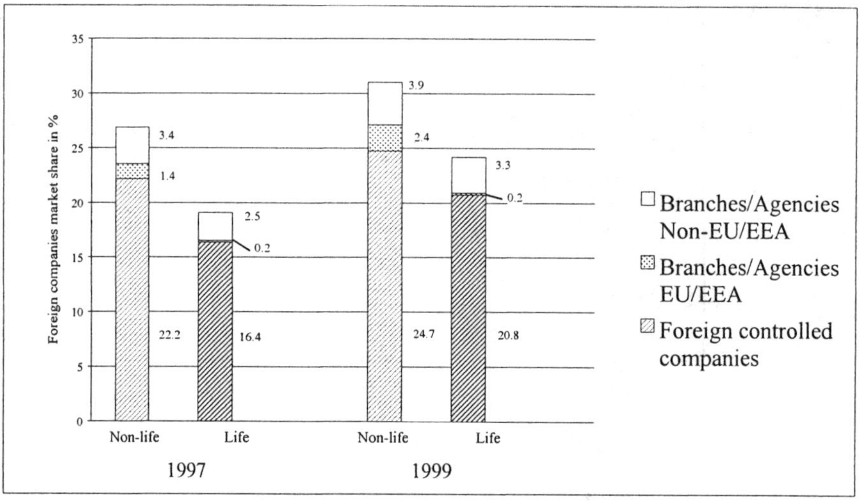

Source: OECD Insurance Statistics Yearbook (2001), own calculations.

One important aspect has not been mentioned so far. The three types of entering a market from abroad (majority stake or take over, branches/agencies, direct sales without physical presence) differ in their potential to break up the structures of the once strongly nationally segmented insurance industry. That is to say that it makes a difference whether a foreign company acquires a domestic company or whether it decides to set up a new establishment or to do direct cross-border business. For the last two cases the decision is mostly combined with new insurance products being offered in the respective countries. Thus, new products have to compete with existing national products. In contrast, the sole change of ownership structures does not necessarily change the diversity of products. An acquirer simply buys the knowledge of local peculiarities. Consequently, benefits for the informed customer are more likely to be reached if the entering company builds up new establishments or enters the market for instance through the internet.[13]

The results on the limited integration of EU insurance markets also hint at the relevance of obstacles to cross-border sales of insurance products. The fact that M&A strategies are dominant can also be interpreted in this way: A merger with a foreign insurance company has the crucial advantage to acquire the necessary know-how about national conditions. Thus, a large extent of regulatory and other national peculiarities should favour M&A relative to greenfield investments.

13 The latter point is touched upon in the last section when assessing the impact of e-insurance on insurance market integration.

Furthermore, the fact of lower integration of life compared to non-life insurance markets suggests that obstacles to integration are particularly severe for life insurance.[14] Therefore, in the next section it is tried to explain these findings by looking at potential obstacles.

4 Remaining Fragmentation and Policy Priorities

Although it has been verified in the previous section that the degree of integration in the European insurance industry is growing it is remarkable that the volume of insurance premiums written by national or local enterprises that are not a part of an insurance group operating on a pan-European scale still amounts to 55%.[15] Even though no benchmark exists for an optimal degree of openness the European insurance market for private risks is still segmented. Furthermore, it has been shown in Section 3 that the life and non-life sectors differ in their degree of openness so that one could suppose barriers being more important with respect to life insurance. This section therefore presents major obstacles to a truly integrated EU insurance market.

In general, obstacles can be grouped into policy induced obstacles and natural obstacles. While it is illusory that natural obstacles will disappear in the medium term and at best fade out in the very long term policy induced obstacles can be diminished by policy action already in the short to medium term. In Table 7 the most relevant obstacles relating to the integration of the single European insurance market are displayed.[16]

Natural Obstacles

Since insurance is essentially based on trust, i.e. the customers confidence in the ability of the insurer to honour its obligations, the average consumer is extremely risk averse. Preferences thus are highly biased towards local structures and established channels of distribution.[17] The more complex an insurance product the lower is the willingness of a customer to sign a contract with an unknown foreign supplier or even without "handshake". According to the ZEW questionnaire (see

---

[14] Since the OECD data set regrettably does not facilitate splitting up the non-life sector into industrial insurance (wholesale business) and the insurance of individual consumers (retail business) the analysed patterns of the non-life sector, especially with respect to the branches/agencies figures, include a combination of an internationalised industrial fraction and a hardly pan-European fraction.

[15] See Gesamtverband der Deutschen Versicherungswirtschaft (2001: 49).

[16] A questionnaire directed to leading EU insurance companies delivered important insights into this topic.

[17] This assessment, of course, does not hold for the insurance of industrial risks and reinsurance.

next page) global players in the European insurance market regard consumer interest in buying products on a cross-border scale as extremely small. Only corporate clients are reported to buy their insurance coverage internationally from one of only a few global insurance companies. Additionally, consumer loyalty to domestic companies, language and other cultural differences are regarded as highly relevant barriers.

Table 7: Obstacles to the integration of the single European market for insurance

Policy induced obstacles	Natural obstacles
▪ Tax treatment of insurance ▪ Regulation and supervision (incl. consumer protection/general good) ▪ Contract law ▪ Marketing rules (distance selling) ▪ Accounting rules	▪ Consumer preferences ("all business is local"): language, culture, loyalty ▪ Information asymmetries ▪ Legal system and tax system in general ▪ Conventions, e.g. the renewal of contracts

Source: Own analysis that is primarily based on a ZEW survey 2001.

On the other side of the market suppliers miss a reliable information basis. Problems that are relevant for every single insurance contract such as information asymmetries are reinforcing with a growing spatial and cultural distance between the insurer and the customer. The legal and tax systems in general are yet additional obstacles that hinder the evolution of a level playing field for the insurance industry. The ZEW survey, though, indicates that some market participants consider solutions to these problems as illusionary.

Conventions regarding the terms of insurance contracts also have an influence on the readiness of policyholders to switch to a rival product, let alone if produced abroad. Price sensitive behaviour, for instance, is favoured in the UK where customers must actively take steps to renew their policies each year. In continental Europe on the contrary the renewal of contracts for the most part is automatic unless a contract is cancelled one to three months ahead.[18]

Policy Induced Obstacles

Taxation

The responsibility for tax policy mainly lies with the EU member states. With respect to insurance one has to differentiate between the taxation of insurance companies and the taxation of an individual policy holder. Since taxation is not

18 See John Kirwan (2000).

harmonised on an EU scale a diversity of both different tax rates and different taxation systems exist.

> ***Questionnaire***
>
> A survey among a few leading players in the European insurance market has been conducted in September/October 2001 by the Centre for European Economic Research (ZEW, Mannheim Germany). The questionnaire contained questions regarding the strategy of market access to other EU markets and the relevance of specific barriers to enter these markets. The analysis in this section partially rests upon information given in the questionnaire.

In fact, the treatment of premiums paid by individuals varies widely among EU countries, e.g. by way of different rates for indirect taxes relevant for premiums. Determined in the Third Insurance Directives, these indirect taxes have to be paid to the host countries and EU member states may even require that a fiscal representative of the insurance company is appointed in the country of the final consumer. The advantages of shopping across borders can be offset by the fact that the taxation regime remains that of the country where the consumer has his residence. The latter aspect has been pronounced by an insurance company in the questionnaire.

Since life insurance products to a significant extent resemble interest-bearing instruments issued by banks the uneven taxation of interests adds to the diversity. Also regarding the taxation of insurance companies a variety of ways in which countries tax insurance business, particularly life insurance, are usual.[19] In 2000, for example, there has been a variation in the income tax rate running from 28% in Ireland and Finland to 40.2% in Belgium. Furthermore, there are many different rules to the deductibility of certain insurance companies reserves (e.g. equalisation reserve and catastrophe reserve).[20] In addition, to avoid double taxation in some EU/EEA countries (Austria, Denmark, Sweden and the United Kingdom) there are differences in taxation treatment between domestic and foreign insurers.[21]

This anecdotal evidence demonstrates that cross-border taxation issues obviously are costly in fields that show no EU harmonisation. Taxation issues therefore are of fundamental strategic importance for an insurance company to either build up offices or subsidiaries, alter their domicile or undertake direct cross-border business. The creation of the International Financial Services Centre (IFSC) in Dublin can be deemed as a logical outcome. The IFSC represents a dynamic place for the development and management of cross-border insurance products. Between 1997

---

19 See OECD (2001b) for a detailed analysis of policyholder and insurance company taxation.

20 See OECD(2001b: 49ff.).

21 See OECD (1999), Liberalisation of International Insurance Operations (1999: 83).

and 1999 cross-border life insurance business through companies domiciled in Ireland quadruplicated.[22] Besides motives of mitigating the tax exposure for pan-EU insurers the IFSC is also used by several North American insurers to penetrate the European market acting from an Irish base.[23]

Even more important than an opaque taxation regime, also discriminatory tax advantages only granted to specific groups have been widespread in the past. While tax competition in general is mostly regarded as desirable, unfair and discriminatory taxation certainly hampers integration. Discriminatory taxation has been present concerning tax deduction of life insurance premiums when deduction is limited to contracts that are effected with an insurer being authorised in the country of the policyholder. Even in 1999 ten EU/EEA countries (Austria, Belgium, Denmark, Finland, Germany, Greece, Luxembourg, Netherlands, Norway, Portugal) granted fiscal advantages of that form.[24] The European Commission in 1997 commented on this problem: "Concerning life insurance products, differences between Member States' direct tax regimes have proved to be a substantial barrier to the development of cross-border activities. [...] The Commission is acting in this field in order to avoid that taxation remains an obstacle to the insurance Single Market."[25] It is instructive to observe that this internet notice has not been modified for four years. According to the Commission's notice the judgement of the Court of Justice has been in a way that permits this form of discriminatory tax deduction if it ensures consistency with the national tax regimes.

The survey confirms the presumption made above since with regard to life insurance business pan-European competition is regarded "tentatively lower". In this special case the market participant explained that assessment by the sluggish behaviour of clients keeping their close ties to their well-known intermediary. Certainly though, market transparency also suffers from the extremely diverse tax provisions, especially within the life insurance sector.

Regulation, Supervision and Consumer Protection

Regulation and prudent supervision of insurance as an highly regulated business within the EU is subject to minimum harmonisation standards. National supervisory authorities therefore are capable of using their scope for discretion. The following aspects are the most relevant:

(a) solvency of the undertaking ("solvency margin"),

(b) establishment of technical provisions,

---

22 See Watson Wyatt (2001), Insurance and financial services review, August, and OECD (2001), Insurance Statistics Yearbook.

23 See IMF (2001), Report on the observance of standards and codes – Ireland: II. Insurance Supervision and International Financial Services Centre, Dublin (2002).

24 See OECD (1999: 40, 132-134).

25 See http://europa.eu.int/comm/internal_market/en/finances/insur/87.htm#11.

(c) assets coverage of the technical provisions (e.g. currency matching rules) (see Vollbrecht, 2001).

Similar to the fiscal arbitrage described above it could be a useful strategy to circumvent tough national provisions. An example for this behaviour can be found in Ireland where Italian insurers open up subsidiaries to circumvent the more stringent solvency margin requirements for life insurers set by the Italian regulatory authorities. These companies to a significant extent re-sell life insurance contracts cross-border to Italy (see Watson Wyatt, 2000). Compared to the problems arising by differing taxation treatment though, a country with a particular tight regulation hurts its own industry. This promotes a convergence in regulatory issues but has no discriminatory effect.

Extensive consumer protection with respect to the general good principle is a basic problem for the retail markets. First, since consumer protection (under the general good principle) is based on the domicile of the consumer the companies have to adapt to the rules of 15 different countries. This means an immense barrier to market entry for SME insurers. Second, national authorities may use their discretionary scope for protectionist regulation. One has to weigh the value of consumer protection against an inferior supply with insurance services. Because there already exists a high level of consumer protection more harmonisation in this field is not premature for the benefit of the consumer. If the level of consumer protection was lowered this could be absorbed by models containing less distortions, e.g. the establishment of powerful pan-European ombudsman rules. The difficulty of credibly obtaining out of court redress is a barrier to the development of cross-border services, particularly in the financial sector since access to redress is vital to consumer confidence. The Commission puts it as follows: "Ultimately the consumer will always have access to the courts. But for cost reasons this is often a last resort. A realistic alternative has been established (FIN-NET) which provides effective and rapid out of court redress on a cross-border basis."[26]

Further policy induced obstacles were also mentioned as relevant in the ZEW survey: the lack of harmonisation of contract law, the freedom of the EU member states to type and number compulsory classes of insurance, the missing global set of accounting rules. Another important barrier has not been identified as relevant. The immense costs for the transfer of small amounts within the EU payment systems certainly prevent retail customers from cross-border deals.[27]

Most policy induced obstacles to a truly Internal Market for insurance in the EU have been identified by EU representatives, in general by adopting the objectives of the Financial Services Action Plan (FSAP) in 1999.[28] The FSAP addresses both

---

26 See http://europa.eu.int/comm/internal_market/finances/general/ecom.htm.

27 See Schüler (2002).

28 See Annex for details concerning the Financial Services Action Plan with relevance to insurance.

wholesale and retail aspects. Also with respect to e-commerce most recently many relevant issues have been taken up by the „Report on e-commerce and financial services to the Financial Services Policy Group" (August 2001). According to statements in the questionnaire policy action has the chief task to solve the legal domicile principle in the field of e-commerce. Furthermore, the political agreement about the Directive for the distance selling of financial services as an essential complement to the e-commerce Directive that became effective in January 2002 has been an important step.

To complete the list of obstacles one should bear in mind that the cross-border data base should be improved. This could be reached by enhancing the co-operation between public authorities in the field of collecting more standardised statistics or even by the centralisation towards a pan-European Financial Services Authority. If no progress occurs in this field every assessment of insurance market integration remains incomplete.

5 Concluding Remarks

"*E-commerce may revolutionise the provision of financial services, especially cross-border within the Internal Market.*" (European Commission, 2001) [29]

A large scale project like that of the single market in insurance needs plenty of time. Actors of Member States and the EU institutions have to identify and remove problems and to agree in practical terms on how to apply the new legislation. Although the data base is far from perfect the analysis allows some general conclusions.

Three generations of Insurance Directives have formally set up the freedoms of establishment and the free movement of services. Of course, countries sustained their national peculiarities in several spheres hence impeding the expansion of cross-border sales. The analysis of the degree of openness and patterns of market entry in European insurance reveals strong differences among countries and among classes of insurance that partly can be explained by the obstacles to a truly single market.

On the supply side, there are obstacles emanating from different national rules (taxation, regulation, contract law, consumer protection). Though only to a slight extent discriminatory, these obstacles are costly and directly hinder cross-border transactions. On the demand side, customers, especially private consumers, are not as price sensitive concerning the purchase of a life insurance contract compared to

---

29 See European Commission, http://europa.eu.int/comm/internal_market/ en/finances/ consumer/ 01-1325.htm).

the purchase of a refrigerator, for example. To a significant extent this is natural in the light of the complexity of many financial products and their characteristic as a good necessitating a large degree of long term confidence in the suppliers' financial strength. Together, supply and demand sided circumstances can to a certain extent be made responsible for the outlined patterns of European cross-border integration. The above analysis suggests that in spite of large cross-border linkages through a wave of mergers and acquisitions the current degree of openness is insufficient, especially for the insurance of private (mass) risks. Admittedly, it should not be expected that the latter business possibly will catch up with the degree of integration in the reinsurance and industrial insurance business.

But at this point technological changes arising through the internet offer a big chance to offset certain obstacles since barriers to market entry are being reduced for smaller insurers, mainly by cost cutting in administration, distribution and claims management.[30] Today, cross-border activities in EU insurance are pursued by only a few international insurers or financial conglomerates. Only these have surmounted the critical mass to do pan-European business. The entry barriers are high for tax reasons besides information asymmetries, consumer protection rules (general good) and consumer preferences. It is costly to deal with a plenty of differing tax and regulation regimes and other national peculiarities. The new setting (e-insurance as an additional or exclusive distribution channel, the Euro as single unit of account) shows up to have the chance for potential competitors with a lower financial size to enter the market. On the demand side, by using the internet not only the costs of a transaction decrease, but also pan-European price transparency is completed as soon as the Euro acquires the unit of account and the means of payment functions by January 2002. Thus overall efficiency might be improved. Actual transactions via the internet, though, are minimal amounting to merely 0.02% of total European premiums (0.2% in the USA).[31] Nowadays, the e-channel joins the group of established distribution channels like direct sales, tied agents, brokers and bank-assurers. The e-channel has to be seen with a great deal of attention since it is well suited to further the integration of the retail markets for insurance products. But it should not be expected that e-insurance proceeds quickly. The propensity to use the internet only slowly expands owing to demographic factors since elderly customers will change their established relationships in purchasing financial products to a far lesser extent than the internet generation.

---

30 See Swiss Re (2000b).

31 See Swiss Re (2000b: 12).

Appendix

Selected Issues of the Financial Services Action Plan: Focus Insurance

The tables in this annex provide extracts from the official EU documentation concerning progress on individual actions in the Financial Services Action Plan (FSAP). The tables show the current situation and provide the Commission's assessment of the degree to which Community institutions and Member States have achieved the objectives set out in the Action Plan until January 2002. Our own assessment has been added in the last column.

Legend:

X	Action has been successfully completed
+	Progress has been achieved in meeting the targets set in the Action Plan
–	No progress (not acute in this excerpt)
**	Own assessment: important for the integration of retail markets

Strategic Objective: Open and secure retail markets

Action	Initial FSAP optimal timeframe	Present timeframe		
Political agreement on proposal for a Directive on the Distance Marketing of Financial Services	Adoption end 2000	Political agreement Oct 2000 Adoption Jun 2002	+	**
Interpretative Communication on the freedom to provide services and the general good in insurance	Issue summer 1999	Issued Feb 2000	X	
Proposal for amendment of Insurance Intermediaries Directive	Proposal mid 2000 Adoption 2002	Proposal Sep 2000 Adoption Dec 2002	+	**
Commission Communication on a single market for payments	Issue summer 1999	Issued Jan 2000	X	
Commission Action Plan to prevent fraud and counterfeiting in payments systems	Issue end 1999	Issued Feb 2001	X	
Commission Communication on an e-commerce policy for financial services	Issue mid 2000	Issued Jan 2001	X	

Strategic Objective: State of the art prudential rules and supervision

Action	Initial FSAP optimal timeframe	Present timeframe		
Adopt the proposed Directive on the Reorganisation and Winding-up of Insurance undertakings	Adoption 2001	Adopted Mar 2001	x	
Adopt the proposal for an Electronic Money Directive	Adoption 2000	Adopted Sep 2000	x	
Amend the solvency margin requirements in the Insurance Directive	Proposal mid 2000 Adoption 2003	Proposal Oct 2000 Adoption Jan 2002	+	
Amendment of the Insurance Directives and the ISD to permit information exchange with third countries	Proposal autumn 1999 Adoption 2001	Proposal Sep 2000 Adopted Nov 2000	x	
Adopting a Directive on Prudential Rules for Financial Conglomerates	Proposal end 2000 Adoption 2002	Proposal Apr 2001 Adoption Dec 2002	+	

Objective: Wider conditions for an optimal single financial market

Action	Initial FSAP optimal timeframe	Present timeframe		
Adopt a Directive for ensuring taxation of interest income from cross-border investment of savings	Political agreement by Nov 1999 Adoption 2000	New Proposal Jul 2001 Adoption Dec 2002	+	**
Implementation of the December 1997 Code of Conduct on business taxation	Ongoing examination in the Code of Conduct Group	Ongoing examination in the Code of Conduct Group	+	**
Review of taxation of financial service products	Discussion in Taxation Policy Group		x	**

Source: European Commission, extracted from the Commissions web-site (http:// europa.eu.int/comm/internal_market/en/finances/actionplan/index.htm) on January, 20, 2002, own additions.

References

Eppendorfer, C., R. Beckmann and M. Neimke (2002), *Market Access Strategies in the EU Banking Sector – Obstacles and Benefits Towards an Integrated European Retail Market*, also published in this volume.

European Commission (2001), http://europa.eu.int/comm/internal_market/en/finances/insur.

European Commission (2001), *Report on E-Commerce and Financial Services to the Financial Services Policy Group*, Brussels.

Farny, D. (2002), Die Marktanteile „ausländischer" Versicherer auf dem deutschen Erstversicherungsmarkt 1993 bis 2000, *Mitteilungen* (1), Institut für Versicherungswissenschaft, Universität Köln.

Gesamtverband der Deutschen Versicherungswirtschaft (2001), *Bericht aus Brüssel* Nr. 30.

Group of Ten (2001), *Report on Consolidation in the Financial Sector*, January.

IMF (2001), *Report on the Observance of Standards and Codes – Ireland: II. Insurance Supervision*.

International Financial Services Centre (IFSC), Dublin (2002), http://www.ifsc.ie.

Kirwan, J. (2000), *The Changing Pattern of European Personal Line Distribution*, paper presented at 22nd UK insurance economists' conference, 29/30 March.

Neimke, M., R. Beckmann and C. Eppendorfer (2002), Deepening European Financial Integration: Theoretical Considerations and Empirical Evaluation of Growth and Employment Benefits, also published in this volume.

OECD (1999), *Liberalisation of International Insurance Operations – Cross-Border Trade and Establishment of Foreign Branches*, Paris.

OECD (2000), *Financial Market Trends* No. 75, Paris.

OECD (2001a), *Insurance Statistics Yearbook 1992-1999*, Paris.

OECD (2001b), *Taxing Insurance Companies*, Tax Policies Studies, No. 3, Paris.

Schüler, M. (2002), Integration of the European Market for E-Finance – Evidence from Online Brokerage, also published in this volume.

Swiss Re (1996), Deregulation and Liberalisation of Market Access: The European Insurance Industry on the Threshold of a New Era in Competition, *sigma* (7).

Swiss Re (2000a), Europe in Focus: Non-Life Markets Undergoing Structural Change, *sigma* (3).

Swiss Re (2000b), The Impact of E-Business on the Insurance Industry: Pressure to Adapt – Chance to Reinvent, *sigma* (5).

Swiss Re (2000c), World Insurance in 1999: Soaring Life Insurance Business, *sigma* (9).

Vollbrecht, J. (2001), Insurance Regulation and Supervision, *Policy Issues in Insurance*, (3), 7-68.

Watson Wyatt (2001), *Insurance and Financial Services Review*, August.

Financial Integration in Europe and Banking Sector Performance

Claudia M. Buch and Ralph P. Heinrich*

Kiel Institute of World Economics, Germany

1 Motivation

Legally, virtually all direct barriers to the cross-border activities of banks in Europe have been abolished in the past decades. Hence, Europe might be considered one of the most integrated banking markets world-wide. However, there is ample evidence suggesting that financial market integration de facto is smaller than one might expect in fully integrated financial markets.[1] This study tries to give an answer to three questions:

- Has integration promoted cross-border banking?
- What are the segmenting barriers to a full integration of financial markets?
- What have been the effects on the performance of banks?

Throughout the study, we try to disentangle policy-induced factors segmenting financial markets (such as taxes, regulations), from those inherent in markets, i.e. 'natural' factors such as preferences, culture, or technology. This distinction is relevant in particular because economic policy can have a direct impact on the former type of barriers, while market-inherent barriers to integration can be affected by economic policy only very gradually and modestly at best.

The remainder of the paper falls into three parts. Section 2 provides stylised facts on the integration of financial markets in Europe, providing also comparative evidence for the United States. The focus is on cross-border capital flows, market shares of foreign banks, and the impact of integration on bank profitability. In Section 3, we provide new empirical evidence on the link between the deregulation of financial markets and banking. We distinguish the impact of deregulation on cross-border banking and the impact of cross-border banking on banking

---

* Acknowledgement: The authors would like to thank participants of seminars at the Kiel Institute of World Economics and the ERF in Brussels for most helpful comments on an earlier draft. All remaining errors remain in our own responsibility.

1 For a review of the literature see Buch (2001).

efficiency. Part four discusses the results, focusing in particular on the benefits of financial integration and potential lessons for economic policy.

2 How Fragmented Are Financial Markets in Europe? Stylised Facts

2.1 Institutional Background

In Europe, financial market deregulation has been shaped both by the abolition of capital account restrictions and the adoption of common legislative standards. Yet, the timing of implementation at the national level has varied quite substantially (European Commission (EU), 1997, Table 1). Although individual countries had opted to liberalise capital flows earlier on, agreements to abolish capital controls on a European-wide level were adopted only in the 1980s (Bakker, 1994). The Single European Act, which was signed in 1986, formally prepared the ground for the removal of all legal obstacles to an internal market. Full implementation into national law was achieved only in the 1990s in the majority of countries.

Table 1: Liberalisation of banking activities in EU member states

	Lifting of capital controls	Interest rate deregulation	First Banking Directive	Second Banking Directive
Belgium	1991	1990	1993	1994
Denmark	1982	1988	1980	1991
France	1990	1990	1980	1992
Germany	1967	1981	1978	1992
Greece	1994	1993	1981	1992
Ireland	1985	1993	1989	1992
Italy	1983	1990	1985	1992
Luxembourg	1990	1990	1981	1993
Netherlands	1980	1981	1978	1992
Portugal	1992	1992	1992	1992
Spain	1992	1992	1987	1994
UK	1979	1979	1979	1993

Source: EU (1997).

First steps towards levelling the playing field for financial institutions across Europe were made in the 1970s by granting the freedom of establishment and passing the First Banking Directive. Since cross-border banking activities remained subject to host-country supervision, the potential for national discretion yet remained substantial. The major step towards closing the remaining gaps was made with the Second Banking Directive, which became effective in 1993. The Directive establishes, among other things, the acceptance of the principles of mutual recognition of banking licenses, of minimum harmonisation, and of home country control. Furthermore, the Directive eliminates the need to get a local banking charter for branches in a foreign country, subjects foreign branches to home country supervision, and abolishes the need for foreign branches to hold a certain amount of endowment capital.

As a result, Europe is one of the most open regions world-wide towards foreign competition in banking. Table 2 gives an overview of the prudential regulations affecting foreign financial institutions. In Europe, there are virtually no restrictions to the market entry of foreign banks in place, indicating a slightly more liberal regime in comparison to high income countries on average and to less developed countries in particular. EU countries as well as developed countries in general also have a lower share of entry applications being denied in comparison to lower income countries.
At the same time, however, the actual share of foreign ownership in Europe is below the average for developed countries, and substantially below the values observed for lower income markets. Despite the substantial deregulation of cross-border banking that has taken place over the past decades, the direct presence of foreign banks (branches plus subsidiaries) on domestic markets remains modest for most EU countries (ECB, 1999).

One reason for the comparatively low market shares of foreign banks in Europe is the typically low profitability of foreign banks in developed market economies (Berger et al. 2000). However, explicit and implicit regulatory barriers play a role as well. Notwithstanding the substantial efforts that have been made at levelling the playing field for financial institutions across Europe and at creating a Single Market for capital, this indicates that substantial indirect barriers to the full integration of financial markets remain. Countries have been able to retain a substantial amount of national flavour in regulating their financial markets and to shield incumbent financial institutions against competitive pressure from abroad. This and the concomitant need to further lower remaining barriers to financial integration has prompted the European Commission to draft a Financial Services Action Plan (European Commission, 1999).

Table 2: Openness of banking system towards foreign competition

	EU	Euroland	Developed countries	High income	Upper middle income	Lower middle income	Lower income
Limits on foreign bank ownership of domestic banks	0.00	0.00	0.08	0.17	0.44	0.19	0.14
Limits on entry of foreign banks	0.00	0.00	0.04	0.07	0.11	0.24	0.14
Concentration ratio	59.19	56.17	60.92	63.75	66.48	72.35	72.91
Foreign bank ownership	16.29	19.97	24.81	33.57	31.72	33.75	33.59
Government-owned banks	9.98	12.97	10.27	10.28	12.32	28.32	35.36
No entry applications	0.00	0.00	0.04	0.09	0.14	0.13	0.00
Domestic	0.21	0.27	0.24	0.31	0.25	0.30	0.11
Foreign	0.08	0.10	0.08	0.16	0.30	0.43	0.22
Fraction of entry applications denied	3.67	3.23	3.21	7.69	11.99	32.22	49.32
Domestic	5.42	3.37	2.13	7.16	8.33	28.04	79.82
Foreign	1.67	2.22	3.21	6.91	16.85	30.83	37.85

All variables are averages by income level or region, respectively. Limits on foreign bank ownership of domestic banks = maximum fraction of banking system assets that can be held by banks that are 50% or more foreign-owned. Bank concentration ratio = fraction of deposits held by the five largest banks. Foreign bank ownership = fraction of banking system's assets that are held by banks which are 50% or more foreign-owned. Government-owned banks = fraction of banking system's assets held by banks that are 50% or more government-owned. No entry applications = dummy variable which assigns a one if applications for licenses have been received in the past 5 years. Fraction of entry applications denied = fraction of applications denied in the past 5 years.

Source: Barth et al. (2001).

Also, a recent report of the Committee of Wise Men states that "*the European Union's current regulatory framework is too slow, too rigid, complex and ill-adapted to the pace of global financial market change. Moreover, [...] existing rules and regulations are implemented differently and [...] therefore inconsistencies occur in the treatment of the same type of business, which threatens to violate the pre-requisite of the competitive neutrality of supervision*" (European Commission, 2001: 7).

However, quantifying the importance of indirect barriers is difficult without having a benchmark case of full integration. Incidentally, the experience of the United States with the integration of financial markets can provide such a frame of reference. Prior to the mid-1990s, the McFadden Act of 1927 effectively restricted interstate branching of commercial banks; intra-state branching was limited by the so-called unit banking system that confined banking activities to a single banking office in some states. Interstate privileges softened subsequently, and by 1994, almost 70% of banking assets were legally accessible from the average U.S. state, an increase from less than 10% in the early 1970s (Berger et al., 1995). The pattern of deregulation has not been uniform across states, however. While some states had lifted barriers to the interregional activities of banks already in the early 1980s, others followed only in the 1990s. In the early 1990s, however, the process of deregulation of regional banking activities was de facto completed (Jayaratne and Strahan, 2000).

Generally, the removal of restrictions to the regional expansion of banks in the United States can be viewed in close relation to the creation of a Single Market in Europe. In both cases, banks were allowed to expand their activities across borders. While also in the US banks have been slow to move into new markets at first (see, for instance, the evidence reviewed in Buch, 2002), cross-border banking has become much more common in recent years. Morgan et al. (2001) show that, in 1995, out-of-state bank holding companies held more than 60% of the banking system's assets in most of the US states.

At the same time, one important difference to the United States is that banking supervision in Europe remains under national responsibility.[2] In Europe, there is no generally accepted institutional link between banking supervision and the responsibility for monetary policy. In some countries, supervision is performed by institutions outside the central banking system, in others, the two tasks are performed under one roof. At the European level, co-ordination of banking supervision takes place through a banking supervision committee at the European Central Bank (ECB) which, however, serves mainly as a place for co-ordination and consultation.

---

2 For a more detailed treatment of regulatory issues at the European level see Lannoo (2000).

In summary then, it is difficult to argue that deregulation of banking activities has proceeded more or less rapidly in Europe as compared to the United States. While intra-European capital controls had been abolished in some countries early on, others followed only in the 1990s. In the United States, there have been no formal capital controls but restrictions to the regional expansion of commercial banks have played a similar role.

2.2 Cross-Border Capital Flows

As EU banking systems have become more and more open internationally, an interesting question is to what extent international asset holdings have been diversified. The International Capital Asset Pricing Model implies that investors should seek to diversify their portfolios to the greatest possible degree, and securities which show a low degree of correlation with the home portfolio should be relatively attractive. Since the member countries of the EU are relatively similar with regard to their state of economic development and since there has been a general convergence process in the run-up to the introduction of the common currency, we might expect to find a relatively small potential for diversification among these countries. If anything, there might be an incentive to diversify into the smaller EU countries which are still undergoing a catching up process and thus provide diversification opportunities. Empirical evidence provided by Buch and Lapp (2000) and Lapp (2001) in fact supports the view that diversification within Europe is not necessarily an optimal strategy while, at the same time, portfolios of German banks were found to be insufficiently diversified.

The lack of evidence in favour of the investment patterns predicted by standard portfolio theory is certainly not confined to Germany. Generally, agents tend to hold the bulk of their financial wealth in assets of their home country and currency (see also Tesar and Werner, 1992). If anything, they diversify their portfolios only within a relatively small regional or cultural surrounding. There is an increasing amount of evidence that, even within national borders, investment patterns are guided by regional and cultural proximity (Coval and Moskowitz, 1999, Grinblatt and Keloharju, 2000). A number of explanations for this home bias in (international) investment portfolios have been offered, ranging from asymmetries in information on financial markets to incomplete integration of goods markets (see Lewis, 1999, for a survey).

Data on the share of EU countries in international asset holdings for the EU countries as well as for the US provides further evidence on the regional bias of investors (Buch, 2001). Generally, the EU member states hold more than one half of their external financial assets within Europe. This holds true for all countries and assets considered with a few exceptions. Austria and the UK, for instance, hold less than 50% of their financial assets within EU, albeit for very different reasons. For Austria, lending to the transition economies of Central and Eastern Europe is of above-average importance, thus likewise reflecting a regional component in investment portfolios. For the UK, to the contrary, the below-average EU-share is the result of the fact that London hosts an international financial centre. As for portfolio investments, Italy and the UK have relatively low shares of EU-investments. Data on the outward stock of FDI have not been available for all countries. While the pattern is similar compared to security holdings for most countries, only Portugal holds a below average share (40%) of its FDI in Europe.

Buch (2001) also reports information for the US as one of the most important international investors. While the share of the EU in the international investment portfolio of the US (about 48%) is somewhat below the average for the EU countries, this gap is yet far smaller than for trade. Only 20% of US trade is with countries of the European Union, as compared to values around 60 to 70% for the average EU country, which could be reflecting the importance of physical transportation costs. Applying a similar reasoning to Europe, one would expect a greater degree of trade integration than financial sector integration among the EU countries. Yet, this holds true only for a few countries (Austria, Portugal, Spain, UK).

The dominance of European countries in international asset holdings does not imply, however, that bilateral financial linkages are important relative to the total size of financial markets. Buch (2001) presents data on the ratio of bilateral asset holdings relative to domestic credit in EU countries. Overall, German and French banks are the major lenders on international banking markets, having accounted for almost 20 and 10%, respectively, of cross-border assets of commercial banks at the end of 1999. Comparing cross-border assets of German commercial banks to domestic credit in the EU countries, however, shows that most bilateral financial linkages are a relatively small fraction of total domestic credit only.

The only two countries which stand out in this regard are Germany and Luxembourg. Cross-border asset holdings of German commercial bank reach shares of 10% or even more of domestic credit in a number of EU countries (Austria, Denmark, Finland, Greece, Italy, Ireland, the Netherlands, United Kingdom). Luxembourg, to the contrary, has liabilities vis-à-vis other EU countries which add up to more than the amount of domestic credit outstanding, Germany alone accounting for about half of these liabilities. Other major sources of intra-EU liabilities have been Belgium, France, and Italy.

Taking a longer-term perspective, Figure 1 plots the evolution of banks' foreign assets and liabilities relative to GDP. From these graphs, a number of interesting features emerge:

First, foreign activities of commercial banks have expanded rapidly after the end of the Bretton-Woods period and the subsequent abolition of capital controls in the early 1970s. Prior to this time, they hardly accounted for more than 5 to 10% of GDP. This is consistent with studies on long-term changes in the degree of capital mobility which find that the degree of integration of international capital markets has started to accelerate in the 1970s (Bordo et al., 1998, Taylor, 1996).

Second, banking systems in Europe show divergent degrees of international openness. Broadly speaking, the countries fall into three groups: banks in highly financially open economies, such as Ireland or the United Kingdom, have foreign assets and liabilities which exceed GDP. The ratio of external assets for most countries is in the range of about 50% of GDP, this group comprising Austria, Denmark, France, Germany, the Netherlands, Portugal, and Sweden. Notwithstanding quite pronounced differences in developments over time, the group of countries which is less integrated into international capital flows and has gross foreign assets or liabilities of only 30% or less of GDP comprises Finland, Italy, and Spain.

Third, outward openness of banking systems seems to have accelerated after 1992 in a few countries such as Germany (which is partly also due to the reunification effect and the resulting increased imports of capital), Ireland, Portugal, or Spain. In others (France, Italy, the Netherlands, Sweden), there has been an upward trend of this measure throughout while others (Austria, Finland, the United Kingdom) have even shown declining shares of banks' foreign assets and liabilities over GDP.

Fourth, net foreign asset positions are relatively small compared to gross positions. This is in line with earlier work looking at countries' international investment positions (see Kraay et al., 2000, or Lane and Milesi-Ferretti, 2000) and is likely to reflect borrowing constraints that become effective if net positions are becoming large.

Figure 1: Foreign assets and liabilities of commercial banks (% of GDP), 1948-1999

_______ gross foreign assets -------- gross foreign liabilities ▬▬▬ net assets

Austria

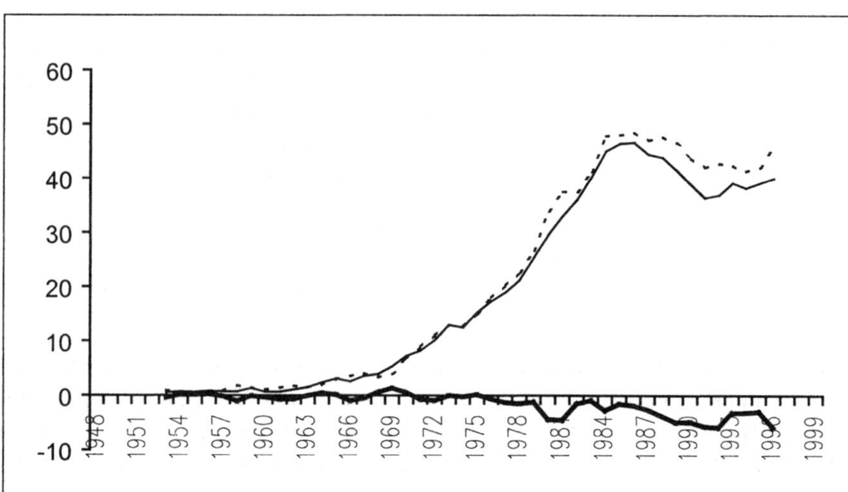

Denmark

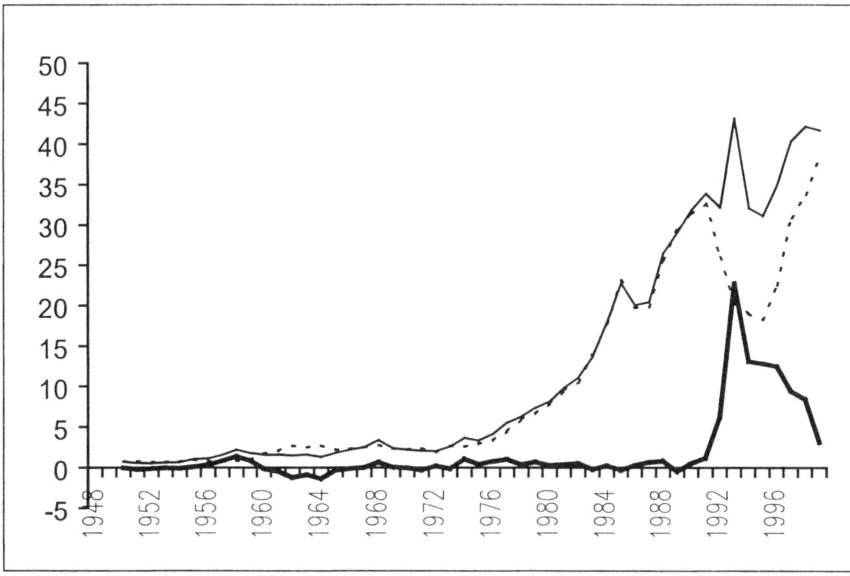

Finland

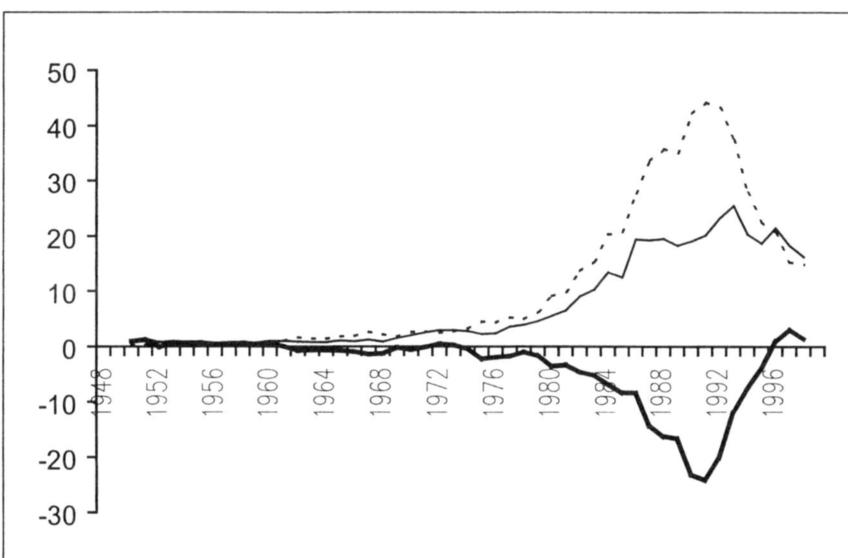

France

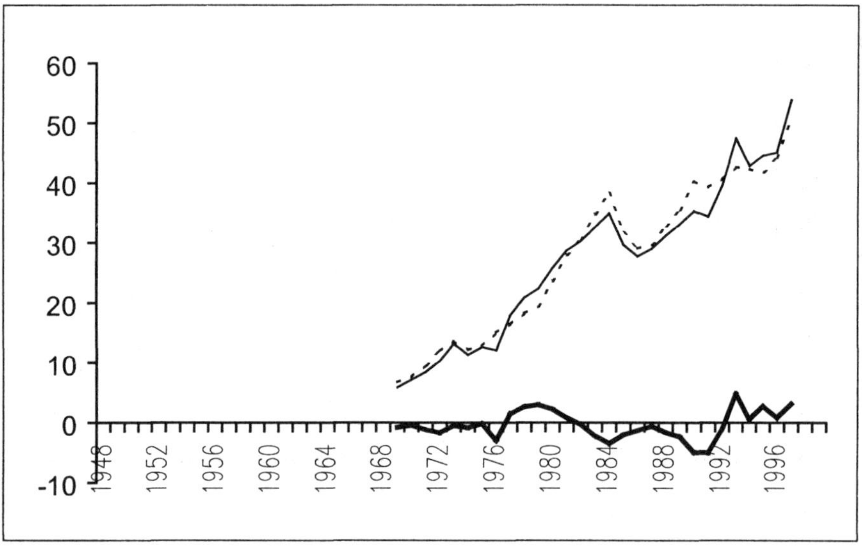

Germany

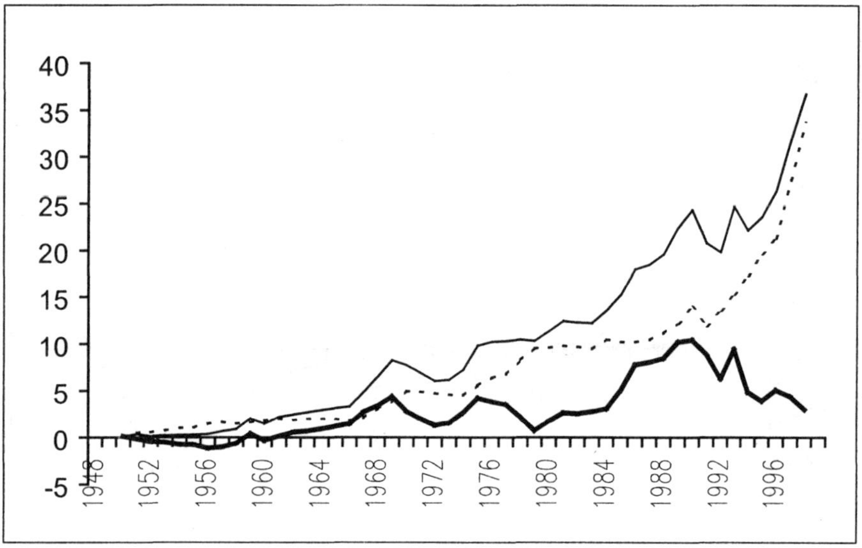

Italy

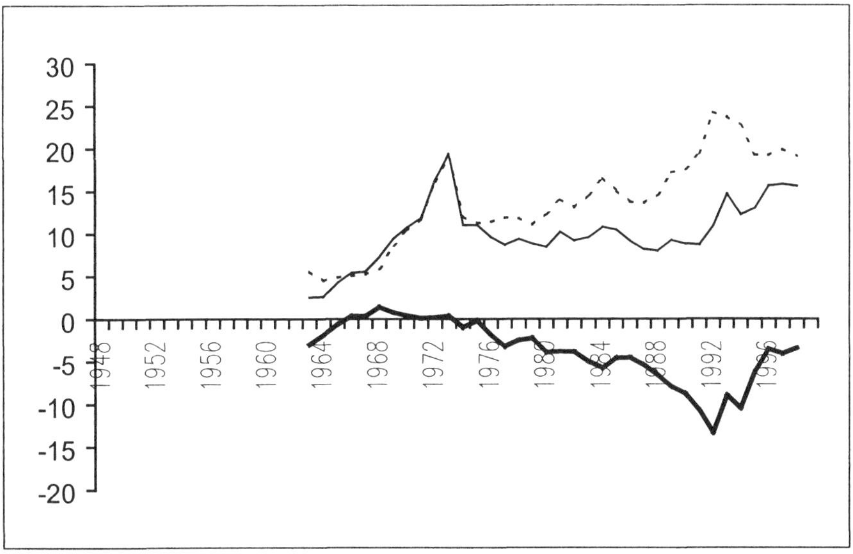

Ireland

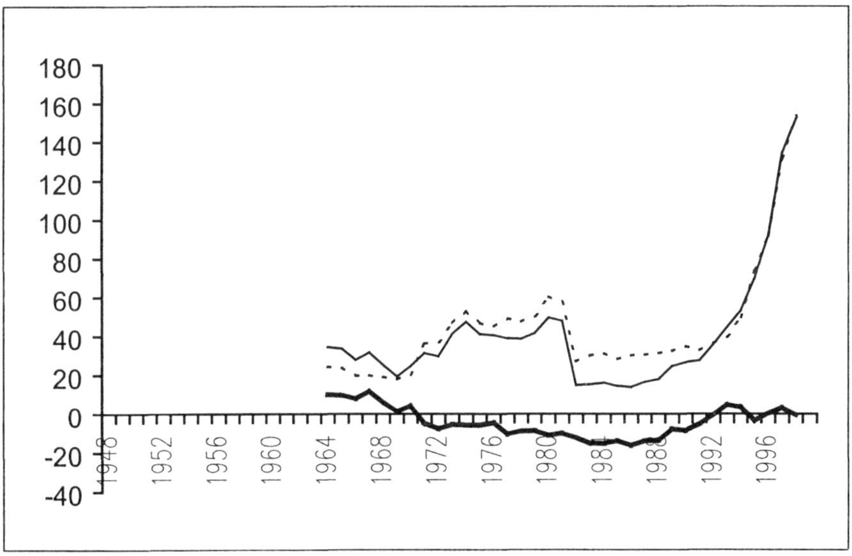

Netherlands

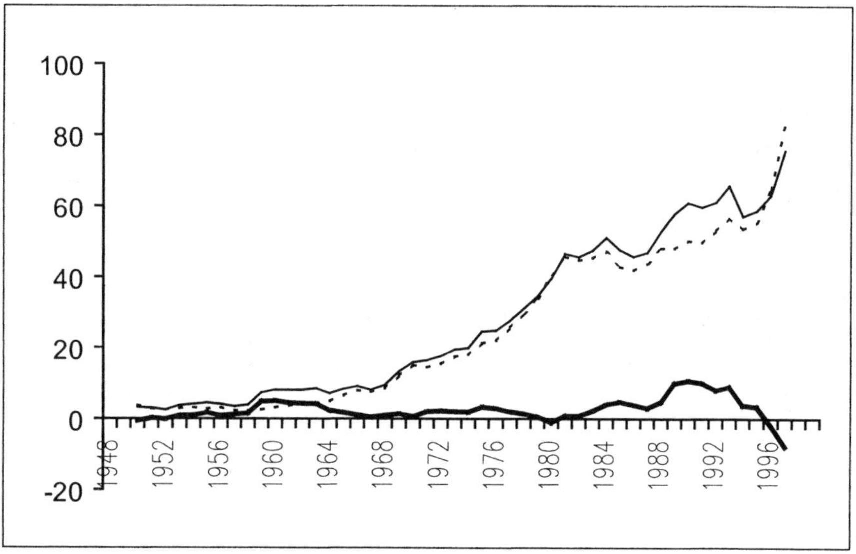

Portugal

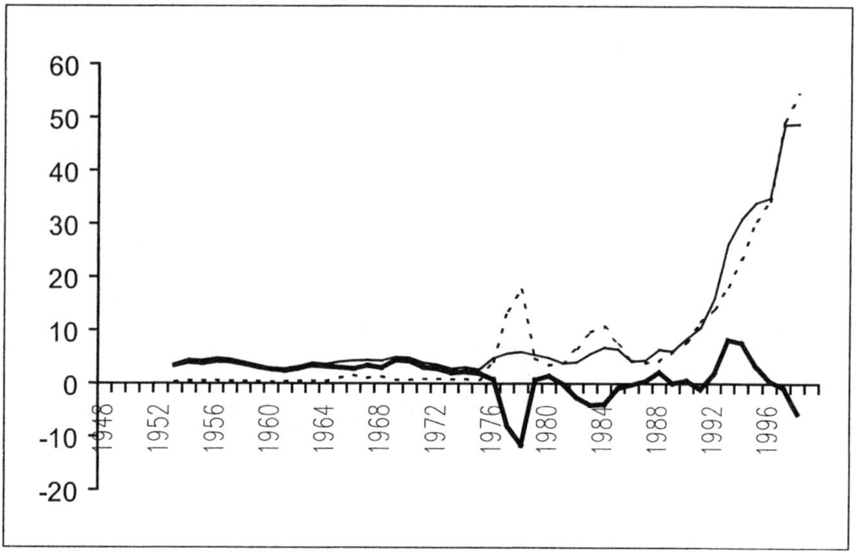

Spain

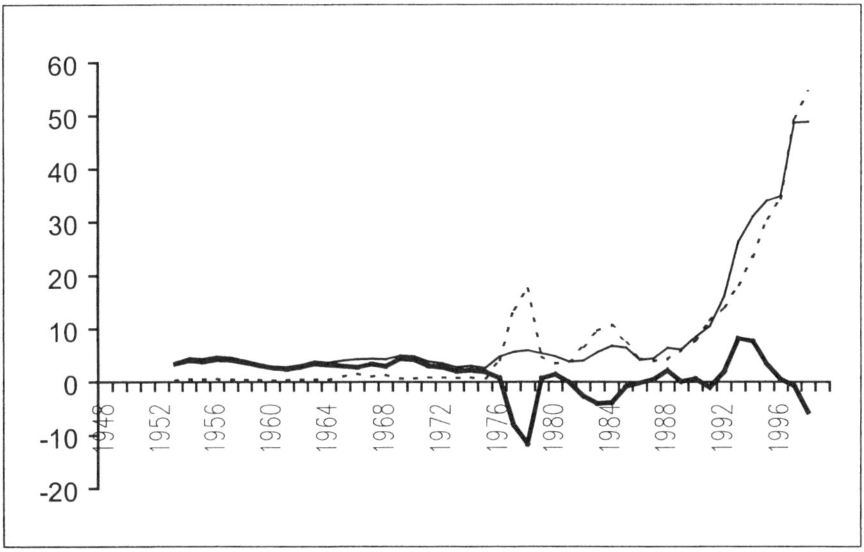

Sweden

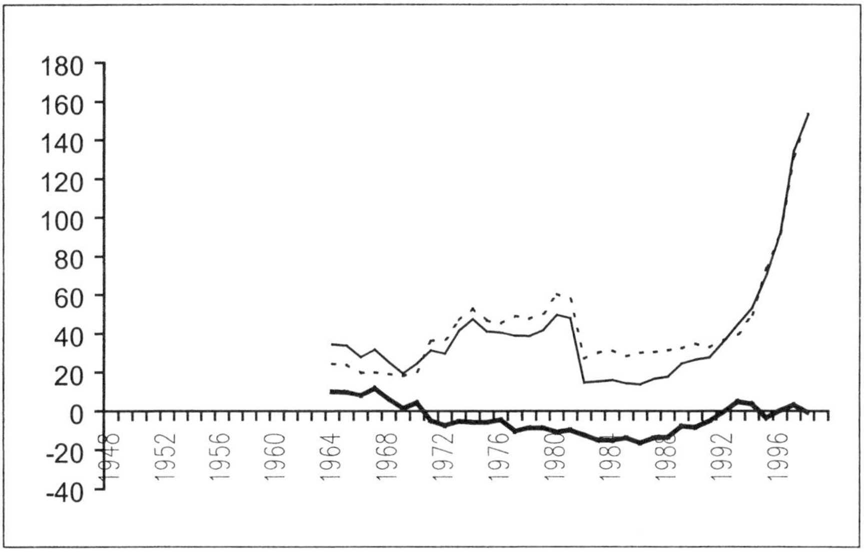

United Kingdom

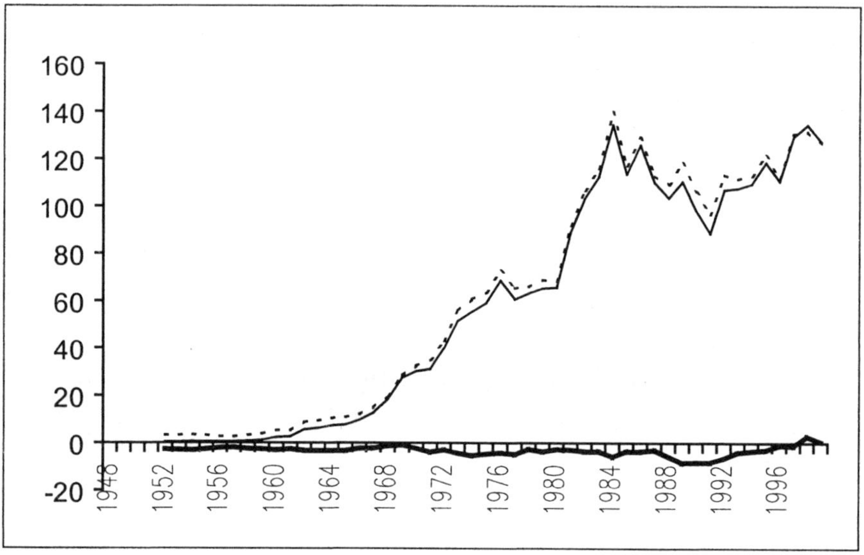

Source: IMF (2001), own calculations.

Generally, changes in the ratio of banks' foreign assets and liabilities to GDP are driven by two factors: changes in the degree of openness of financial systems and changes in the importance of the banking system relative to GDP. In order to isolate these two effects, Buch (2001) presents data on the importance of claims and liabilities towards non-residents relative to the balance sheet total of EU financial institutions in the 1990s. Two results are striking: First, the importance of foreign assets and liabilities relative to their balance sheet total again varies quite substantially between the EU member countries. At the bottom end of the scale, banks in Italy and Spain have assets and liabilities vis-à-vis non-residents of only 10 to 15% of their balance sheet total. For the majority of the countries, this share is around 20 to 25%. Second, changes in these ratios have been relatively modest for most countries during the 1990s, and there has been no consistent time trend across countries. To some extent, the increase in the ratio between foreign assets of the banking systems relative to GDP thus reflects the increase in the ratio of total banking system assets to GDP.

2.3 Market Shares of Foreign Banks

In contrast to the rapid increase of foreign assets and liabilities of commercial banks, market shares of foreign banks in EU countries are relatively small (Figure 2). The UK, Ireland, and Luxembourg are exceptions. These are countries which host international financial centres and have a very liberal regime towards foreign banks.

The experience of Western Europe with relatively low market shares of foreign banks is in contrast to evidence from several emerging markets where, after entry had been liberalised in general, foreign banks found it much easier to acquire market shares. Several factors are responsible for this:

First, mergers and acquisitions (M&As) are one important channel through which entry in the banking sector occurs. So far, however, M&As in Europe have taken place mainly on a national level. Between 1985 and 2000, 84% of all merger cases involved domestic financial institutions only, as compared to 5% involving two European institutions, and 11% of mergers between European and non-European institutions (ECB, 2000). Hence, domestic banking systems seem to have consolidated and strengthened first, thus reducing the profitability of entry.

Second, the low frequency of bank mergers between (developed) EU countries and the limited entry of foreign banks is also a response to the limited success of entry. Empirical studies tend to show that international bank mergers have a relatively small probability of being successful and that foreign banks in developed countries tend to perform worse than their domestic counterparts (Berger et al., 2000).

Figure 2: Market shares of foreign banks (share of total assets), 1990-1997

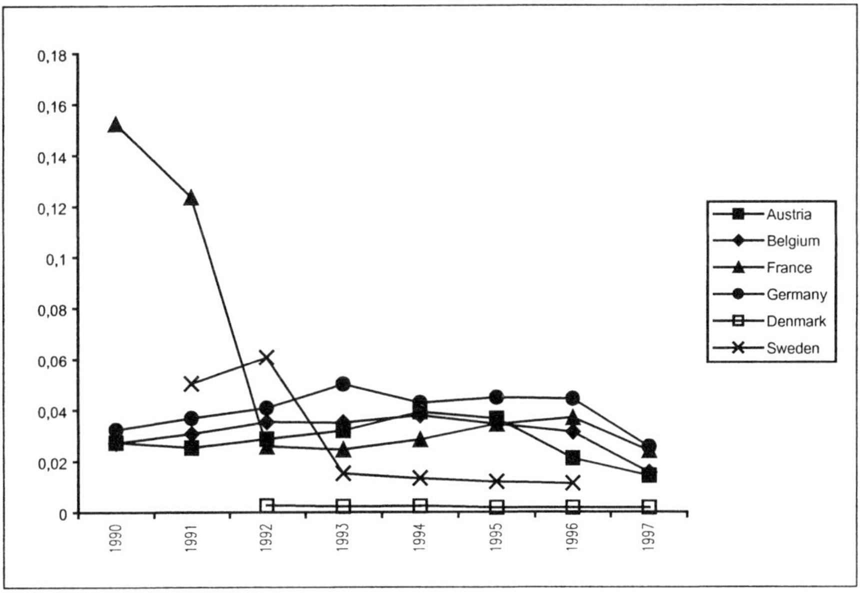

Figure 2: continued

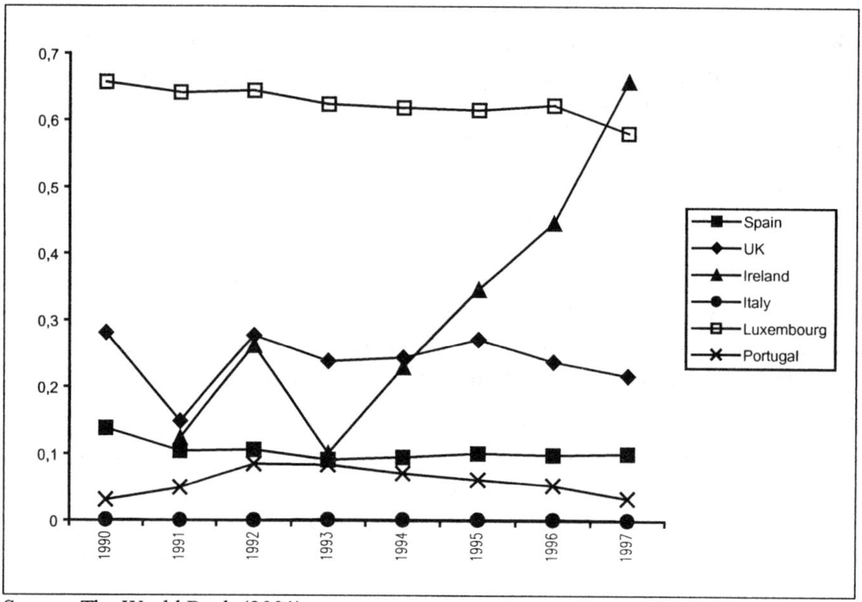

Source: The World Bank (2001).

2.4 Bank Profitability and Efficiency

Mainly, an increase in the openness of banking systems in Europe has thus occurred through increased capital flows rather than the market entry of foreign banks. The question is to what extent these changes have affected the profitability of the European banking industry. Correlations between the return on equity across European countries suggest that there remains a considerable degree of segmentation of banking markets. On average, the profitability of banks across EU countries (as measured by their return on equity) has been virtually uncorrelated in the past. Using data on the correlation of the return on equity for European banks for the years 1979 through 1996 as provided by Berger et al. (2000a), we find an average correlation coefficient of 0.05. In integrated markets, we would expect a much closer link. Average return correlations for profits of banks across US regions, for instance, are substantially higher (0.44) (Berger and DeYoung, 2001).

Table 3: Performance indicators of banks in Europe and in the US in the 1990s

Data are for all banks with the exception of Greece, Portugal, the United Kingdom and the United States (commercial banks only) and Denmark (commercial and savings banks). Volatility of profits and provisions has been measured through the coefficient of variation = standard deviation / sample mean.

a) Profits before tax in percent of average assets

	1990	1991	1992	1993	1994	1995	1996	1997	1998	1999	Average	CV
Austria	0.44	0.40	0.41	0.34	0.49	0.42	0.39	0.43	0.43	0.46	0.42	0.09
Belgium	0.29	0.25	0.23	0.37	0.34	0.33	0.39	0.38	0.44	0.45	0.35	0.20
Denmark	-0.27	-0.01	-1.20	0.65	...	1.41	1.23	1.05	0.97	0.86	0.52	1.54
Finland	0.29	0.40	-0.78	-2.63	-1.42	-1.19	-0.37	0.41	0.86	0.54	-0.39	-2.70
France	0.36	0.39	0.28	0.12	0.02	0.15	0.18	0.28	0.35	0.47	0.26	0.51
Germany	0.48	0.58	0.57	0.58	0.52	0.57	0.53	0.47	0.71	0.38	0.54	0.15
Greece	0.46	0.87	1.60	1.15	1.06	0.31	0.26	0.79	0.99	1.20	0.87	0.46
Italy	1.00	0.94	0.70	0.81	0.28	0.36	0.5	0.33	0.90	1.02	0.68	0.41
Netherlands	0.55	0.53	0.58	0.68	0.70	0.75	0.78	0.74	0.61	0.78	0.67	0.14
Spain	1.31	1.38	1.08	0.36	0.77	0.82	0.86	0.94	0.95	0.96	0.94	0.29
Portugal	...	...	...	0.98	0.71	0.65	0.77	0.88	0.83	0.8	0.80	0.13
UK	0.72	0.4	0.31	0.76	1.15	1.17	1.14	1.15	1.23	1.35	0.94	0.37
Average EU	0.51	0.56	0.34	0.35	0.42	0.48	0.56	0.65	0.77	0.77	0.54	0.27
US	0.77	1.33	1.76	1.73	1.81	1.85	1.93	1.81	2.03	1.38	1.64	0.22

Table 3 continues

Table 3 continued

b) Net provisions in percent of average assets

	1990	1991	1992	1993	1994	1995	1996	1997	1998	1999	Average	CV
Austria	0.39	0.5	0.52	0.66	0.58	0.51	0.44	0.44	0.39	0.37	0.48	0.18
Belgium	0.22	0.31	0.38	0.24	0.14	0.24	0.22	0.23	0.22	0.14	0.23	0.29
Denmark	1.21	1.49	1.79	1.76	0.92	0.76	0.49	0.34	0.34	0.28	0.94	0.60
Finland	0.26	0.27	-0.01	-0.06	-0.01	-0.03	-0.01	-0.02	0.01	-0.02	0.04	3.02
France	0.26	0.28	0.50	0.68	0.57	0.59	0.39	0.28	0.23	0.12	0.39	0.45
Germany	0.46	0.35	0.40	0.46	0.54	0.36	0.34	0.34	0.32	0.29	0.39	0.19
Greece	0.33	0.45	0.69	0.32	0.34	0.39	0.26	0.55	0.65	0.57	0.46	0.31
Italy	0.65	0.55	0.64	0.78	0.80	0.78	0.69	0.72	0.49	0.39	0.65	0.20
Netherlands	0.24	0.29	0.27	0.24	0.18	0.16	0.18	0.19	0.24	0.17	0.22	0.20
Spain	0.57	0.64	0.72	1.43	0.77	0.50	0.49	0.43	0.44	0.24	0.62	0.49
Portugal	…	…	…	0.86	0.58	0.40	0.43	0.42	0.61	0.43	0.53	0.29
UK	0.95	1.27	1.24	0.87	0.33	0.30	0.20	0.18	0.24	0.23	0.58	0.73
Average EU	0.50	0.58	0.65	0.69	0.48	0.41	0.34	0.34	0.35	0.27	0.46	0.29
US	1.03	0.78	0.47	0.28	0.30	0.37	0.41	0.41	0.39	0.33	0.48	0.48

Source: OECD (2001).

Table 3 provides comparative evidence on the performance of commercial banks in Europe and in the United States, using profits before taxes in percent of assets as a measure of profitability (Panel a) and net provisions in percent of assets as a measure of asset quality (Panel b). Generally, panel a shows that net profits have been much lower in the EU countries (average of 0.54% of assets) throughout the 1990s than in the United States (average of 1.64%). With regard to the volatility of profits, measured through the coefficient of variation, however, the regions are similar (0.27 versus 0.22). For net provisions, the picture looks somewhat different: Whereas the averages are fairly close (0.46% of assets for Europe versus 0.48 for the United States), the volatility of provisions was higher throughout the 1990s in the United States than in Europe (coefficient of variation of 0.48 versus 0.29).

Before trying to explain differences in the profitability of banks and the possible impact of deregulation, we review briefly the empirical evidence on bank profitability in Europe. Studying the situation prior to the implementation of the Second Banking Directive, Molyneux et al. (1994) find a lack of integration of European banking markets. They are using the so-called Panzar-Rosse-statistic (*H*) which calculates the responsiveness of banks' total revenues to changes in input prices. If banks operate in a highly concentrated banking sector under conditions of monopoly or perfect oligopolistic collusion, they respond to changes in input prices, and *H* would be zero or negative. In perfectly competitive markets, banks act as price takers, and *H* would be unity.

Using essentially the same methodological approach, Bikker and Groeneveld (2000) argue that the results of Molyneux et al. (1994) are relatively unstable because they do not take into account the gradual changes in competition that have occurred in European banking. Adjusting for this and using data for the years 1989 through 1996, Bikker and Groeneveld (2000) generally obtain more stable results and conclude that the Second Banking Directive has not increased the degree of competition in European banking. Rather, the degree of competition appears to have been rather fierce already prior to the creation of the Single Market.

Casu and Molyneux (2000) use a different empirical methodology by analysing to what extent the performance of banks in Europe deviates from an estimated efficient frontier. Their results are generally consistent with the other studies in that they find, if anything, only minor improvements in the efficiency of banks in Europe following the Second Banking Directive. However, their finding that efficiency levels are relatively low overall and are, moreover, strongly influenced by country-specific factors is in contradiction to the conclusions of Bikker and Groeneveld (2000) that competition is and has been relatively intense throughout.

The importance of country-specific conditions is stressed also in Pastor et al. (2000). These authors are estimating a common frontier for banks from 10 European countries for the year 1993, taking into account factors such as regulatory or demographic factors unique to the individual country which might affect banking performance. One result is that differences in domestic conditions do indeed have a significant impact on relative banking performance. They distinguish three groups of banks: Facing relatively adverse economic conditions in their home markets, banks in Denmark, Portugal, and Spain yet achieve relatively high efficiency scores. Facing relatively favourable conditions on their home market, banks in France and Italy do not seem to be able to perform efficiently at home while banks in Belgium, Germany, Luxembourg, and the Netherlands do. In the case of these latter countries, the ability of domestic banks to exploit favourable conditions on their home market might thus explain difficulties of foreign banks to enter.

3 Cross-Border Integration of Banking: New Empirical Evidence

This section presents new empirical evidence on the determinants of cross-border banking. The aim of this section is two-fold. We intend to assess empirically (i) what the effects of deregulation on cross-border banking have been and (ii) how this has affected the efficiency of banks.

3.1 Deregulation and Cross-Border Banking

Earlier empirical evidence on the factors driving the international expansion of banks provides relatively strong support for the notion that policy-induced as well as market-inherent barriers prevent a greater integration of financial markets. Buch (2000) uses a panel dataset for bilateral assets and liabilities that banks in advanced market economies hold in a large cross-section of countries. Evidence is available for the years 1983 through 1999, hence the dataset allows the impact of changes in regulations to be analysed.

The paper finds that the EU's Single Market program and the Basle Capital Accord tended to have a positive impact on intra-EU asset holdings and lending to OECD countries, respectively. In addition to regulations, information costs as proxied through distance, a common language, or a common legal system seem to have a significant impact on international investment decisions of banks. This supports evidence on the determinants of international asset portfolios that finds a strong explanatory power for distance (as a measure of information costs) (Portes and Rey, 2001, Ghosh and Wolf, 2001).

Generally, information costs appear to be the main factor segmenting international financial markets. Yet, when weighing the relative importance of information costs and regulations, results differ between countries. While banks from some countries prefer to expand into markets to which they have close cultural ties, others prefer to access markets with relatively low regulatory entry barriers. In particular banks from Spain seem to exploit comparative advantages stemming from the presence of a common language and a common legal system.

In this paper, we provide complementary evidence on the determinants of international activities of banks. The focus is on the link between deregulation and international banking. Table 4 provides an overview of the data that we use.

Table 4: Data definitions and sources

Variable	Definition	Source
Foreign assets and liabilities	Gross foreign assets and liabilities of commercial banks, relative to total assets of banks	OECD (2001)
Market shares of foreign banks	Assets of foreign banks in percent of total banking system assets.	World Bank (2001)
Market size	GDP in billion US-Dollar and the size of the population (in millions) are used to control for country size. The expected effect is negative: large countries would be less open to foreign competition and/or capital flows than smaller countries.	IMF (2001)
State of development	The state of development is measured through GDP per capita. The expected effect is positive for gross foreign assets: more developed countries are likely to be more open for foreign capital and foreign competition. However, the fact that more developed countries typically have lower spreads may reduce their attractiveness for foreign competitors.	IMF (2001)
Trade openness	Trade openness is measured as the sum of exports and imports relative to GDP.	IMF (2001)
Deregulation	Four dummy variables are used to control for deregulation trends: (1) The Basle Capital Accord of 1988 has tended to raise the equity requirements for international banks. The isolated effect on gross assets would be negative. (2) EU membership. (3) The EU's Single Market program was addressed by including a dummy variable which was set equal to 1 after the implementation of the Second Banking Directive. (4) Alternatively, we used a combined EU dummy taking a zero value for non-members, a 1 for members prior to the implementation of the Banking Directive, and a 2 for members thereafter.	

Table 5: Results of panel unit root tests

	Levels			First differences		
	LL	Modified LL	IPS	LL	Modified LL	IPS
Foreign assets / total assets	2.29	3.76	0.98	3.56	-7.62*	-2.51*
Foreign liabilities / total liabilities	4.76	1.96	3.07	1.60	-6.33*	-2.56*
Profit before taxes	-3.14*	1.13	-3.78*	-6.65*	-21.46*	-7.82*
Net interest income	12.95	120.75	5.32	-9.49*	-12.03*	-8.89*
Net non-interest income	1.29	8.04	1.19	0.10	-11.35*	-8.35*
Gross income	2.93	3.11	1.47	-3.11*	-15.13*	-8.08*
Operating expenses	4.53	0.90	3.71	-3.34*	-7.45*	-5.99*
Provisions	-13.06*	-14.03*	-5.60*	-7.69*	-15.82*	-6.95*

This Table presents the results of unit root tests for the time series under study. We are using three different tests. First, Levin and Lin (LL) (1993) have adjusted the standard ADF-tests for unit roots to panel data, allowing for time trends and short-run dynamics. As in the ADF-test, the Null that the variable contains a unit root is tested against the alternative that the variable is stationary. Second, Breitung (2000) has suggested a modified version of this test. His test corrects for a bias in the *t*-statistic, which occurs if more than one lagged endogenous variable is included, by estimating the model in deviations from the mean. The third test we use is the one proposed by Im, Pesaran, and Shin (IPS) (1997) which gives more flexibility with regard to the autocorrelation coefficient under the alternative hypothesis by performing ADF-tests for all cross-sections and averaging over the estimated coefficients. We report results for a specification with a constant term and two lagged endogenous variables (one for the first differences of the profitability measures) but without a linear time trend. Results are very invariant in qualitative terms to varying the lag length or including a trend. * denotes significance at the 5 percent level.

Based on two panel unit root tests that we employed, the hypothesis that our dependent variable is non-stationary could not be rejected (Table 5). Therefore, we estimated the model in first differences. More specifically, we estimate the following equation:

$$\Delta \log y_{it} = \Delta \log X_{it}\beta + \Delta R_{it}\gamma + \delta d_i + \varepsilon_{it},$$

where y_{it} are foreign assets and liabilities of the banking systems, X_{it} is the vector of controls for market size, state of development, and trade openness, R_{it} is the vector of regulation dummies, d_i is a country fixed effect, and ε_{it} is the disturbance term.

Regressions were run on a panel of OECD countries, using annual data for the period 1979-1999. Most of our banking data were taken from the publication *Bank Profitability – Financial Statements of Banks*, published by the OECD (OECD, 2001). This dataset was complemented by macroeconomic data from the *International Financial Statistics* of the IMF (IMF, 2001). Due to data limitations, the final sample had to be restricted to include the following countries: Austria, Belgium, Czech Republic, Denmark, Finland, France, Germany, Hungary, Iceland, Ireland, Italy, Luxembourg, the Netherlands, New Zealand, Norway, Poland, Portugal, Spain, Sweden, Switzerland, and Turkey.

Table 6: Determinants of banking sector openness

	Full sample			EU members		
Dependent variable	Foreign assets and liabilities (1)	Foreign assets (2)	Foreign liabilities (3)	Foreign assets and liabilities (4)	Foreign assets (5)	Foreign liabilities (6)
log GDP per capita	0.594 (0.463)	0.282 (0.583)	0.715 (0.484)	0.641 (0.448)	0.536 (0.565)	0.574*** (0.179)
log GDP	-0.863* (0.489)	-0.855 (0.630)	-0.685 (0.477)	-0.901* (0.528)	-0.901 (0.672)	-0.686*** (0.204)
log trade openness	-0.327 (6.256)	-0.533** (0.274)	-0.192 (0.356)	0.107 (0.204)	0.004 (0.230)	0.250 (0.226)
BIS	0.055* (0.031)	0.063 (0.058)	0.018 (0.024)	0.032 (0.026)	0.020 (0.040)	0.036* (0.022)
EU membership	-0.128 (0.071)	-0.015 (0.079)	-0.246*** (0.086)			
Second Banking Directive	0.097 (0.073)	0.109 (0.087)	0.093 (0.061)	0.071 (0.066)	0.095 (0.078)	0.053 (0.057)
Adjusted R^2	0.127	0.097	0.149	0.121	0.106	0.206
Period	1979-99	1979-99	1979-99	1979-99	1979-99	1979-99
N*T	284	284	288	146	146	146

Equations are specified in first differences. All dependent variables are specified in logs and normalised by total assets. Robust standard errors in brackets. *** (**, *) = significant at the 1 (5, 10) percent level. BIS = dummy for Basle capital adequacy standards, 0 until 1987, 1 thereafter; EU membership = 0 for non-members, 1 for members. Second Banking Directive = 0 before, 1 after implementation of the directive. The regressions include country fixed effects.

Table 6 reports estimation results on the determinants of the openness of the domestic financial sector. The first column measures openness by the sum of the foreign assets and foreign liabilities of the domestic banking system normalised by total assets. The significantly negative coefficient on the GDP suggests that, in larger countries, economic and financial interaction with the rest of the world tends to be less important quantitatively than in smaller countries. While this result is as expected, the coefficients on the other two control variables, GDP per capita and trade openness, are insignificant, and the latter also does not have the expected sign. Thus our priors that richer countries have more open banking systems, and that openness to trade (measured here as the sum of exports and imports over GDP) and openness of banking systems are positively associated are not confirmed.

Of our three variables capturing changes in the regulatory environment, neither EU membership per se nor the implementation of the Second Banking Directive appear to have had a significant effect on the openness of banking industries. By contrast, the introduction of the BIS capital adequacy standards exhibits a significant coefficient, and its sign is positive. One might have expected that, by requiring banks to hold more risk-adjusted capital, the BIS standards would make banks more hesitant to expand internationally. A possible explanation for the positive coefficient could be that the new standards were lower for credits to debtors from OECD countries than for other international credits. Thus banks might have responded by shifting their international lending from non-OECD countries to now relatively cheaper OECD member countries.

To investigate this issue further, columns 2 and 3 use as dependent variables the shares of foreign assets and foreign liabilities separately. If the introduction of the BIS standards had an asymmetric effect on lending inside and outside the OECD area, then the coefficient on the BIS dummy should differ in sign or at least significance across these two specifications. Specifically, foreign assets, which include assets held outside the OECD area, should be negatively affected, whereas foreign liabilities might be affected positively to the extent that lending is redirected towards the OECD area. However, our results do not confirm this conjecture, as the coefficient on the BIS dummy is insignificant and positive in both equations.

In the last three columns of Table 6, we investigate the effects of deregulation within the EU only. While these equations exhibit a slightly better fit in terms of the control variables, in particular with a positive sign on the trade variable and a significant coefficient on GDP per capita in at least one specification, the regulatory variables again do not really help to explain the pattern of the international integration of banking industries. In particular, the implementation of the Second Banking Directive does not have any significant effects within the EU sample. The only, albeit weak, piece of evidence in favor of an impact of regulation on integration comes from the fact that the BIS dummy is marginally significant and positive in the regression on foreign liabilities (column 6). As discussed above, this might reflect a reorientation of international lending away from countries penalised by the BIS standards. Overall though, the evidence suggests that deregulation has not had a strong impact on the degree of openness of the EU banking systems.

3.2 Deregulation and Banking Efficiency

After having analysed the link between deregulation and cross-border banking, we turn to the link between deregulation, foreign presence, and banking sector efficiency. We use a similar estimation strategy as in the previous section to identify the determinants of efficiency. An earlier study by Claessens et al. (2000) using firm-level data from 80 countries for the years 1988-1995 found that foreign bank entry significantly reduced domestic bank profitability, net non-interest income, and overhead expenses. No significant effects were found for net interest income and loan loss provisions. To the extent that high profits and high income reflect market power, and to the extent that high overheads reflect operational inefficiency, these results imply that foreign entry improves the efficiency of the domestic banking sector. Efficiency improvements may essentially come from two sources. Foreign banks may import best practices from abroad which domestic banks then copy. And foreign entry increases competitive pressure, thereby forcing domestic rivals to cut prices and costs.

We use the same dataset as before, i.e. aggregated, annual data on the profitability of banks to replicate the analysis of Claessens et al. (2000) for OECD countries. As dependent variables, we use the net interest margin, net non-interest income, profits before taxes, overhead costs, and loan loss provisions, all normalised by total banking sector assets. As explanatory variables, we include the number of foreign banks as a percentage of all banks as a proxy for financial sector openness[3] and deregulation (Basle and EU) dummies, as well as the ratio of equity over total assets, the ratio of non-interest income over assets, the ratio of overhead expenses of assets, GDP per capita, growth, inflation, and real interest rates as controls. Following Claessens et al. (2000), the equations are specified in first differences.[4] After eliminating missing observations, the following countries were included in the regressions: Austria, Australia, Belgium, Canada, Czech Republic, Denmark, Finland, France, Germany, Greece, Hungary, Iceland, Ireland, Italy, Japan, Luxembourg, the Netherlands, New Zealand, Norway, Poland, Portugal, Spain, Sweden, Switzerland, Turkey, the United Kingdom, and the United States.

Our results are given in Table 7. The alternative specifications explain between 18.5 and 34% of the variance in the data. The ratio of equity to assets has a positive and frequently significant impact on the three profit measures in columns (1)

---

3 This proxy was taken from Worldbank (2001). Since this variable was available only for the period 1990-1997, we had to restrict the analysis to this period. We also ran similar regressions using the market share of foreign banks in terms of total assets or gross foreign assets and liabilities of commercial banks as alternative proxies for openness, but the results were inferior to those reported in the table.

4 Because profitability measures can take on negative values, we do not take logs of our dependent variables. We experimented with semi-logarithmic specifications, but found them statistically inferior to the ones reported in Table 7.

through (3). However, the required real rate of return, as proxied by the real interest rate, remains mostly statistically insignificant. Also, the inflation rate often enters with a negative sign. These last two results are in contrast to the findings of Claessens et al. (2000). Country size as proxied by GDP has a positive effect on the net interest margin, while the level of economic development as measured by per capita GDP has a negative, although frequently insignificant effect.

Taken together, these results suggest the following. First, higher profits in larger countries might be due to economies of scale. Second, a stronger regulatory environment in more developed countries seems to lead to lower market power and hence lower profits. However, in specifications not shown in the table, we also attempted to capture scale and competition effects with a proxy for market concentration, and failed to find consistently significant effects. By the same token, including measures of the development of financial market which might exert competitive pressure on banks, such as stock market capitalisation or turnover relative to GDP, the size of the private and public bond markets relative to GDP, or the volume of new equity and bond issues, did not systematically improve the model.

In contrast to the findings of Claessens et al. (2000), the presence of foreign banks does not appear to significantly reduce profits or costs in our aggregate data for OECD countries. One reason for the discrepancy could be that Claessens et al. are looking at the efficiency of domestic banks only, whereas our aggregate data include both domestic and foreign banks. In addition, the result of Claessens et al. may be driven primarily by the non-OECD, less developed countries in their sample. Given earlier findings that foreign banks tend to be less efficient than local banks in developed countries (De Young and Nolle, 1996, Mahajan et al., 1996, Vander Vennet, 1996, Hasan and Lozano-Vivas, 1998, Miller and Parkhe, 1999, Parkhe and Miller, 1999), positive efficiency effects on domestic banks would have to come primarily via increased competitive pressure in our sample. Possibly, this effect has been stronger in non-OECD countries whose banking markets may have been less competitive prior to foreign entry. Moreover, a priori the causality between foreign entry and the efficiency of the domestic banking industry could also go the other way. It is conceivable that foreign banks enter preferably those markets where efficiency has been low and where competition has been weak. Thus, positive or insignificant coefficients on foreign bank presence may to some extent reflect self-selection of foreign entrants into inefficient markets.

As for the regulatory environment, the Second Banking Directive had a significantly negative effect on loan loss provisions in our sample, but had no significant impact on either overhead costs or profitability measures. These results thus broadly confirm earlier assessments of a limited impact of the Second Banking Directive (Bikker and Groeneveld, 2000, Casu and Molyneux, 2000). As to the issue whether this can be attributed to previously high competitive pressure in the EU banking industry as compared to the rest of the OECD, our results suggest otherwise. After controlling for the impact of the Second Banking Directive, EU members have significantly higher pre-tax profitability and net non-interest income, but no cost advantage, suggesting the presence of anti-competitive rents.

Table 7: Determinants of banking sector efficiency

	Net interest margin (1)	Net non-interest income (2)	Profit before taxes (3)	Overhead costs (4)	Loan loss provisions (5)
Equity	0.110*	0.015	0.266***	0.147**	-0.141*
	(0.967)	(0.069)	(0.105)	(0.069)	(0.0833)
Overhead costs	0.128**	0.490***	-0.687***		0.305**
	(0.066)	(0.113)	(0.193)		(0.156)
GDP per capita	-0.0003*	-0.0002	-0.0003	-0.0003	-0.0002
	(0.0002)	(0.0003)	(0.0002)	(0.0003)	(0.0001)
GDP	$4.06\text{x}10^{-6}$**	$5.76\text{x}10^{-6}$	$2.53\text{x}10^{-6}$	$2.71\text{x}10^{-6}$	$2.12\text{x}10^{-6}$
	$(1.85\text{x}10^{-6})$	$(3.8\text{x}10^{-6})$	$(3.25\ \text{x}10^{-6})$	$(3.27\text{x}10^{-6})$	$(3.46\text{x}10^{-6})$
Inflation	0.001	-0.001**	-0.0003**	$-8.92\text{x}10^{-6}$	0.000
	(0.0004)	(0.0004)	(0.0002)	(0.001)	(0.0001)
Real interest rate	0.0005	-0.0008*	-0.0004	-0.000	0.0001
	(0.0004)	(0.0004)	(0.0003)	(-0.0002)	(0.0002)
Number of foreign banks/all banks	0.007	0.0004	0.025*	-0.026	-0.018
	(0.012)	(0.016)	(0.014)	(0.022)	(0.012)
Dummy for 2nd Banking Directive	-0.0008	-0.001	-0.0003	-0.0003	-0.002**
	(0.001)	(0.0008)	(0.0009)	(0.001)	(0.001)
EU membership dummy	0.0005	0.003*	0.005***	0.001	-0.002
	(0.002)	(0.002)	(0.002)	(0.006)	(0.002)
Adjusted R^2	0.354	0.448	0.391	0.345	0.393
Period	1990-97	1990-97	1990-97	1990-97	1990-97
N*T	144	144	144	144	144

Equations are specified in first differences. Robust standard errors in brackets. *** (**, *) = significant at the 1 (5, 10) percent level. Net interest margin is interest income less interest expenses; net non-interest income is non-interest income less expenses related to non-interest income; profits before taxes is net interest margin plus net non-interest income less overhead costs and loan loss provisions; equity is capital plus reserves. These variables are all normalised by total assets.

It should be noted, though, that market power and the associated rents can also be the result of banks' investments into monitoring. That is, by spending resources to overcome information asymmetries between lenders and borrowers, banks may gain informational advantages over potential competitors and hence may gain market power. To the extent that monitoring facilitates the banks' lending decisions and thereby improves the allocation of capital, those improvements would have to be set against possible distortions caused by market power. Viewed from this perspective, care needs to be exercised before interpreting declines in profitability as evidence of gains in overall efficiency. However, if increased competitive pressure and the resultant erosion of market power really forced banks to scale back their monitoring activities, the associated inefficiency in the allocation of capital should presumably show up as a deterioration of asset quality and hence as an increase in loan loss provisions. We do not find any evidence of this in our data.

4 Summary of Results and Policy Implications

The degree to which financial markets in Europe are integrated with each other is of concern to policy-makers, researchers, and practitioners for several reasons. Countries which are closely linked financially might expose themselves to spillovers of financial crises. Monetary and fiscal policies are constrained by the interregional mobility of capital. And, not least, the efficiency of the financial system is affected by the degree to which it is integrated into international capital flows and by the degree to which it is exposed to competitive pressure from abroad. Therefore, the purpose of this paper has been to analyse financial linkages in Europe, in particular in Europe's banking systems, and to single out factors potentially segmenting financial markets.

Showing the changing degree of integration of markets and the importance of bilateral financial linkages, however, is a difficult task. Recent data on the allocation of financial assets of EU countries show that the bulk of assets is held within Europe. Also, the degree of openness of financial systems of the EU countries has increased over the past decades. This might suggest that the potential for spillover effects within the region are large. Compared to total domestic credit, bilateral financial linkages among EU countries, however, still remain small. The notable exception are claims of Germany as the largest creditor in Euroland on a number of smaller member countries.

In contrast to the relatively rapid increase in foreign assets and liabilities of commercial banks, market shares of foreign banks have so far remained small in most EU countries. Analyses of the correlation of returns across European banking markets suggest that there remains a considerable degree of segmentation. Evidence from the US also shows that particularly retail markets feature quite significant "natural" barriers to entry. While banks have expanded relatively quickly after geographical deregulation, the scale of their regional expansion seems to have been restricted nevertheless. Essentially, the evidence from the US confirms that retail banking is a local business.

We complement the available empirical evidence on the determinants of international integration of the banking industry and the impact of integration on efficiency by using panel data on OECD banking industries for the period 1979-1999. Apart from controlling for market size, level of economic development and trade links, we focus particularly on the impact of changes in the regulatory environment on financial openness. The introduction of the Basle capital adequacy standards generally raised the capital requirements for international lending, and also introduced different minimum standards for credits to borrowers from OECD and from non-OECD members. To the extent that the new standards were binding, they should have made foreign lending more expensive, and particularly so to borrowers from non-OECD countries. We find some evidence consistent with the notion that the introduction of the Basle standards has not only led to a reduction in foreign lending, but also to some substitution from non-OECD to OECD borrowers. By contrast, EU membership per se does not seem to have an impact on financial openness. However, we find some tentative evidence for a positive, if delayed impact of the implementation into national law of the Second Banking Directive.

In contrast to some prior research, a larger foreign presence in a domestic banking market does not appear to lead to improvements in industry-wide efficiency in our sample. This is consistent with earlier findings that foreign banks are often less efficient than their domestic counterparts in developed countries, but it also suggests that in OECD countries, the – fairly low – levels of foreign entry observed so far have not significantly increased competitive pressure. With respect to the regulatory environment, EU membership, if anything, appears to be associated with higher profit levels, suggesting that competitive pressures have been below average in the EU. However, we do find some limited evidence that the implementation of the Second Banking Directive has led to efforts to raise the quality of loan portfolios.

Although there are several avenues along which the empirical analysis presented in this paper could be extended and modified, there are several results which are fairly robust and which can be used to derive implications for economic policy:

First, even though substantial progress towards liberalisation of financial markets in Europe has been made and even though many direct policy-induced barriers to financial integration have been abolished, financial markets are likely to show a greater degree of segmentation than those of a national monetary union in the future. This is because there remains a substantial amount of indirect policy-induced barriers to integration such as government ownership in the financial sector and country-specific financial sector regulations which tend to favour incumbent financial institutions. Moreover, "natural", market-inherent barriers to integration will remain important that stem from differences in preferences or from information costs. This also implies that, while there certainly is scope for economic policy to further contribute to greater integration, some degree of segmentation of financial markets will remain. The Financial Services Action Plan (FSA) spells out a number of initiatives intended to further reduce information costs within the EU.[5] However, in light of the evidence on the limits to financial market integration even within a single country like the United States, expectations for significant further increases in market integration emanating from these initiatives should not be exaggerated.

Second, the persistence of barriers to the integration of financial markets has implications for macroeconomic policy. In imperfectly integrated markets, macroeconomic policies retain degrees of freedom, and regional factors are important in shaping policy decisions. While, for instance, money markets and bond markets are integrated to a considerable degree internationally, banking markets are much more segmented. Moreover, the integration of financial markets can be considered a relatively gradual process. While some forms of capital are relatively mobile internationally, the bulk of capital tends to be invested locally. This has two implications for policy-makers: On the one hand, markets for securitised financial assets punish unsustainable economic policies relatively quickly. On the other hand, policy-makers do retain quite some leverage, in particular with regard to taxing those forms of capital that cannot easily move across borders.

Third, the results of this paper also have implications for banking supervision. There has been an intensive debate in the theoretical literature focusing on the possible links between deregulation, the geographical expansion of banks' activities, and the resulting increased competitive pressure on the incumbent financial institutions. Since increased competition tends to put downward pressure on interest rate spreads, it could be argued that banks are likely to cut down on their monitoring activities and to increase their risk-taking in response to deregulation. Banking supervision, in turn, would have to respond by tightening controls and by possibly re-designing regulations.

The need to reform banking supervision may appear particularly acute in Europe not only because increased competition may make banking more risky but also because, currently, banking supervision in Europe is organised in a relatively heterogeneous way. At the same time, structural changes in the composition of the banking sector affect the effectiveness of banking supervision. On the one hand, the increasing integration of financial markets and the positive effects that deregulation has had on cross-border banking has affected the operations of many,

---

5 These include most notably the initiative to give EU companies the option to use International Accounting Standards and to enhance the comparability of financial reports issued by EU companies, the European passport for fund management companies, the initiative to establish codes for best practice with regard to the provision of information to consumers, and the initiative for enhanced disclosure of the activities of banks and other financial institutions.

notably larger banks. On the other hand, the activities of many, in particular smaller banks, remain confined to relatively small regional market niches. Hence, banking regulations must continue to take account of the fact that regional shocks will remain pervasive. Just as it is difficult to draw a clear distinction between national and international banks, the dividing line between different types of financial institutions becomes increasingly redundant. Generally, however, the expansion of banks into new fields, both geographically and by type of activity, necessitates a tighter co-ordination of banking supervision internationally. The steps in this direction spelled out in the EU Financial Services Action Plan are therefore welcome.

Fourth, banking supervisors not only have to decide how to supervise incumbent financial institutions, the degree to which foreign banks should be allowed to enter national financial markets has always been an important policy issue as well. Currently, this issue may seem of lesser importance in developed market economies, where entry has de facto been liberalised, than in emerging markets. Yet, also in developed countries, implicit barriers such as state-ownership in banking remain important deterrents to foreign entry. Notwithstanding the difficulties that all foreign banks are facing in entering a new market, superior skills and privatisation programs have drawn many foreign banks to emerging market economies. Both of these factors are much less evident when deciding to enter a banking market of a relatively mature market economy. If competition in the host country is relatively fierce already and if profit margins are relatively low accordingly, it may simply not be profitable for a bank to incur the fixed cost of entering that market. Hence, low market shares of foreign banks need not necessarily reflect a lack of competition but, quite to the contrary, might be reflecting relatively fierce competition.

References

Bakker, A.F.P. (1994), *The Liberalization of Capital Movements in Europe,* Amsterdam.

Barth, J.R., G. Caprio Jr. and R. Levine (2001), *The Regulation and Supervision of Banks Around the World: A New Database*, http://www.worldbank.org/research/projects/bank_regulation.htm

Berger, A.N. and R. DeYoung (2001), The Effects of Geographic Expansion on Bank Efficiency, *Journal of Financial Services Research*, Forthcoming.

Berger, A.N., A.K. Kashyap and J.M. Scalise (1995), The Transformation of the U.S. Banking Industry: What a Long, Strange Trip It's Been, *Brookings Papers on Economic Activity* 2, 55-218.

Berger, A.N., R. DeYoung and G.F. Udell (2001), Efficiency Barriers to the Consolidation of the European Financial Services Industry, *European Financial Management* 6, Forthcoming.

Berger, A.N., R. DeYoung, H. Genay and G.F. Udell (2000), Globalization of Financial Institutions: Evidence from Cross-Border Banking Performance, *Brookings-Wharton Papers on Financial Services* 3, 23-158.

Berger, A.N., S.D. Bonime, D.M. Covitz and D. Hancock (1999), *Why Are Bank Profits so Persistent? The Roles of Product Market Competition, Informational Opacity, and Regional/Macroeconomic Shocks*, Board of Governors of the Federal Reserve System. Washington, D.C.

Bikker, J.A. and J.M. Groeneveld (2000), Competition and Concentration in the EU Banking Industry, *Kredit und Kapital* 33 (1), 62-98.

BIS (Bank for International Settlements) (2001), *Quarterly Review: International Banking and Financial Market Developments*, Basle.

Bordo, M.D., B. Eichengreen and J. Kim (1998). *Was There Really an Earlier Period of International Financial Integration Comparable to Today?* NBER Working Paper 6738, Cambridge.

Breitung, J. (2000), The Local Power of Some Unit Root Tests for Panel Data, in: Baltagi, B. (Ed.), *Nonstationary Panels, Panel Cointegration, and Dynamic Panels,* Advances in Econometrics, Vol. 15, Amsterdam, 161-178.

Buch, C.M. (2000), *Information or Regulation: What Is Driving the International Activities of Commercial Banks?* Kiel Working Paper 1011, Kiel.

Buch, C.M. (2001), *Cross-Border Banking and Transmission Mechanisms – The Case of Europe,* Kiel Working Paper 1063, Kiel.

Buch, C.M. (2002), Financial Market Integration in the US – Lessons for Europe? *Comparative Economic Studies* (forthcoming).

Buch, C.M. and S. Lapp (2000), Bank Portfolios in Euroland, in: Moser, T. and B. Schips (Eds.). *EMU, Financial Markets, and the World Economy,* Boston.

Casu, B., and P. Molyneux (2000), *A Comparative Study of Efficiency in European Banking,* School of Accounting, Banking and Economics, University of Wales (Bangor), Mimeo.

Claessens, S., A. Demirguc-Kunt and H. Huizinga (2000), The Role of Foreign Banks in Domestic Banking Systems, in: Claessens, S. and M. Jansen (Eds.), *The Internationalization of Financial Services: Issues and Lessons for Developing Countries,* London.

Coval, J.D. and T.J. Moskowitz (1999), Home Bias at Home: Local Equity Preference in Domestic Portfolios, *The Journal of Finance* 54 (6), 2045-2073.

DeYoung, R. and D.E. Nolle (1996), Foreign-Owned Banks in the U.S.: Earning Market Share or Buying It? *Journal of Money, Credit, and Banking* 28 (4), 622-636.

ECB (European Central Bank) (1999), *Possible Effects of EMU on the EU Banking Systems in the Medium to Long Term,* Frankfurt.

ECB (European Central Bank) (2000), *Mergers and Acquisitions Involving the EU Banking Industry – Facts and Implications*, December, Frankfurt.

EU (European Commission) (1997), *Credit Institutions and Banking. The Single Market Review,* Subseries 2, Vol. 3, Office for Official Publications of the European Communities, Luxembourg.

EU (European Commission) (1999), *Implementing the Framework for Financial Services: Action Plan,* COM(1999)232, 11.05.99, Luxembourg.

EU (European Commission) (2001), *Final Report of the Committee of Wise Men on the Regulation of European Securities Markets*, Brussels, February 15.

Ghosh, S. and H. Wolf (2001), *Proximity Bias in International Capital Flow,* mimeo, The World Bank, George Washington University and National Bureau of Economic Research, Cambridge.

Grinblatt, M. and M. Keloharju (2000), *Distance, Language, and Culture Bias: The Role of Investor Sophistication,* Yale ICF Working Paper 00-04.

Hasan, I. and A. Lozano-Vivas (1998), *Foreign Banks, Production Technology, and Efficiency: Spanish Experience*, Paper presented at the Georgia Productivity Workshop III, Athens, Georgia.

IMF (International Monetary Fund) (1999a), *Balance of Payments Statistics Yearbook. Washington* D.C.

IMF (International Monetary Fund) (1999a), *Direction of Trade Statistics Yearbook*, Washington D.C.

IMF (International Monetary Fund) (1999b), *Results of the 1997 Coordinated Portfolio Investment Survey*, Washington D.C.

IMF (International Monetary Fund) (2001), *International Financial Statistics,* Washington, D.C.

Im, K.S., M.H. Pesaran and Y. Shin (1997), *Testing for Unit Roots in Heterogeneous Panels,* University of Cambridge, Revised version of the DAE Working Paper No. 9526.

Jayaratne, J., and P.E. Strahan (2000), The Effects of Entry Restrictions on Bank Performance in the United States, in: Harker, P.T. and S.A. Zenios (Eds.), *Performance of Financial Institutions: Efficiency, Innovation, Regulation,* Cambridge.

Lapp, S. (2001). Das Anlageverhalten deutscher Investoren, Kiel University, Dissertation, mimeo.

Levin, A. and C.-F. Lin (1993), *Unit Root Tests in Panel Data: Asymptotic and Finite-Sample Properties. University of California San Diego,* Unpublished Working Paper (revised).

Mahajan, A., N. Rangan and A. Zardkoohi (1996), Cost Structures in Multinational and Domestic Banking, *Journal of Banking and Finance* 20 (2), 238-306.

Miller, S.R. and A. Parkhe (1999), *Home-Country Environment as a Source of International Competitiveness: An Analysis of the Global Banking Industry,* Michigan State University, East Lansing.

Molyneux, P., D.M. Lloyd-Williams and J. Thornton (1994), Competitive Conditions in European Banking, *Journal of Banking and Finance* 18 (3), 445-459.

OECD (Organisation for Economic Cooperation and Development) (2000), *International Direct Investments* (CD-Rom), Paris.

OECD (Organisation for Economic Cooperation and Development) (2001). *Bank Profitability – Financial Statements of Banks* (CD-Rom), Paris.

Parkhe, A. and S.R. Miller (1999), *Is There a Liability of Foreignness in Global Banking ? An Empirical Test of U.S. Banks' X-Efficiency,* Michigan State University, East Lansing.

Pastor, J.T., A. Lozano-Vicas and I. Hasan (2000), *Cross-Border Performance in European Banking,* New York University Salomon Center, Working paper S-00-14, New York.

Portes, R. and H. Rey (2001), *The Determinants of Cross-Border Equity Flows: The Geography of Information*, Princeton University and CEPR, mimeo.

Rhoades, S.A. (1997), Research on IO Topics in Banking: An Introduction and Overview. *Review of Industrial Organization* 12, 1-8.

Taylor, A.M. (1996), *International Capital Mobility in History: The Savings-Investment Relationship*, NBER Working Paper 5743, Cambridge.

The World Bank (2001), *Financial Structure and Economic Development Database,* http://www.worldbank.org/research/interest/data.htm

Vander Vennet, R. (1996), The Effects of Mergers and Acquisitions on the Efficiency and Profitability of EC Credit Institutions, *Journal of Banking and Finance* 20 (9), 1531-1558.

Market Access Strategies in the EU Banking Sector – Obstacles and Benefits Towards an Integrated European Retail Market

Carsten Eppendorfer, Rainer Beckmann and Markus Neimke*

Ruhr-Universität Bochum, Germany

1 Introduction

Over the last years, competition in the European banking sector has intensified considerably. The following factors have been decisive for that evolution: the *liberalisation* of the European financial sector, *technological progress* as well as an amplified *diversification of savings and assets*. The introduction of the Euro goes along with an accelerated integration of the market for financial services and leads to a further increase in competition and structural changes in the banking sector (Deutsche Bundesbank, 1999, Galati and Tsatsaronis, 2001). However, timeframe and depth of this structural change vary noticeably between the different sections of European banking. While the money market and the market for wholesale products (wholesale banking) already form a common European market, there still is an extensive segmentation of national markets for retail products (retail banking). Responsible for this low degree of integration in retail markets are a number of *natural barriers,* such as language or culture, as well as *politically induced* market access *barriers* such as regulations or taxation, which make cross-border trade in financial services more difficult (ECB, 1999a). Further deregulation and harmonisation towards an integrated European retail market are suitable to increase customer benefits by fostering product diversification and lower prices.

Within the framework of this study, firstly, different market access strategies of the banking sector are systematised. Then it is analysed, to which extent different strategies contribute to the integration of European retail markets. By examining the banks *Banco Santander Central Hispano* (Spain), *Nordea Group* (Sweden), *BNP Paribas* (France), as well as *HSBC* (England), market access strategies of four European top banks are illustrated in case studies. Secondly, motives, problems as well as consequences accompanied with these strategies are discussed. Thirdly, it is examined in detail which politically induced market access barriers

* Acknowledgement: We thank Prof. K.-O. Hammarkvist, Stockholm and Julien Carmona, Paris for valuable information and comments.

currently complicate cross-border trade in financial services and which steps towards a further harmonisation and integration are taken on EU level. Finally, consumer benefits of a future integration of European retail markets are discussed briefly.

2 Importance of Different Market Access Strategies

Basically, the variety of market access strategies in the banking sector can be summarised under four main headings. *Direct cross-border sales* mean trade of financial services without any physical presence of banks in target markets. This category comprises telephone banking, conventional mail marketing and, in particular, internet banking. The second strategy is the establishment of *branches* or *subsidiaries* in the target country. *Mergers* and *acquisitions* (M&As) constitute the third strategy (ECB, 1999a). These are usually followed by considerable modifications in the organisational and legal structure of the respective companies. Finally, market access can be achieved by *co-operations* and *strategic alliances*. Here, it is decisive that there is only a minority stake.

Direct Cross-Border Sales

Different market access strategies in the banking sector differ in the extent of their contribution to the integration of European retail markets. A low contribution is achieved by direct cross-border sales of financial services. Merely 2.8% of all credits to private non-banks occurred in 1999 were in the "cross-border" category. Their growth rate of 23.5%, however, appeared higher than the growth rate of domestic credits, which was 9.2% (ECB, 2000a).

Branches and Subsidiaries

The market share of foreign branches and subsidiaries (Table 1) – measured in relation to total bank assets – in 1997 was less than 10%. Merely 3.4% in European mean applied to branches. Higher market shares occurred only in Belgium (28.2%), Ireland (45.4%) as well as in Luxembourg (90.9%). The small market share of foreign branches and subsidiaries confirms the assumption that banking operations in Europe concentrate on domestic markets to a considerable extent (ECB, 1999a and ECB, 1999b). Up to now, the "Freedom of establishment" for branches in Europe also had no essential impulse on further integration.

Mergers and Acquisitions

Since the beginning of the 1990s, a substantial consolidation process within the banking sector can be observed. In particular, *mergers* and *acquisitions* led to a decreased number of banking institutions all over Europe. The amount of *mergers* and *acquisitions* in the European banking sector in 1997 was about 280, compared to 440 in 1999. In the same period, the aver age value of *mergers* and *acquisitions* tripled from 200 to 600 million Euro (ECB, 2000a and ECB, 2000b).

Table 1: Market share of foreign branches and subsidiaries from Europe in 1997 (as a percentage of total domestic assets)

	Austria	**Belgium**	**Finland**	**France**	**Germany**	**Greece**	**Ireland**	**Italy**	**Luxembourg**	**Netherlands**	**Portugal**	**Sweden**	**Spain**	**UK**	**EU**
Market share of foreign branches	0.7	9.0	7.1		0.9	11.1	17.7	3.6	19.4	2.3	2.5	1.3	4.8	22.5	3.4
Market share of foreign subsidiaries	1.6	19.2	--	n.a.	1.4	1.8	27.8	1.7	71.1	3.0	6.8	--	3.4	1.0	n.a.
Market share of total foreign branches and subsidiaries	**2.3**	**28.2**	**7.1**		**2.4**	**13.0**	**45.4**	**5.3**	**90.9**	**5.3**	**9.4**	**1.3**	**8.2**	**23.4**	**n.a.**

Source: ECB (1999a) and ECB (1999b).

Up to now, however, the consolidation process concerned to a large extent the respective domestic market. In 1999, merely 19.5% of mergers and acquisitions within the European banking sector occurred cross-border, which means an increase in comparison to the 1997 figure of 16% (OECD, 2001). Also taking into consideration cross-border mergers and acquisitions with *non*-European countries, the share is noticeably higher. This higher share is in particular attributed to the entry of European banks in *Emerging Markets* (ECB, 2000b). The trend of entering foreign markets by mergers and acquisitions to increase one's own market share still seems to intensify. The trend is accompanied by an increasing number of *co-operations* and *strategic alliances*. In comparison to other entry strategies, mergers and acquisitions seem to contribute most significantly to the integration of European retail markets in the future. The appendix shows the most important mergers and acquisitions within the European banking sector since the introduction of the Euro.

In addition to mergers and acquisitions within the banking sector, a number of cross-industry mergers and acquisitions involving banks can also be observed (*conglomerates*). In particular, large banks diversify their business fields with the objective of reaching broad market coverage in financial services (*one-stop finance*) (Willman, 2000a). Not only capital investment companies (e.g. fund companies), but also insurance companies are the target objects of mergers and acquisitions in the banking sector. Up to now, however, mergers and acquisitions mainly were carried out within the banking sector. The share of domestic and cross-border conglomerates amounts to only 23% of all mergers and acquisitions with banking companies in the 1990s (OECD, 2001). An overview of the main types of M&A is given in Table 2.

Table 2: Main types of European M&As in the banking industry

	Within banking industry	Cross industry
Within border	**Domestic bank M&As** M&As involving credit institutions located in the same country. Examples: • Banco Santander/Banco Central Hispanoamericano (1999) • BNP/Paribas (1999) The most dominant type of M&As in the European banking industry: 60.7% of all European banking M&A transactions between 1990 and 1999 took place within the domestic banking industry (1990: 44%, 1995: 45.8%, 1999: 61.4%)	**Domestic conglomeration** M&As involving credit institutions and insurances and/or other financial institutions all located in the same country. Examples: • Credit Suisse/Winterthur (1997) • Citicorp/Travelers Group (1998) Less dominant than domestic M&As within the banking industry: 16.1% of all banking M&A transactions between 1990 and 1999 were domestic cross-industry transactions; after an increase in the mid-nineties (1990: 16%, 1995: 22.9%, 1999: 12.5%) there have been declining shares in the last years.
Cross-border	**International bank M&As** M&As involving credit institutions located in different countries, one of which is an EU country. Examples: • Deutsche Bank/Bankers Trust (1998) • HypoVereinsbank/Bank Austria (2000) • Nordea Group (2000) Less dominant than domestic bank M&As but the most increasing type of M&As involving the banking industry: 16.1% of all banking M&A transactions between 1990 and 1999 were cross-border bank M&As (1990: 30%, 1991: 10%, 1993: 10.8%, 1995: 20.1%, 1999: 19.5%)	**International conglomeration** M&As involving credit institutions located in an EU country and insurances and/or other financial institutions located in another EU or third country. Examples: • Deutsche Bank/Morgan Grenfell (1997) • Dresdner Bank/Kleinwort Benson (1995) Less dominant type of European M&A transactions in recent years and at present: 7.1% of all transactions involving the European banking industry between 1990 and 1999 were international cross-industry transactions; after increasing shares in the mid- 1990s (1990: 8%, 1995: 11.2%) there has been a decline during the last years (1997: 9.6%, 1998: 8.5%, 1999: 6.5%).

Sources: Following ECB (2000b) and OECD (2001).

Prospect of Future Relative Importance of Strategies

There are different assessments of the *future* importance of the various market access strategies with respect to the integration of the European retail market. However, there seems to be consensus with regard to the fundamental tendencies. For instance, *direct cross-border sales* of financial services – for example by internet – seems to be limited in spite of technological progress. In particular, different product definitions or missing proximity to customers are responsible here (Haberer, 1993 and Schüler, 2002).

The expansion of a new *branch network* abroad remains unattractive for financial reasons (fixed costs), because of existing overcapacities as well as due to new sale technologies (Crowder, 1999; The Economist, 1998; Ackermann, 1998 and Haberer, 1993). Furthermore, such "greenfield" investments are accompanied by high time exposures – not only concerning the setup of new brand names. Yields occur with a considerable time lag, which counteracts the interests of shareholders.

Presumably, *mergers* and *acquisitions* will represent the most important market access strategy in the future, too. However, due to disproportionate risks, a noticeable increase of cross-border mergers and acquisitions will not occur until consolidation on the domestic market has been completed (Nairn, 2000). In this context, *co-operations* and *alliances* are taken as a strategy which is accompanied by lower risks. In particular, co-operations and alliances provide access to the distribution channels of foreign partners. While the trend to diversification in the field of large banks (*one-stop finance*) will be continuing, small and medium banks will increasingly specialise regionally and by the products offered and will unwind most parts of small customer business. For this reason, long-term integration of European retail markets seems to be limited – against the background of an extensive integration of money markets and wholesale markets (ECB, 1999a). Last but not least, the share of retail business by banks is regressive due to increasing disintermediation. An increasing importance of retail banking is only expected in the markets of Eastern Europe.

3 Case Studies

After the analysis of their macroeconomic importance we now examine different market access strategies of European banks within the framework of case studies of individual enterprises. For this purpose, market access strategies of *Banco Santander Central Hispano (BSCH),* with their head offices in Spain, *Nordea Group*, headquartered in Sweden, *BNP Paribas* (France), as well as the *HSBC,* with head offices in England, are analysed.

Banco Santander Central Hispano

Banco Santander Central Hispano (BSCH) is among the ten largest European banks, with a market capitalisation of EUR 47 billion (2001) and 126,000 employees world-wide (Table 3). The market access strategies pursued by BSCH comprise direct cross-border sales, the foundation of branches, as well as mergers and acquisitions. For the purpose of direct sales of financial services, the group set up the European Internet Bank *Patagon* as well as the phone bank *Santander Direkt*. The world-wide branch network currently contains 10,800 branches in 42 countries. Mergers and acquisitions can be classified as the most important market access strategy of the BSCH within Europe. A cross-border expansion took place here particularly in the Portuguese, the German as well as in the Italian market. Mergers and acquisitions were complemented through the exchange of know-how with various European partners in the form of co-operations and strategic alliances. Offering a wide range of products through various channels of distribution can be considered as a goal of BSCH's market access strategy. The internet will take an important position in the future sales of financial services (BSCH, 2001).

Nordea Group

The merger of Merita (Fin) and Nordbanken (Swe) in 1998 was the first cross-border merger of two European top banks of the same size (Table 4). The consortium expanded in 2000 by the merger of MeritaNordbanken and Unidanmark (DK). After an acquisition of Christiania Bank og Kreditkasse (Nor) was rejected first by the Norwegian government, in 2000 MeritaNordbanken, Unidanmark and Christiania Bank og Kreditkasse finally formed Nordea Group, which represents the largest bank consortium in Northern Europe, with a market capitalisation of approx. EUR 20 billion (2001), 1,481 branches and 37,630 employees. The main motives to form Nordea were different kinds of synergies (e.g. economies of scale and scope) as well as an increased market share in the Nordic market, including also Estonia, Latvia, Lithuania and Poland. Nordea Group pursues a multi-channel distribution strategy that contains one of the most successful phone (e.g. WAP banking in co-operation with Nokia) and internet services of the world, offering almost complete services of the Nordea Group. The cross-industry merger of Unidanmark and the insurer Tryg-Baltica (DK) forced the selling of insurance products (household and general insurance), too (one-stop finance). Using a multi-channel distribution strategy, e.g. the common internet bank (Solo Internet Bank), existing barriers to market access ought to be bypassed. In the context of politically induced barriers to market access, especially different national supervision institutions, different consumer protection rules (e.g. different deposit guaranty systems or cross-border management of bank secrets) and different national tax legislation (e.g. Denmark) are mentioned by Nordea Group.

Table 3: Market access strategy of Banco Santander Central Hispano (BSCH)

General company data	• One of the European top-10 banks (€ 47 bn market capitalisation per 31 March 2001); • More than 10,800 branches in 42 countries; • More than 126,000 employees world wide;			
Pan-European strategy	• Joint ventures and exchange of expertise with large European partners, e.g. by co-operations and strategic cross-border alliances with Société Générale (F), Royal Bank of Scotland (GB), San Paolo-IMI (I) and Commerzbank (Ger); • Creation of the pan-European Internet bank Patagon.com; • Expansion of Patagon in Latin America (planned);			
Recent cross-border expansion activities				
Target countries	Portugal	Germany	Italy	Spain
Date of first entry	1993	1995	1998	1999
Entry method	1993: Acquisition of Banco de Comércio e Indústria and change of brand to Banco Santander Portugal in 1998; 1999: Acquisition of Banco Totta & Açores and Crédito Predial Portugues;	Acquisition of CC-Bank by Banco Santander; Setting up of the subsidiary Santander Direkt Bank (telephone bank) by Banco Santander; Integration of the operations of Open Bank (acquired by Patagon.com) and Santander Direkt Bank under the Patagon.com brand (planned);	Co-ownership of Finconsumo (acquisition of 50% by BSCH);	Acquisition of Banesto; Domestic Merger of Banco Santander and Banco Central Hispanoamerica with brand BSCH (but no full consolidation of operations);
Products offered	Full banking service	Full banking service	Loans and credit	Full banking service
Distribution channel	Multi-channel	Mainly direct via telephone- or online-banking	Multi-channel	Multi-channel

Source: Following Datamonitor (2000) and BSCH (2001).

Last but not least, Nordea Group could strongly contribute to the integration of financial services market in Northern Europe due to the smaller cultural and social differences between the northern in comparison to the southern countries in Europe. However, after the consolidation process is completed and all synergies are realised, further expansion, following real trading patterns with direction south (e.g. Germany, Netherlands) is the natural way to go (Nordea, 2001).

BNP Paribas

BNP Paribas (F) is among the ten largest European banks, with a market capitalisation of EUR 41.9 billion (2001) and 80,000 employees world-wide (Table 5). BNP Paribas was formed by a domestic merger of BNP (F) and Paribas (F) in 2000. In the 1980s, Paribas entered the Spanish market by establishing a new branch net. These branches were sold in 2000 due to high fixed costs against the background of a relatively low market share. For the same reason Paribas sold its branches in Belgium and the Netherlands in 1997. Currently, BNP Paribas only in France operates through a branch net of its own. Cross-border distribution predominantly is conducted through branches of European partners. For instance, market access to Germany was obtained by a joint venture of BNP Paribas and Dresdner Bank in 2000.

Furthermore BNP Paribas distributes retail products via the subsidiaries *Cardif* (bank insurer) and *Cetelem* (consumer bank). Cardif predominantly sells through branches (direct marketing or telemarketing) of pan-European partners (banks, finance companies, commercial firms and insurers). In France Cardif co-operates with *Crédit du Nord*, *Banque Directe*, *Banque Hervet* as well as *Cartol*. Cetelem distributes a complete range of financial products through branches of foreign partners (co-operations and alliances with retail banks and financial institutions) such as *Savings Bank of Florence* (Ita), *Caixa Galicia* (Spa) *Dresdner Bank* (Ger) and others. Via partnerships with *Ikea*, *Carrefour* or *Conforama* Cetelem also conducts point-of-sale finance. A further pan-European strategy comprises the constitution of product specialists (e.g. for online brokerage or mortgages), who co-operate with partners abroad. These different kinds of co-operations and alliances are suited to bypass barriers to market access. Here in particular different national tax legislation or accounting standards, as well as different consumer protection regulations are noted by BNP Paribas (BNP Paribas, 2001).

Table 4: Market access strategy of Nordea Group

General company data	• MeritaNordbanken, Unidanmark and Christania Bank form the Nordic financial group Nordea (almost € 20 bn market capitalisation per August 2001); • Nordea Group has a strong distribution network throughout the Nordic and Baltic Sea region which comprises 1,481 branch offices or Internet-service centres with 37,630 employees; • Nordea is present in 22 countries including 14 countries outside the Nordic and Baltic Sea region;			
Pan-European strategy	• "One-bank-shopping-concept": to provide a single point of entry for customers to enable them to get access to the entire supply of services of all integrated banks; single brand Nordea for all banks from December 2001; • Branches network in the Nordic region, representative offices and co-operation with local banks in the most important European cities and countries; • Integrated Internet-banking: Solo as a full-service Internet bank;			
Recent expansion activities				
Target countries	Finland and Sweden	Denmark	Norway	Sweden
Date of first entry	1998	2000	2000	2001
Entry method	Merger between Merita (Fin) and Nordbanken (S) into MeritaNordbanken with Nordic Baltic Holding as the bank's holding company;	Acquisition of Unidanmark by MeritaNordbanken;	Acquisition of Christiania Bank og Kreditkasse to form Nordea Group;	Acquisition of Postgirot (Swe) by Nordea;
	– **2000**: Integration of Christiania Bank og Kreditkasse (K-Bank) (Nor), Merita Bank (Fin), Nordbanken (Swe) and Unidanmark (DK) into **Nordea Group**;			
Products offered	• Allfinance (incl. lifeinsurance products in all Nordic countries and non lifeinsurance products in Norway, Denmark and Finland) • Cross-selling potential due to the integration into Nordea			
Distribution channel	Multi-channel (branches, telephone, internet)			

Source: Following Datamonitor (2000) and Nordea (2001).

HSBC

With 23 million customers and approx. 6,500 offices in 78 countries, *HSBC* is one of the largest providers of financial services in the world (Table 6).

HSBC started as a colonial bank in Hong Kong from where the company expanded to Asia and the rest of the world. On the European market, HSBC was represented noticeably only in England for a long time. Market shares in Luxembourg, Spain and France were low. With the take-over of *CCF* in 2000, the enterprise gave up its strategy of organic growth and acquired large market shares in France. While in England HSBC concentrates on mass market, the take-over of CCF targets personal asset management of customers in the middle and upper wealth bracket. The joint venture of HSBC and Merrill Lynch marks the first connection of this kind world-wide. The offer of Merrill Lynch-HSBC contains broker as well as retail services, whereby all services are offered exclusively over the internet (HSBC, 2001).

Table 5: Market access strategy of BNP Paribas

General company data	• One of the European top-10 banks (market capitalisation at 31 Dec 2000: € 41.9 bn; • Operations in 87 countries in Europe, Asia and United States; • 80,000 employees, including 61,000 in Europe, including 49,000 in France; • Network of 2,200 branches in France, 13.1 million retail customers in the EU;			
Pan-European strategy	• Set-up of Multichannel Bank; • Cross-selling between the various business units and with other divisions of the Group;			
Recent expansion activities				
Target countries	France	Germany	Spain	Pan-European
Date of first entry	2000	2000	1980's	1990s
Entry method	Merger between BNP and Paribas to create BNP Paribas; 1998 merger between Compagnie Financière de Paribas, Banque Paribas and Compagnie Bancaire to form Paribas; 1993 Privatisation of BNP	Joint venture between BNP Paribas and Dresdner Bank	Establishing a branch network (sold in 2000)	Different market access strategies (e.g. "Cardif-model", "Cetelem-model")
Products offered	Full banking service	Consumer finance	Private Banking (only wealthy customers)	Full banking service
Distribution channel	Multi-channel	Multi-channel	Traditional	Multi-channel

Source: BNP Paribas (2001).

Table 6: Market access strategy of HSBC

General company data	• One of the European top-10 banks (more than € 125 bn market capitalisation per August 2001); • 6,500 offices in 78 countries;				
Pan-European strategy	• Global online banking and investment services: creation of the Merrill Lynch-HSBC online bank; • Focus on private banking business; • Focus on expansion by organic growth complemented with strategic acquisitions;				
Recent expansion activities					
Target countries	Luxembourg	Spain	United Kingdom	France	Greece
Date of first entry	1977	1982	1992	1881	2001
Entry method	Independent start-up (HSBC Luxembourg)	Independent start-up (HSBC Spain);	Midland Bank becomes wholly owned member of the HSBC Group; Midland bank was renamed HSBC bank in 1999; 2000: partnership with Merrill Lynch to create a global online banking and investment services company (Merrill Lynch-HSCB);	2000: Acquisition of Crédit Commercial de France (CCF);	Acquisition of the Barclays branches;
Products offered	Private banking with focus on wealthy customers		Full banking service	Private banking with a more comprehensive product range than in other countries	Private banking
Distribution channel	Traditional		Multi-channel		Traditional

Source: Following Datamonitor (2000) and HSBC (2001).

4 What Can We Learn from These Case Studies?

From the viewpoint of individual enterprises, the cases of *Banco Santander Central Hispano*, *Nordea Group*, *BNP Paribas* as well as *HSCB* clarify which important role mergers and acquisitions play within the integration of European retail markets. The case studies confirm the macroeconomic observation on the different importance of varying strategies to market access. All of the examined banks pursue multi-channel distribution strategies. However, important cross-border market shares are predominantly acquired by mergers and acquisitions (e.g. acquisition of *CCF* by *HSBC*, merger of *Merita* and *Nordbanken*) as well as co-operations and alliances (e.g. *BNP Paribas*). In addition, particularly the foundation of telephone and internet banks (e.g. *Patagon*, *Santander Direkt Bank*, *Solo Internet Bank* or *Merrill Lynch-HSBC*) are of increasing importance. A considerable technical progress with regard to communication technologies accelerates this development. The foundation of branches or subsidiaries is – for the reasons mentioned above (fixed costs, problems in establishing new brand names, yields with significant time lags) – of no considerable future importance. The example of *BNP Paribas* demonstrates, that there is even a trend to decrease the number of branches.

As mergers and acquisitions is the most important strategy the motives and risks accompanied by different forms of mergers and acquisitions are summarised in Table 7. Economies of scale and economies of scope are regarded as the most important *motives* for the execution of mergers and acquisitions. In addition to these cost-sided arguments, higher market shares as well as product and risk diversity are particularly important (Nairn, 2000).

Risks result in particular from the integration of different enterprise cultures and business fields. Furthermore general factors affecting all companies include risks and represent barriers to market entry. For instance, "*natural barriers*" such as different cultures or different consumer preferences are of high relevance, as are "*politically induced barriers*" such as different national tax-legislation or different regulations (Buch, 2001). Due to low natural barriers *Nordea Group* became the largest bank consortium in Northern Europe, and likewise *Banco Santander Central Hispano* strongly expanded only in Southern Europe (Nairn, 2000). Because of different politically induced barriers to market access, all of the examined banks follow a multi-channel strategy in cross-border trade (e.g. *BNP Paribas*). However, politically induced barriers of market access are often responsible for the failure of market access (ECB, 2000a).

Table 7: Motives and risks with four types of Mergers & Acquisitions (M&As)

	Within banking industry	Cross industry
Within border	**Domestic bank M&As** Main motives: • Cost benefits from economies of scale, e.g. • by reduction of surplus staff and overlapping branches or mutual use of administrative functions; • Increasing market share; Main risks: • Pricing of the strategic risks; • Operational risks after the transaction, mainly related to the integration of personnel, information and risk management, customer and account systems etc.	**Domestic conglomeration** Main motives: • Cost benefits from economies of scope through cross-selling; • Revenue enhancement due to product diversification; • Risk diversification; Main risks: • Increased ex ante risks because of different business area; • Reputation risks (failure of one company may lead to declining reputation of the whole conglomerate); • Increased integration difficulties due to different fiscal and accounting treatment etc.
Cross-border	**International bank M&As** Main motives • Achieving access and presence in an international market with a larger customer base (market share); • Possibility of reaching the critical mass to offer specific services; Main risks: • Increased ex ante risks because of cultural barriers or differences (unknown market, regulations and practices); • Different fiscal and accounting treatment and reporting requirements.	**International conglomeration** Main motives: • Cost benefits from economies of scope through cross-selling; • Access and presence in international financial markets; • International product diversification; Main risks: • Increased ex ante risks due to a different business area; • Different fiscal and accounting treatment and reporting requirements; • Reputation risks.

Source: Following ECB (2000b).

Table 8 shows cases of withdrawn mergers and acquisitions. As can be seen in addition to *disagreements* of the involved parties, rejection by *governments* or *regulatory institutions* as well as *regulatory uncertainties* often prevent successful market access.

Table 8: Withdrawn M&As in the banking industry

Year	Involved banks		Reasons for failure
1999	Bank of Ireland (Irl)	Alliance and Leicester (UK)	Disagreements of the involved parties;
1999	BNP (Fra)	Société Générale (Fra)	Rejection by French banking regulators
2000	Dresdner Bank (Ger)	Deutsche Bank (Ger)	The Dresdner Bank broke off the merger talks due to Deutsche Bank's insistence that Dresdner sell off its investment bank Kleinwort Benson in whole or in pieces;
2001	Unicredito (Ita)	Commerzbank (Ger)	Disagreement on valuation and price of the transaction;
2001	SEB (Swe)	Föreningsspar-banken (Swed-bank) (Swe)	Rejection by the European Commission due to objections with regard to antitrust law;
2001	UnoFirst (created out of merger of Enba's (parent company of Irish Internet-only bank First-e) (IRL) and BBVA's (UK) internet subsidiaries)		Collapse due to some disagreements with respect to ownership of the tech-nology, regulatory uncertainty, the sharp fall in high-tech stocks and a reassessment of the short-term potential of Internet banks (according to *Busi-ness&Finance online*);

Sources: Financial Times Deutschland (2001a), Financial Times Deutschland (2001b), Business&Finance (2001) and BBC News (2001).

Beyond the case studies, empirical evidence with regard to different barriers to market access, stems from Questioning of leading Pan-European Banking Groups conducted in 2001 (Figure 1). Natural obstacles like language or consumer preferences noticeably hinder market access. In contrast market infrastructure or market attractiveness seem to be of minor relevance. Within the politically induced barriers especially different tax legislation seems to be of particular importance. Both, tax legislation and regulations specific to each country represent – with different levels of importance – the most important obstacles for all of the above-mentioned market access strategies of banks and thus to the integration of European retail markets. Furthermore, politically induced barriers – unlike natural barriers – can be removed by political decisions to increase the potential of future *integration* and consumer *benefits*. Therefore, politically induced barriers are now discussed in more detail.

Figure 1: Relevance of different barriers to market access in regard to retail bank products

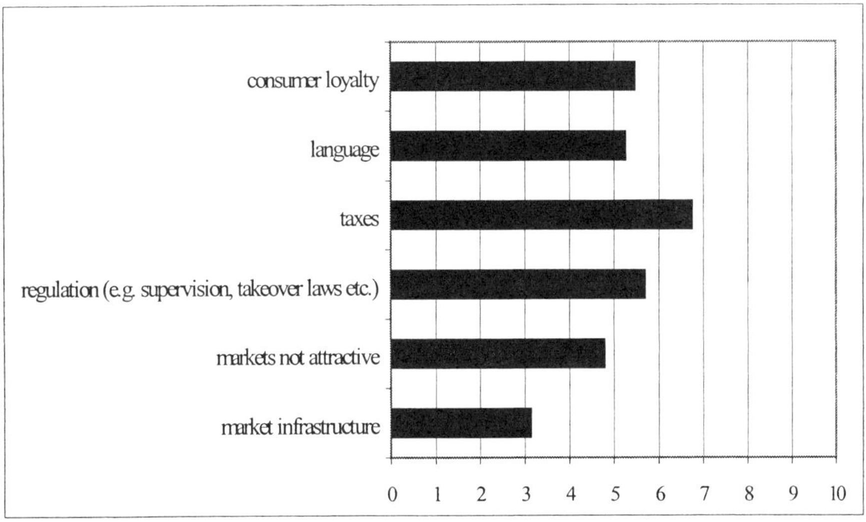

The importance of different barriers is measured by using a scale from 10 (highly relevant) to 1 (no relevance at all). Source: Questioning of leading Pan-European Banking Groups (2001).

5 Politically Induced Barriers of Cross-Border Bank Activities

Legal regulation with the purpose of creating a common European market for financial services of the banking sector are based on a line of decisions and directives of the last thirty years (Figure 2). In addition to the "Freedom of establishment", arrangements relating to bank supervision are of considerable importance with regard to market access decisions of banks. Bank supervision is based on two elements: firstly, on *national responsibility* (principles of supervision by the home country and the mutual recognition of admission), and secondly, on the *cross-border co-operation* of national supervisory institutions. Furthermore, a *minimum harmonisation* of regulations should be guaranteed (ECB, 2000a).

Figure 2: EU Financial Services Directives (Single Market Program)

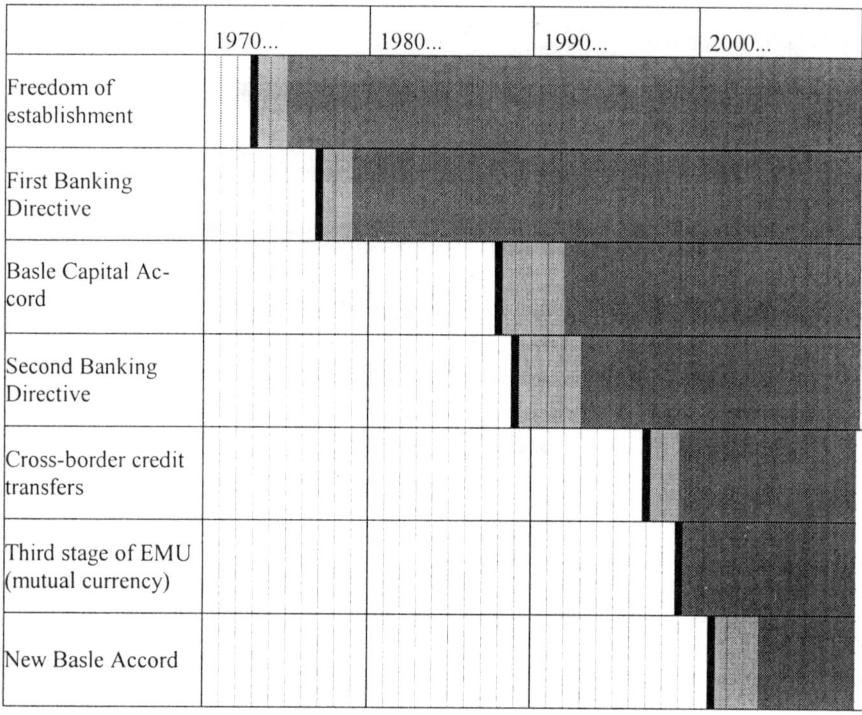

Source: EU (2001a) and EU (2001b).

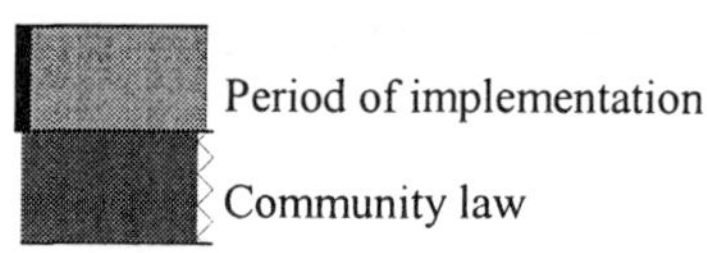

Since 1999, the European Union is improving the general conditions for further integration of the market for financial services within the framework of the "Financial Services Action Plan (FSAP)". In addition to the retail and wholesale market, measures also concern the position of the European financial market in relation to non-European financial markets. An overview is given in Table 9.

Table 9: Objectives of the Financial Services Action Plan (FSAP)

Strategic objective	Actions in order to achieve the strategic objective are needed to ...
A single EU wholesale market	• enable corporate issuers to raise capital on competitive terms on an EU-wide basis; • provide investors and intermediaries with access to all markets from a single point-of-entry; • allow investment service providers to offer their services cross-border without encountering unnecessary obstacles or administrative or legal barriers; • to establish a sound and well integrated prudential framework within which asset managers can put funds at their disposal to their most productive use; • create a legal certainty so that securities trades and settlement are safe from unnecessary counterparty risk;
Open and secure retail markets	• equip consumers with the necessary information and clear rights to permit their full and active participation in the single financial market; • identify and counteract unjustified insistence on non-harmonised consumer-business rules as an obstacle to cross-border provision of services; • create legal conditions in which new distribution channels and distance technologies can be put to work on a pan-European scale; • encourage the emergence of cost-effective and secure payment systems which enable citizens to effect small-value cross-border payments without incurring exorbitant charges;
State-of-art prudential rules and supervision	• eliminate any gaps in EU prudential framework, arising from new forms of financial business or globalisation; • set rigorous and appropriate standards so that the EU banking sector can successfully manage intensification of competitive pressures; • enable the EU to assume a key role in setting high global standards for regulation and supervision, including financial conglomerates;
Wider conditions for an optimal single financial market	• eliminate disparities in tax treatment • create an efficient and transparent legal system for corporate governance

Source: Following Europäische Kommission (1999) and European Commission (2001).

From the perspective of European banks, however, there is still a line of obstacles which hinders cross-border trade in financial services (Questioning of leading pan-European banking groups, 2001 (Figure 1) and Schröder, 2001). For instance, the principle of mutual recognition often is not applied in practice. Although the supervision by the home country is valid for foreign branches, solvency control, for instance, is under the supervision of the host country. This makes expansion of a branch network abroad complicated. The strategies of *Banco Santander Central Hispano*, *Nordea Group*, *HSBC* and especially of *BNP Paribas* confirm the problems of creating a branch network abroad.

Furthermore – as stated e.g. by *BNP Paribas* – consumer protection regulations differ within European countries. For cross-border sales of financial services, this calls for compliance to additional requirements in the respective countries. Additional information costs arise and thus hinder cross-border sales – for example via internet – especially of small and medium-sized enterprises. Such obstacles are often used to protect domestic markets. In contrast, large enterprises – as shown in the cases of *Nordea Group* (Solo Internet Bank) as well as *HSBC* (*Merrill Lynch-HSBC*) – use the internet to bypass certain barriers to market access. Different national supervision practice (different competences of the respective national institution as well as different reporting requirements for companies) set up such barriers – in particular with regard to cross-border mergers and acquisitions. Neutrality of competition is not guaranteed. In the long run, harmonisation in the form of a single European supervisory institution for all kinds of financial services possibly could become advisable (ECB, 2000a and Schröder, 2001).

In addition to these regulative obstacles, different national tax legislation and other legal differences represent market access barriers (Questioning of leading pan-European banking groups, 2001, Figure 1). For instance, credit collaterals are evaluated differently among European countries, hindering the allocation of cross-border credits. Mergers and acquisitions as the most important strategy of banks examined in this study can be seen as a way to deal with that kind of barrier. In addition, different national accounting standards for companies, bankruptcy principles and take-over arrangements obstruct market access by mergers and acquisitions. A common European take-over directive failed in the EU-parliament in 2001 (Table 10). Due to an uncommon take-over legislation as well as missing harmonisation of company and taxation legislation, a trend towards co-operations, strategic alliances as well as joint ventures – e.g. *BSCH* with *Société Générale* (F), *Royal Bank of Scotland* (GB), *San Paolo-IMI* (I) and *Commerzbank* (D) or *BNP Paribas* with *Dresdner Bank* (D) – can be recognised. Further harmonisation and a stronger institutional co-ordination of these politically induced market access barriers are useful to accelerate the integration of retail markets in Europe and to achieve further consumer benefits.

Table 10: Take-Over Directive (turned down by European Parliament on 04.07.2001)

Motivation and objectives	• a minimum level of protection for minority shareholders of companies subject to take-over bids which is equivalent throughout the EU; • a basic level of disclosure and information to guarantee greater transparency during the take-over bid
Proponents and their arguments	• British, Danish, French and Swedish MEPs (Members of European Parliament) generally supported the directive; • they argued that this directive would have made the European corporate sector more dynamic and fairer by requiring shareholders' support before companies took steps to fight off take-over bids, thus facilitating hostile take-overs;
Critics and their arguments	• German MEPs in particular, but also Italian and Spanish MEPs were against the directive; • they argued that there was no effective possibility for management of the target company to place defensive measures to frustrate a bid without consulting their shareholders; • they further argued that this directive did not secure a level playing field for shareholder rights in the EU (there are for example 'Golden Shares' with special rights to vote in some European countries) with competitive disadvantages possibly arising for some European countries;
Follow-up	• according to the European Commission a new version of the directive is unlikely to be ready before 2002.

Source: Union Network International (2001).

6 Consumer Benefits of an Integrated European Retail Market

The integration of the European retail markets is associated with a number of benefits for consumers. From a macroeconomic point of view, the integration first leads to an accelerated development of financial markets (Buch, 2000 and Lemmen, 1998). Through different channels of transmission, the development of financial markets has positive effects on growth in a second step. Important channels in this context are an improved allocation of savings capital as well as the reduction of losses of saving capital. In addition, higher national income and increasing growth also lead to a decreasing rate of unemployment (Neimke, Eppendorfer and Beckmann, 2002).

Table 11: Price changes for corporate and retail customer deposits since the full implementation of the Single Market Program (1992-1997)

Country / **Product area**	**Belgium**	**Denmark**	**France**	**Germany**	**Greece**	**Ireland**	**Italy**	**Netherlands**	**Portugal**	**Spain**	**United Kingdom**	**EU**
Corporate customer deposits (large firms)	-27	-18	-42	-31	-28	-40	-11	-22	-29	-26	-21	**-25**
Corporate customer deposits (small firms)	-27	-13	-35	-29	-30	-37	-8	-30	-30	-29	-19	**-24**
Retail customer deposits	-27	-31	-35	-30	-30	-37	-4	-32	-25	-28	-11	**-23**

Price defined as margin between rate paid to customer and money market rate (Changes in margin due to business cycle effects excluded): -50 is 'large decrease', -25 is 'small decrease', 0 is 'no change', 25 is 'small increase', and 50 is 'large increase', Source: European Commission (1997).

From the consumers' point of view, increasing integration can be expected to have positive effects on prices, product variety and the quality of services. Stronger competition in the banking sector and lower operating costs conditional on new information and communication technologies go along with stronger price pressure on financial services. Interests and fees for services decrease, differences between the European countries are reduced. Table 11 provides an overview of price changes for deposits since the implementation of the *Single Market Program* in 1992. Simultaneously, banks are forced to enhance the quality of financial services. Competition in conjunction with technological progress leads to increased financial innovations and therefore to higher product variety. New technologies also offer consumers more time flexibility, as they do no longer have to rely on branch opening hours to conduct their business (Leyshon, 2000).

In spite of the limits that are put on the integration of retail markets in the long run, the potential of integration is by far not exhausted. Problems originate from different regulation and taxation that represent barriers to market access for the banking sector and thus for cross-border trade in financial services. Further deregulation and harmonisation steps towards a common European financial market are needed to benefit consumers substantially.

7 Conclusions

Over the past years, European financial markets have integrated considerably. However, significant differences still persist with regard to different sectors of financial markets. Within the banking sector, the money market as well as the market for wholesale products already form common European markets. However, there still exists an extensive segmentation of national markets for retail-products. Responsible for this low degree of retail market integration are a line of natural and politically induced barriers to banks' market access. In this paper market access strategies were examined based both on aggregate data for the banking sector and case studies of individual banks (*Banco Santander Central Hispano*, *Nordea Group*, *BNP Paribas* and *HSBC*). Four main strategies were considered in particular: *direct cross-border sale* (telephone- or internet banking), the establishment of *branches* and *subsidiaries*, *mergers* and *acquisitions*, as well as *co-operations* and *strategic alliances*. It can be observed, that in the last years, especially mergers and acquisitions followed by co-operations and strategic alliances strongly contributed to the integration of the European retail markets. Each of the examined strategies, however, still has to deal with considerable barriers to market access. In particular, such barriers are: differences in national tax legislation, national consumer protection rules, national accounting standards and bankruptcy principles, solvency control, take-over directives and national supervision. In order to bypass existing barriers, European banks have to adjust their strategies. For a stronger integration of European retail-markets, further harmonisation of legislation and supervision seems to be necessary. A further integration push would especially lead to an increase of consumer benefits through lower prices and a higher product variety of financial services.

References

Ackermann, J. (1998), Intensiver Wettbewerb um Kunden und Kapital, *Neue Züricher Zeitung*, 30.06.1998.

BBC News (2001), Business: The Company File Plan to Create Europe's Largest Bank Fails, *BBC Online Network*, http://bbc.co.uk.

BNP Paribas (2001), http://www.bnpparibas.com, September 1.

BSCH (2001), http://bsch.es, October.

Buch, C. (2000), *Financial Market Integration in the US: Lessons for Europe?*, Kiel Working Paper No. 1004, Kiel.

Buch, C. and G. L. DeLong (2001), *Cross-Border Bank Mergers: What Lures the Rare Animal*, Kiel Working Paper No. 1070, Kiel.

Business&Finance (2001), Enba/BBVA $1.5bn Banking Merger Collapses, http://businessandfinance.ie, April.

Crowder, N. (1999), Die europäische Bankenlandschaft wird sich verändern, *Frankfurter Allgemeine Zeitung*, Frankfurt, January 28.

Datamonitor (2000), *Retail Banking Frontrunners in Cross-Border Expansion: Banking Without Frontiers*, New York.

Deutsche Bank (2001), http://www.group.deutsche-bank.de, September 1.

Deutsche Bundesbank (1999), *Mögliche Auswirkungen der WWU auf die Bankensysteme der EU auf mittel- bis langfristige Sicht*, Frankfurt.

EU (2001a), http://www.europa.eu.int/scadplus/leg/de/s08000.htm, August.

EU (2001b), htttp://www.europa.eu.int/eur-lex/de/lif/ind/de_analytical_index_06.htm, August.

Europäische Kommission (1999), *Finanzdienstleistungen, Umsetzung des Finanzmarktrahmens: Aktionsplan*, Mitteilung der Kommission, Luxembourg, May 11.

European Commission (1997), Credit Institutions and Banking, *The Single Market Review*, Subseries 2, Vol. 3, Office for Official Publications of the European Communities, Luxembourg.

European Commission (2001), Progress on the Action Plan for Financial Services, http://www.europa.eu.int/comm/internal_market/en/finances/actionplan/annex.pdf, August.

ECB (1999a), Banking in the Euro Area: Structural Features and Trends, *ECB Monthly Bulletin*, April, 41-53.

ECB (1999b), *Possible Effects of EMU on the EU Banking Systems in the Medium to Long Term*, Frankfurt, February.

ECB (2000a), EMU and Banking Supervision, *ECB Monthly Bulletin*, Frankfurt, April, 49-64.

ECB (2000b), *Mergers and Acquisitions Involving the EU Banking Industry – Facts and Implications*, Frankfurt, December.

ECB (2000c), *The Euro: Integrating Financial Services*, Frankfurt.

Financial Times Deutschland (2001a), Unicredito und Commerzbank brechen Verhandlungen ab, http://www.ftd.de, September 11.

Financial Times Deutschland (2001b), Schwedische Bankenmerger gescheitert, http://www.ftd.de, September 20.

Fortis (2001), http://www.fortis.com, September 1.

Galati, G. and K. Tsatsaronis (2001), The Impact of the Euro on Europe's Financial Markets, *BIS Working Paper* No. 100, Basle.

Haberer, J.-Y. (1993), Die künftige Konkurrenz amerikanischer und japanischer Banken nicht ignorieren, *Handelsblatt*, May 13.

Heinemann, F. and M. Jopp (2002), *The Benefits of a Working European Retail Market for Financial Services*, Bonn.

HSBC (2001), http://hsbc.com, October.

Intesa Bci (2001), http://www.intesabci.it, September 1.

Lemmen, J. (1998), *Integrating Financial Markets in the European Union*, Cheltenham.

Leyshon, A. (2000), *Financial Services Mergers and Acquisitions: Consumer Impacts*, University of Nottingham.

Nairn, G. (2000), New Online Opportunities for Banks in the Euro Zone, *Financial Times*, May 3.

Neimke, M., C. Eppendorfer and R. Beckmann (2002), Deepening European Financial Integration: Theoretical Considerations and Empirical Evaluation of Growth and Employment Benefits, published also in this study.

Nordea (2001), http://nordea.com, October.

OECD (2001), Group of Ten, Report on Consolidation in the Financial Sector, January.

Schröder, U. (2001): Defizite bei der Verwirklichung der Grundfreiheiten: Auf dem Wege zu einem europäischen Finanzmarkt, Tagung des AEI Bonn mit HWWA Hamburg: *Der unvollendete Binnenmarkt*, Hamburg, June 21.

Schüler, M. (2002), Integration of the European Market for E-Finance – Evidence From Online Brokerage, published also in this study.

SEB (2001), http.//www.seb.se, September 1.

The Economist (1998), *Europe's Lovesick Bankers*, London, January 10, 59-60.

Union Network International (2001), http://www.union-network.org, July 20.

Willman, John (2000a), Scope for Further Mergers and Acquisitions, *Financial Times*, May 26.

Willman, John (2000b), Freeze Or Jump? That is the Question, *Financial Times*, May 26.

The Benefits of Creating an Integrated EU Market for Investment Funds

Friedrich Heinemann*

Centre for European Economic Research (ZEW), Mannheim, Germany

1 Introduction

The European investment fund industry is looking back at a period of high growth. Assets of European UCITS[1] almost tripled from 1.21 trillion Euros by end 1995 to 3.56 trillion by end 2000 (see Figure 1). In the same period the ratio of European investment funds (UCITS and other types) assets relative to GDP has grown from 23% to 52%. On a per capita basis this represents an increase from 4,000 Euro in 1995 to 11,600 Euro in 2000.[2] Even in the depressive phase at the stock exchanges in the first half of 2001 the industry proved its robustness – and could still realise a moderate positive growth rate of 2% in terms of UCITS' net assets (FEFSI, 2001b).

In spite of the recent growth slowdown the long-run potential remains high. The fund industry is going to benefit from stable trends such as the shift of savings towards more sophisticated capital market products and the need for long-run capital formation of an ageing population.

While the growth rates seem to suggest a smooth development of the sector, there remains one major shortcoming: The EU market for investment funds is not an EU market in the true sense. National markets so far remain highly dominated by domestic fund companies. The reasons for the fragmentation are not obvious given the fact that important regulatory measures to open the markets date back to 1985 when the UCITS directive took effect.

---

* Acknowledgement: I am indebted to Diana Mackay, European Fund Information Services, London, for providing data on cross-border notifications of European investment funds.

1 UCITS stands for "undertakings for collective investment in transferable securities" as defined in the Directive 85/611/EEC which was to establish the internal market for investment funds.

2 All data are from FEFSI (2001). Note that FEFSI reports aggregate data for its member countries which in addition to EU countries include Switzerland, Norway, Czech Republic, Hungary and Poland.

Figure 1: Data on the European market for UCITS

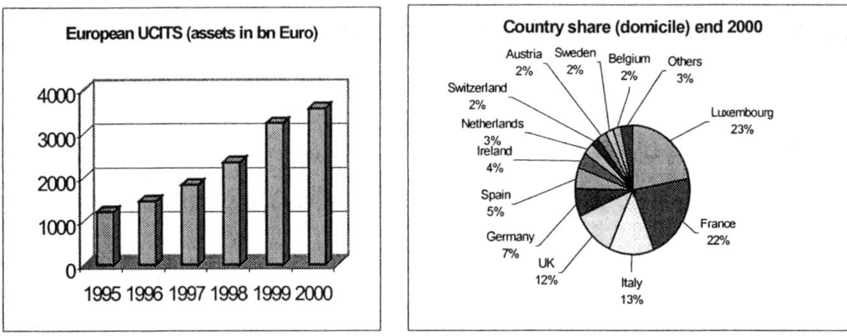

Source: FEFSI (2001). German special funds (set up for institutional investors, not sold to the public) not included. Together with special funds the German share comes close to that of France and Luxembourg.

The lasting relevance of national borders is less easy to understand compared to other financial services like credit or insurance where obvious information problems hinder cross-border sales. Information problems do not seem to be that relevant for open end funds: Fund rankings by companies such as Standard & Poor's are easily accessible and provide comparisons in regard to the quality of domestic and foreign products.

National fragmentation is costly. It restricts choice of consumers to the products of the national market. Competition is less intense than it would be with a truly unified market. In addition, disadvantages arise from small average fund size in EU countries compared to the US. Since substantial cost shares of running a fund (advertising, research, accounting and legal obligations) have a fixed character, an increasing size of assets opens leeway for falling relative operating costs. Because in the present situation, similar fund products cannot be pooled for all EU countries but have to be set up in national variants, these economies of scale cannot be realised. An increasing integration would therefore benefit consumers through a triple effect. First, choice would increase. Second, average fund sizes could grow leading to economies of scale. Third, the increasing competitive pressure should shift a major part of these cost savings towards consumers.

It is the purpose of this study to quantify the corresponding potential benefits for European fund investors and to contribute to a better understanding of integration obstacles. To this end, an extensive study on the determinants of fund expenses executed by the Securities Exchange Commission in 2000 based on a large sample of US funds is exploited in this paper.

The analysis proceeds in the following way. Section 2 describes recent trends for the EU fund industry concerning size, growth and integration. Section 3 presents results on potential costs savings through an increase in average fund size. Section

4 looks into the present obstacles to further integration. Section 5 concludes by assessing priorities for regulators and the industry itself to overcome the fragmentation.

2 EU Fund Industry: Borders Matter

The growth of the EU fund industry should not obscure the fact that the market is far from being a unified market. Assessing the degree of integration, a two-step approach is helpful. For a successful cross-border marketing of funds two kinds of hurdles have to be overcome:

- First, the regulatory obligations need to be fulfilled by registering a fund with the authorities in the target market (type one integration).[3]
- Second, market success has to follow. The fund has to find investors in the target market willing to shift money from domestic to foreign funds (type two integration).

Integration of type one (notification procedure) is a necessary but not a sufficient condition for type two integration (market success). The data base to assess type one integration is much better than for type two. Data on number of cross-border fund notifications obtained from European Fund Information Services, London, allow at least a rough quantification to which extent the notification hurdle is overcome. Data on the market success of foreign funds are not available on such a consistent basis.

Figure 2 shows for each country the number of funds notified and the domicile of these funds. At first view, the data seem to indicate that type one integration of European fund markets is large since in most countries (except Denmark, France and Spain) there are more foreign than domestic funds available. However, this is an incomplete picture. Foreign funds are by far dominated by funds domiciled in Luxembourg, Dublin and other tax preference locations. These funds often are of the "round trip" type: Although being cross-border in a formal sense they are designed for a particular national market and the choice of the domicile results from tax reasons.

The figure immediately reveals a particular type of fragmentation costs carried by consumers in small European countries. These investors suffer from a lack of choice among products. While investors in big markets can choose among thou-

---

3 A fund fulfilling the UCITS definition must be accepted by each EU supervisory authority. Nevertheless, the notification procedure can be costly and time consuming – see Section 4.

sands of products, availability is restricted to a few hundred in countries like Denmark, Greece, Portugal and Norway.

Figure 2: Number of funds available in national markets (31 March 2001)

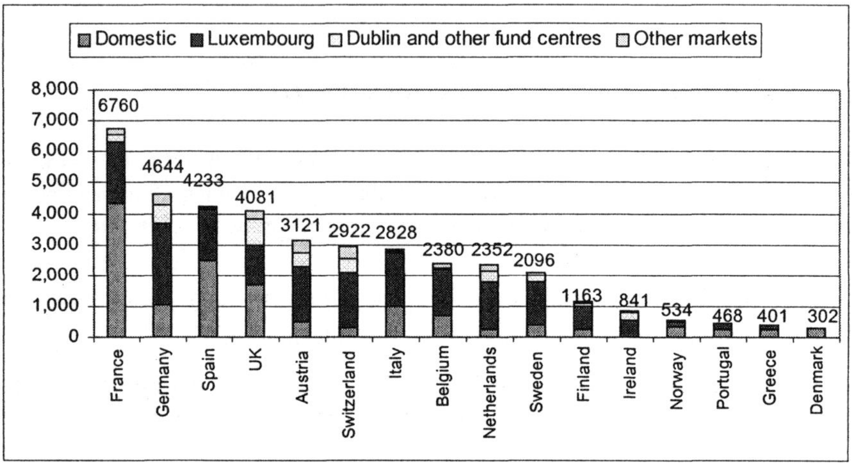

Source: European Fund Information Service, London, derived from Lipper data. The category "Dublin and other fund centres" includes the Channel Islands, Bermuda, Liechtenstein and the Netherland Antilles.

The national fragmentation of markets also becomes obvious by asking:

- to how many EU countries are domestic funds being exported and
- from how many EU countries are funds imported?

Figure 3 counts the number of import and export markets from the perspective of each EU country. There are only three countries – Luxembourg, Ireland and the UK – whose funds are sold at least in two thirds of all member countries. Many national fund industries do practically not export their domestic funds. In no EU country there are today funds available from more than 6 other EU domiciles. While this finding may partly be influenced by the Luxembourg effect – beneficial tax domiciles are used for cross-border funds – these findings nevertheless show the closeness of national markets.

So far the analysis was solely based on data in regard to step one of cross-border strategy, i.e. the existence of a cross-border notification. However, a notification with the target market's authorities does not guarantee market success. A matrix on EU market penetration of cross-border funds is not available. Fund management groups treat this kind of information as secret.

Figure 3: Inward and outward openness of EU countries' fund sectors

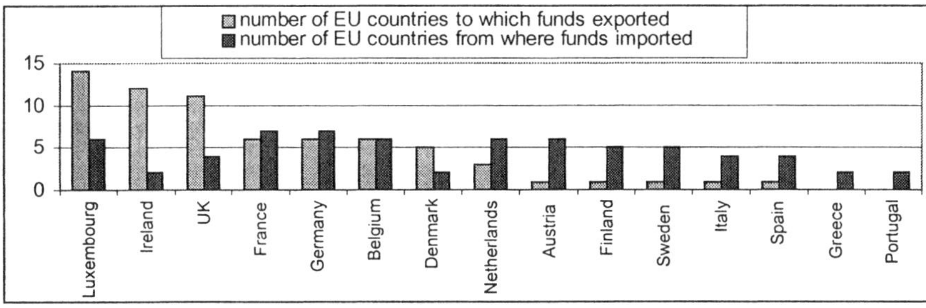

Source: Calculations based on matrix of cross-border notifications from European Fund Services, derived from Lipper data. An import/export relationship between two EU countries is counted if there are at least 5 fund notifications in a field.

Data on foreign funds market shares as published in different research documents are not consistent. In an unpublished paper of summer 2001, European Fund Services estimates the market share of pure foreign funds (round-trippers are excluded) in Germany for mid 2000 at a level of around 13% in terms of assets. Foreign market shares in France, Italy and Spain are estimated to be not higher than 5% in the same source. In Sweden, foreign funds' market share is reported to be even below 1%. Moody's (2000) estimates the market share of foreign funds in Germany with 2.4% of assets much lower and with 7.6% for Italy a bit higher. Even these contradicting bits of information clearly show that the large shares of foreign funds in nationally registered products (see Figure 3) is by far no indicator for market shares. All available asset based data show that true foreign funds still play nothing but a minor role.

3 Quantifying Potential Economies of Scales

On average funds domiciled in the EU are much smaller than US funds: While at the end of the first quarter 2001 a typical EU fund has assets of 176 million Euro[4], the average US size is 910 million Euro, and thus five times larger. Fund size differs considerably between EU countries (see Figure 4) – the extremes are Italy with 417 million and Finland with only 56 million.

---

4 FEFSI reports for the end of 2000 even a larger discrepancy: an average of 140 million Euro for a European and 875 million Euro for a US fund. These FEFSI calculations include, however, also funds from non-EU European countries.

Figure 4: Average fund size (million Euro, end of March 2001)

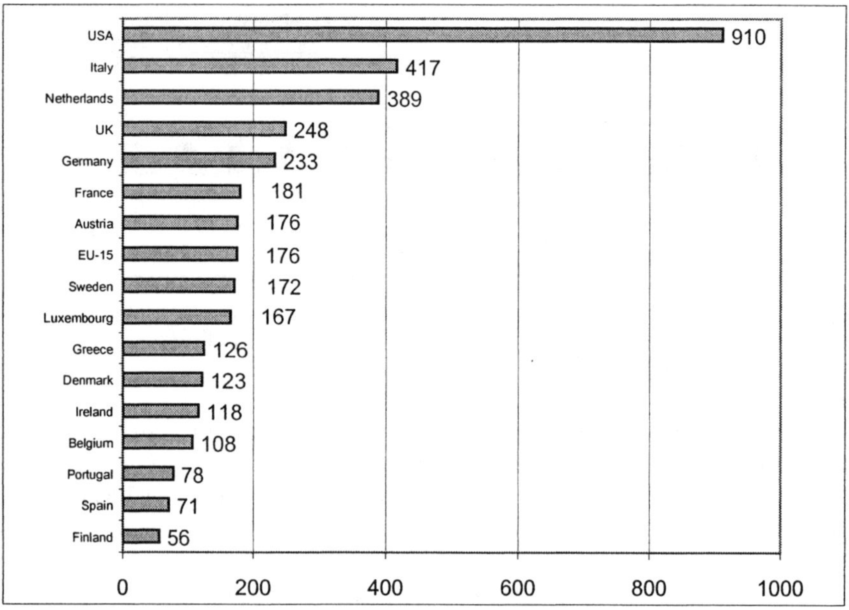

Own calculation based on fund asset data by FEFSI and data on number of funds by European Fund Service derived from Lipper data. Included are only publicly offered, open-ended funds. A fund is attributed to the country of domicile independently from where it is sold.

The smaller European size is an obvious consequence of market fragmentation. If borders did not play a role in selling funds, average fund size and country size should not be correlated as they obviously are. With separation of markets, a national product is largely restricted to national consumers, implying the correlation between country and fund size.

Fund size is a significant driving force for average costs. This intuitively appealing hypothesis was supported by a thorough study of the US Securities Exchange Commission in 2000 (SEC, 2000). Based on 1999 data for almost 9,000 funds the study explores the determinants of fund costs.[5] Included in these expenses are management fees, but not sales loads and no transaction costs for a fund's selling and buying of securities.[6]

5 Money market funds are excluded from the database.

6 The reason for excluding sales loads lies in data problems: For a sensible integration of these costs on an annual basis one would need to know average holding periods for each fund. Apart from that data on effectively paid sales load are not obtainable. The exclusion of sales load should not bias the SEC analysis' results too much since the basic regression includes a dummy for load/ no-load funds.

Figure 5: Fund expense ratio in % depending on size of assets

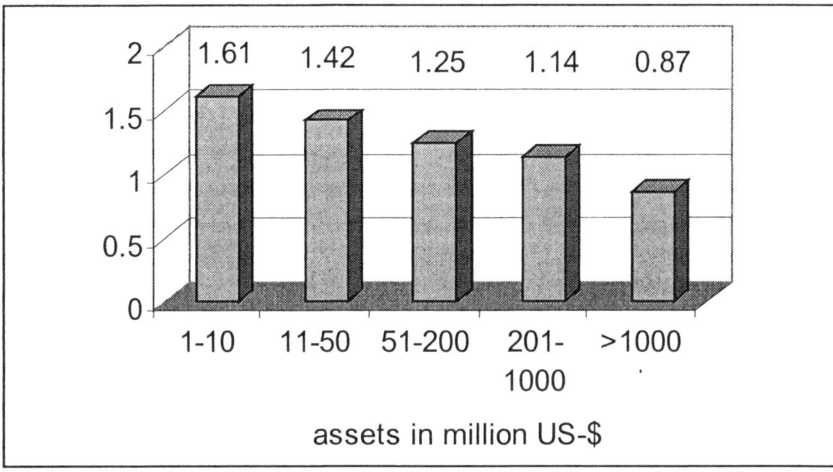

Source: SEC (2000), data base: 9,000 open-ended US funds, without money market funds. Expense ratio does not include sales loads.

While the descriptive view already reveals a negative correlation between volume of assets and expenses (see Figure 5), this finding alone would not provide a robust basis for the analysis, since a multitude of determinants explain the costs of running a fund and could bias the results: Equity funds are more expensive than bond funds. Funds investing in domestic assets are cheaper than internationally investing funds etc. More reliable than the simple descriptive view are therefore the results of a multivariate regression.

Such a cross-section regression is included in SEC (2000). Among others the following control variables are included in the specification: volume of fund assets, portfolio turnover, fund age and several dummies for fund category (equity, bond, specialty, international), index and no-load funds. A crucial result for the purpose of this paper is: The volume of a fund's assets turns out to have a highly significant negative impact on fund expenses. Figure 6 depicts the economies of scale associated with these regression coefficients. It shows that ceteris paribus a 10/50/100 million $ fund has a cost disadvantage compared to a 1 billion $ fund of 44/28/22 basis points.

Since a study of a comparable data base and quality does not exist for the European fund industry, these US findings are the best available basis for a quantification of the potential benefits from larger European fund sizes. Of course, cost structure of US and EU fund sectors are not completely identical due to differences in regulation, competition and investors' preferences. Nevertheless, the assumption seems well justified that basic features of the cost structure are comparable between both markets.

Figure 6: Cost disadvantage to fund size of 1 billion US-$ (in basis points)

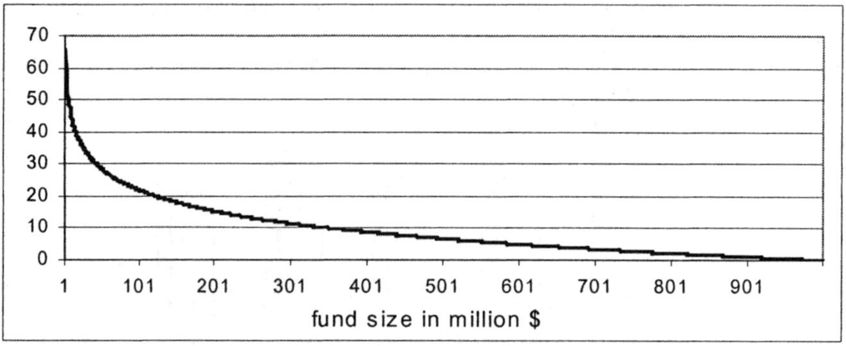

Calculated from regression results in SEC (2000). The underlying relationship between fund size and costs holds ceteris paribus, i.e. for the comparison of two funds where all other cost driving determinants are identical.

The assessment of the cost savings potential through pooling of funds in a unified EU fund market comes to interesting results. In the logic of the economies of scale argument, consumers in those countries with the smallest funds today could expect the largest benefits from European fund pooling. Figure 7 shows the potential savings in basis points for different EU markets for various scenarios on average fund size. The 400/600/800 million $ scenario assumes that average EU fund size reaches half/three quarters/total of the present US level.

Figure 7: Cost savings under different fund size scenarios (in basis points)

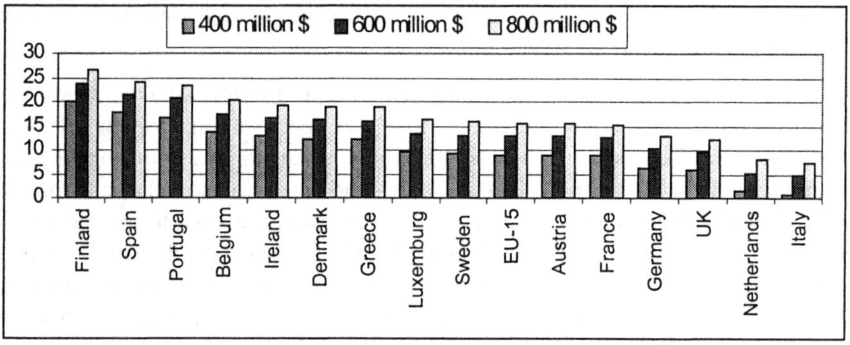

Calculations based on regression results from SEC (2000). Note that country assignment refers to domicile of funds. Particularly in the cases of Ireland and Luxembourg this is not equivalent to target market of funds.

The cost savings associated with these scenarios are not trivial in absolute numbers. Figure 8 gives an indication based on the present size of the EU fund sector and the above quantified economies of scale: Annual costs of managing European funds could be cut by around five billion Euro if the average US fund size could be realised (which is about 800 million $). Of course, these numbers can only be regarded as a rough indication of benefits. One major shortcoming is the static perspective of the analysis that is based on the present size of European fund markets. Even under the present fragmentation and inefficient cost structure this financial segment is growing. If efficiency gains through pooling could be realised this should lead to a further acceleration of growth. In this sense these benefit estimates can be regarded as conservative.

There is no reliable way to quantify how these cost savings would be distributed between the industry (profit margin increase) and the private investors (increase in net returns). Since integration of fund markets would lead to an intensification of competition among fund companies the chances should not be bad for investors to gain a significant part of these cost savings.

It should also be pointed out that another dimension of benefits from pooling EU funds does not shine up in these data: the larger choice for investors from small EU countries if most funds were sold pan-European.

Figure 8: Potential annual savings of fund expenses in EU (in million Euro)

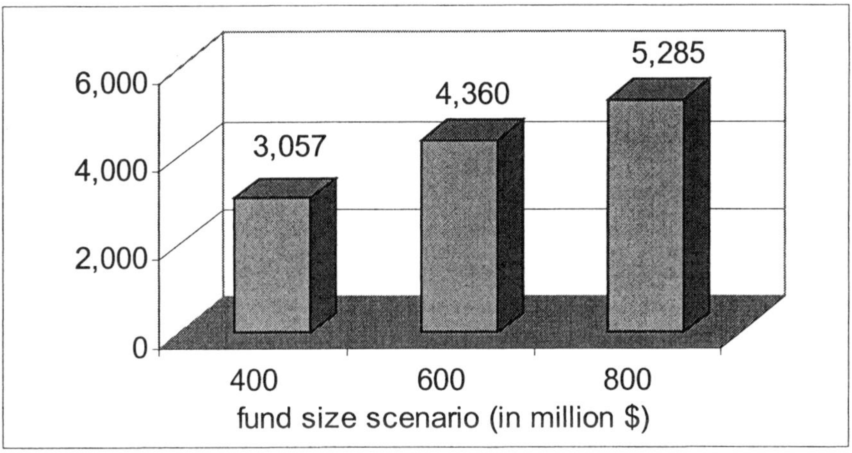

Calculation based on FEFSI data on the size of EU fund markets as per end of March 2001, assumption is that economies of scale correspond to the findings of SEC (2000).

4 Obstacles to Cross-Border Sales of Funds

Based on the above analysis there can be no doubt that a unified EU fund market would be beneficial for consumers. In contrast to that finding it is less obvious how this aim can best be reached. Although many obstacles have been identified it is far from clear which of these obstacles are most important. For purposes of analytical stringency, a basic distinction should be made between "policy induced" and "natural" obstacles. Policy induced hurdles to cross-border sales of funds can directly be dismantled by appropriate adjustments of EU and national legislation. Natural obstacles resulting from consumers preferences or the inherent characteristics of a market are not under the direct control of policy makers. It should be stressed that "natural" as used here is not to be understood as unalterable. It might be the case that market trends or changes in consumer behaviour tend to overcome existing "natural" obstacles.

4.1 Policy-Induced Obstacles: Regulation and Taxation

The fund industry itself as represented by its European association FEFSI or the US counterpart ICI stresses very much the importance of the policy-induced obstacles. This analysis can be summarised in the following way:[7]

Although the UCITS Directive in 1985 intended to provide a convenient passport for pan-European sales of funds its success remained so far limited. Reasons are:

- *Innovations leaving UCITS definition outdated:* The European fund passport is limited to those products fulfilling the Directive's definition of UCITS. Here the legislator always lags behind market development. Examples are money market funds, "funds of funds" or certain index funds (those that conflict with the issuer ceilings, Herring, 2001) that so far have not been included in the UCITS definition.
- *The burden of registration in the target market*: The UCITS Directive is interpreted and implemented differently in member states. According to the Directive a fund must be authorised for sale by local authorities in the target market. Registration procedures vary by country. ICI (2000) reports for example that in Italy registration takes typically up to six months. Further examples highlight the burden of the diffuse registration procedures (Moody's, 2000): In Spain an official translation of the fund prospectus is obligatory. The Netherlands require a detailed tax history of a fund.
- *Host country responsibility for advertisement and marketing:* Article 44 (2) of Council Directive 85/611/EEC of 20 December 1985 (last amendment from November 2000) states: "Any UCITS may advertise its units in the Member

---

7 For a recent summary of these associations' views see FEFSI (2001c) and ICI (2000).

State in which they are marketed. It must comply with the provisions governing advertising in that State." Thus one single pan-European marketing strategy for a fund is impossible due to different national restrictions for this strategy.

- *Tax discrimination of foreign funds*: In a multitude of ways national tax laws discriminate against foreign funds (FEFSI and Pricewaterhouse Coopers, 2001). An extreme example is Denmark where a discriminatory taxation of capital gains of foreign funds practically precludes the market entry of foreign funds (see Table 1 for details). Fortunately, in many countries tax discriminations are of a milder nature for foreign funds that are registered.

Table 1: Significant discriminatory tax barriers to the sale of foreign UCITS in their territory

Country	Description of discriminatory tax measure
Austria	Existing income tax regime
Belgium	i. Tax on distributions to individual investors ii. Participation exemption iii. Benefit from foreign tax credits
Denmark	Foreign fund legislation
Finland	none noted
France	Plan d'Epargne en Actions ('PEA')
Germany	i. Existing foreign investment fund law ii. New tax reform measures
Greece	Investment funds legislation which penalises foreign UCITS
Ireland	Taxation of Irish investors in offshore UCITS
Italy	Capital gains tax
Luxembourg	None noted
Netherlands	Reclaim of foreign withholding tax
Portugal	Different income tax regimes for individual investors
Spain	None noted
Sweden	None noted
UK	i. Offshore fund legislation ii. UK Imputation tax system

Source: FEFSI/Pricewaterhouse Coopers (2001: 15), including all tax law changes up to April 2001.

From a fund company's perspective, the registration and advertising related obstacles lead to a fixed cost problem for entering a new EU target market. These fixed costs will make an entry only profitable if there is sufficient potential in the target country. The findings on cross-border notifications in Section 2 are consistent with this view. Foreign funds are much more present in the big fund markets. Attempts to simplify entry costs would therefore be particularly promising for opening up the markets of the smaller countries.

It is, however, questionable whether even the best regulatory changes could really produce a fast integration of fund markets. The experience of markets such as Germany or France poses some challenging questions: Here the significant presence of foreign funds prove that the fixed cost problem is of less relevance for these markets. Thousands of foreign funds have overcome the registration and advertisement hurdles but their market success is limited. Explanation attempts must therefore also look at the natural barriers.

4.2 Natural Obstacles: Consumer Preferences and the Features of Existing Distribution Channels

A natural obstacle to cross-border sales of funds in Europe could result from consumer preferences. It is, however, doubtful whether consumers really have a preference for investment funds from domestic companies. According to research cited by Mackay (2001) the criterion fund performance is today a top criterion in fund selection while much less interest is paid to the domicile of a fund. In addition, ranking lists of fund performance are today easily available through the Internet and these rankings include registered foreign funds. Thus it is hard to explain the present pattern of the market from consumer preferences or information problems alone – factors that may play a larger role for other financial services.

Moody's (2000) convincingly assigns large importance to a further natural obstacle resulting from the existing distribution channels. Still the major part of funds is sold over the bank counter. Banks still often advise their customers with a bias towards fund products of the own group. Therefore, foreign funds still lack distributive capacities preventing a breakthrough even after overcoming the regulatory hurdles of the registration procedure.

The distribution obstacle is natural in the sense that legislators do not have direct instruments to overcome it. However, ongoing market trends can be expected to alleviate the problem in the future.

First, the expected restructuring of distribution channels towards direct internet sales and independent fund shops ("fund supermarkets") will work towards structures less biased towards domestic products (see Figure 9). These newly emerging channels operate on the 'open architecture' approach where distributors offer other groups' funds to their clients (Warland, 2002). Second, as a by-product of cross-border M&As in banking the domestic bias in this sector is being reduced. Third, the bias for domestic funds might also decline within domestic banks. Consumer sophistication is increasingly pushing the demand for third party products. Banks have to react and to offer a more neutral assistance in fund selection or otherwise risk to lose market share.

Figure 9: Dominating fund distribution channels for the German market 1998 and 2005 Forecast

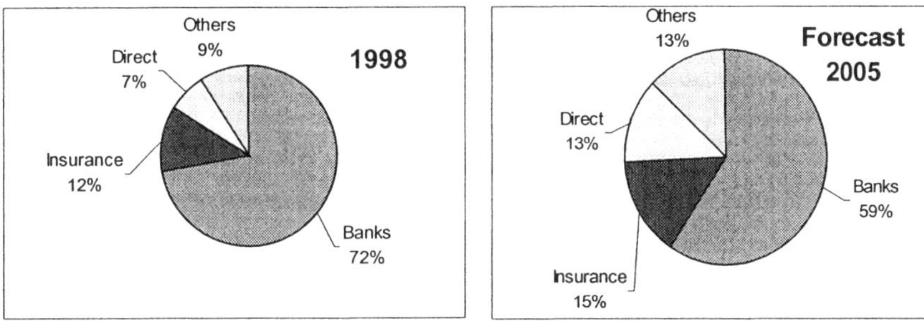

Source: Bundesverband Deutscher Investmentgesellschaften.

5 Policy Priorities

Even if market trends will successfully open the big EU countries for foreign funds this will not help the smaller countries to the same extent. Here the limited market potential will prevent foreign suppliers from paying the "entrance ticket" in form of the costly registration procedure. Therefore, it is of particular importance for the smaller markets that the policy-induced obstacles are overcome.

The present legislative activities promise some limited progress in this regard: The UCITS directive is in the process of modernisation.[8] If these changes take effect problems with the restricted UCITS definition in regard to money market funds, "funds of funds" and index funds will be overcome. The adjustments will further introduce a fully harmonised simplified prospectus alleviating the fixed cost problem of entering another EU market.

The Lamfalussy approach to financial market legislation (the establishment of a 4 level regulatory approach, see Lamfalussy Report, 2001) is also relevant in the UCITS context. If the new procedures prove to be successful in speeding up legislation this could shorten time lags between fund market developments and

8 COM (2000) 329 and COM (2000) 331.

UCITS directives. The ongoing adjustments are an impressive example for the slow reaction speed: The two initiatives to modernise the fund directive date back to summer 1998 and did only pass at the end of 2001.

Less progress is made concerning the problem of host country control in regard to advertising. In particular, the e-Commerce Directive[9] will not help the fund industry to overcome national borders through the Internet (FEFSI, 2001c): Although the spirit of the e-Commerce Directive is to establish the country of origin approach in the regulation of a server, a derogation concerns the host country control in the marketing of UCITS. Thus, the EU fund industry remains confronted with the problem that each pan-European marketing strategy can be challenged by national authorities in each EU member country on grounds of consumer protection.

In regard to discriminatory fund tax practices there is hardly any progress. The Code of Conduct for Business Taxation is not helpful to overcome the UCITS problems. The Code of Conduct addresses tax practices aimed at attracting foreign business to a Member State rather than measures of keeping foreign business out of a market – which is the problem in the fund market (FEFSI and Pricewaterhouse Coopers, 2001). At least for some countries like Denmark all other attempts to open the country for foreign funds will be in vain as long as the most serious forms of tax discrimination are not abolished.

So far European legislators have not addressed a further topic which might be promising given the above insights on distribution linked obstacles: Pressing fund distributors to behave less biased in selling funds. Of course, it is not easy to design measures that could foster more neutral fund selection. The problem is that substantial additional regulatory costs must be avoided since these are not in the interest of the consumers. Nevertheless, given the large relevance of the distribution obstacle for the fragmentation of fund markets legislators should devote more thoughts and efforts to this issue.

References

FEFSI (2001a), *The State of the European Investment Funds Industry*, Brussels, download: http://www.fefsi.org.

FEFSI (2001b), *Quarterly Statistical Release*, No. 6, September, Brussels, download: http://www.fefsi.org.

FEFSI (2001c), Annual Report 2000-2001, Brussels, download: http://www.fefsi.org.

---

9 Directive, 2000/31/EC.

FEFSI and Pricewaterhouse Coopers (2001), *Discriminatory Tax Barriers in the Single European Investment Funds Market: A Discussion Paper*, Report to the European Investment Funds Industry, London, June, download: http://www.fefsi.org.

Herring, F. (2001), *European Licence for all Funds*, Vision + Money Special, The Financial Markets Magazine of Deutsche Börse AG, October, 26-30.

ICI Investment Company Institute (2000), *Questionnaire Response to Committee of Wise Men on the Regulation of European Securities Markets*, download: http://www.ici.org/eu_ucits_wise_com.html.

Lamfalussy Report (2001), *Final Report of the Committee of Wise Men on the Regulation of European Securities Markets*, Brussels, February 15.

Mackay, D. (2001), *Mutual Funds Trends and Developments*, Presentation ICI General Members Meeting, May.

Moody's Investors Service (2000), *Moody's Global Fund Update: Cross-Border Distribution of Funds – Hurdles and Developments*, August.

SEC US Securities and Exchange Commission, Division of Investment Management (2000), *Report on Mutual Fund Fees and Expenses*, Washington, download: http://www.sec.gov/news/studies/feestudy.htm.

Warland, P. (2002), *European Fund Opportunities – Not for the Fainthearted*, JP Morgan Chase client publication, London.

Integration Benefits on EU Retail Credit Markets – Evidence from Interest Rate Pass-Through

Friedrich Heinemann and Martin Schüler

Centre for European Economic Research (ZEW), Mannheim, Germany

1 Introduction

Competition benefits consumers in many ways. On credit markets, benefits arise from the speed of interest rate adjustment. With low competition banks are slow to pass declining market rates through to debtors. With high competition banks are forced to react in a faster way – otherwise they risk to lose market shares. Since integration of the EU markets for financial services intensifies competition it should, therefore, also speed up pass-through of interest rate changes.

Based on this consideration it is the objective of this study to quantify the potential benefits from further integration by focusing on interest rate pass-through. The link between market and lending interest rate has extensively been studied for monetary policy purposes (see survey below). However, to the authors' knowledge this study is the first to use it to develop benefit indicators for further financial retail market integration.

The quantification of benefits follows a straightforward strategy. If borders played no role for EU credit markets significant national differences in adjustment speed between market and retail rates should vanish. Thus, perfect integration would imply convergence of pass-through speed between national markets. Of course, no one can forecast exactly to which level this convergence would lead. In our study we work with the assumption that pass-through speed converges to the level of the national market that is adjusting fastest today. This assumption allows to simulate retail interest rates for different countries and to compare these simulated series with actual series. This comparison is the base for our suggested new indicator of integration benefits.

This indicator extends the literature on financial market integration which suffers from its wholesale perspective: Wholesale oriented indicators often hint at a high level of integration of the EU financial market. This result is in sharp contrast to the obvious incomplete integration of retail markets. Since our indicator is based on a central price indicator of European retail financial markets – retail lending rates – it should help to get a more complete picture of the degree of integration.

Indeed it can be shown that based on the experience from the second half of the nineties debtors in some countries could have gained substantial interest rate savings in periods of rate declines. Since the pass-through is asymmetric – i.e. it is faster if this is for the bank's advantage – this also indicates a net consumer gain over the whole interest rate cycle. The findings on heterogeneous pass-through also support the view that today retail financial markets are much less integrated in Europe than many indicators based on capital market links seem to suggest.

The analysis proceeds in the following way. In Section 2, the pass-through literature is surveyed, followed by a discussion of the relationship between market integration and interest rate adjustment. After the presentation of some descriptive results (Section 3) the core quantitative part follows in Section 4. Section 5 concludes.

2 The Concept of Interest Rate Pass-Through in Monetary and Integration Economics

2.1 Short- and Long-Run Links

The main objective of the existing interest rate pass-through literature is a better understanding of a central bank's interest rate policy. This literature's focus is the response of bank lending rates to changes in the money market rate which is an important part of the monetary transmission mechanism. Two groups of studies can be distinguished: Those taking the possible long-run relationship (cointegration) between lending and money market rate into account and those that do not.

Studies with a Short-Run Focus

Studies with a main focus on the short-run link between money market and lending rates (e.g. Borio and Fritz, 1995, Cottarelli and Kourtelis, 1994, and Donney and Degryse, 2001) usually employ the following autoregressive distributed lag model for lending rates:

$$L_t = c + \beta_0 M_t + \sum_{i=1}^{k} (\alpha_i L_{t-i} + \beta_i M_{t-i}) + \varepsilon_t \tag{1}$$

where L_t and M_t are lending rate and money market rate at time t, respectively. k is defined as the model's optimal lag-length and ε_t is an error term. The coefficient β_0 measures the short-run or impact effect of changes in the money market rates on lending rates. A value of β_0 of less than one displays lending rate stickiness, i.e. sluggish adjustment of lending rates to money market rates. Equation (1) has to be estimated in differences if the interest rate series exhibit unit roots in order to avoid spurious results.

Studies Taking Account of the Long-Run Link

Equation (1) implies that a long-run link between money market and lending rate can be calculated as

$$\theta = \frac{\sum_{j=0}^{k} \beta_j}{1 - \sum_{i=1}^{k} \alpha_i} \tag{2}$$

thus, in the long-run equation (1) becomes

$$L_t = \theta_0 + \theta M_t + u_t \tag{3}$$

Equation (3) states the cointegration equation, i.e. the long-run relationship between the lending rate and the money market rate. This long-run relationship can be incorporated in the model. By doing so, one gets the following error correction specification:

$$\Delta L_t = c + \beta_0 \Delta M_t + \sum_{i=1}^{k} (\alpha_i \Delta L_{t-1} + \beta_i \Delta M_{t-i}) + \gamma (L_{t-1} - M_{t-1}) + \varepsilon_t \tag{4}$$

where Δ is the first difference operator. According to equation (4) changes in the lending rate, over time, are due to two sources. First, with a lag, changes in the lending rate are due to changes in the money market rate. Second, they are due to deviations from the long-run relationship. Moazzami (1999), Sander and Kleimeier (2001) and Mojon (2000) follow this road.

By estimating equation (4) the short-term impact multiplier as well as the long-run multiplier and its standard error can directly be obtained. Estimation of equation (4) is computationally more efficient compared to estimation of the standard pass-through model (Moazzami, 1999). Therefore, if cointegration between the money market rate and the lending rate is present, estimating the error correction specification is preferable.

2.2 Main Findings

In general, pass-through studies display three major results.[1] First, the short-run impact multiplier typically is below one, indicating that lending interest rates adjust sluggishly to money market rates. Second, they find significant asymmetry in the stickiness of upward and downward movements of retail rates. Finally, there

1 See appendix 1 for a summary of results.

are considerable differences in pass-through coefficients and speed of adjustments across countries.

Sluggish Adjustment

A bank will only adjust its rate when the optimal rate differs by such an amount from the existing rate that the revenues from changing the rate exceed the costs of change. Such costs may arise from different sources which leads to several explanations as to why retail interest rates are sticky (Nabar et al., 1993):

- Asymmetric information between banks and borrowers can lead to adverse selection and moral hazard. In this case an optimal interest rate exists that maximises a bank's expected return on loans. Borrowers accepting a higher rate than this optimal rate are likely to be poorer than borrowers on average and existing borrowers are likely to choose riskier projects when facing such a higher rate. This explains that an increase in loan rates above this optimal rate may actually reduce the bank's expected return.
- There are "menu costs" that may prevent banks from adjusting retail rates instantly. These administrative costs may involve, for example, labour, computing and notification costs.
- Banks may be interested in long-term relationships with their customers and as a consequence change loan rates upward less often than justified by the movement in the underlying cost of funds. Banks and customers have an implicit risk-sharing arrangement that includes that banks keep retail interest rates more fixed than the money market rate. In return, bank customers are willing to pay a mark-up for this insurance.
- Banks can react to a change in money market rate not only by changing the interest rate. The true loan price can adjust along other dimensions such as collateral, commitment and fees.
- Rate stickiness can result from the fact that the retail interest rates have a longer maturity than the money market rate. Banks will not adjust their rates instantly when there is uncertainty about the future development of market rates.[2]
- A lack of competition among banks or between banking finance and direct finance such as commercial papers may lead to sluggish adjustment of retail rates. Banks in concentrated markets are able to increase their profit margin by postponing a decrease in rates. In this context the cost of lowering rates would be the foregone monopoly rent – an opportunity cost.

---

2 However, this point is of no relevance in our case, since we take long-term market rates as costs of fund for long-term retail rates, see Section 2.4.

Asymmetry in the Stickiness

There are a number of studies that find significant asymmetry in the stickiness of upward and downward movements of retail rates (e.g. Mester and Saunders, 1995, and Mojon, 2000). The pass-through to credit rates is higher in periods of increasing money market rates than in periods of decreasing market rates. The opposite holds true for deposit rates.

Consumers face costs of switching banks. This reduces the interest rate elasticity of the credit demand curve and the deposit supply curve. Thus, the maximisation of banks' income may result in this asymmetric pass-through.

Besides, when concentration in the banking market is lower this interest rate cycle asymmetry of the pass-through is less pronounced (Hannan and Berger, 1991, Neumark and Sharpe 1992).

Heterogeneity in the Pass-Through Across Countries

As appendix 1 reveals there are also substantial differences in the pass-through across countries. Mojon (2000) undertakes a number of regressions in order to analyse which observable features of the institutional and financial structure can explain these differences across countries.[3] His findings reveal the following: The volatility of the money market rate as a feature of the *monetary policy regime* has a negative effect on the pass-through to credit rates. Obviously, changes in the money market rate are more likely to be passed through to retail rates if they are perceived to be permanent. In contrast, as with nominal prices, the pass-through to lending rates is higher when inflation is high.

Both *competition among banks and from direct finance* affect the pass-through significantly. The competition intensity among banks leads to faster adjustment of credit rates when the market rate is falling and of deposit rates when the market rate is rising. As an indicator for the competition from direct finance, the volume of short-term securities – that can also be seen as a substitute to traditional bank deposits – has a positive impact on the pass-through, i.e. competition from direct finance increases the speed of adjustment.

Finally, higher staff costs, which are taken as an indicator for the *rigidity of bank costs* lead to a smaller degree of pass-through to credit rates.

---

3 Mojon (2000) performs a panel regression for the countries in the Euro area. A similar approach was undertaken, for example, by Cottarelli and Kourelis (1994), that tested the impact of banking market structure on a cross-section of pass-through elasticities estimated for 31 countries. They found the following indicators of financial structure to significantly lower the speed of adjustment of bank rates to money market rates: the absence of money market for negotiable short-term instruments, relatively high volatility of the money market rate, restrictions of international capital flows, the existence of barriers to entry, and public ownership of the banking system.

2.3 Pass-Through and Financial Market Integration

As explained above national differences in pass-through speed are caused by a multitude of factors. Nevertheless, an unequivocal statement about the impact of market integration on the link between market and lending rates is possible: Integration fosters convergence of pass-through speed between national markets. Reasons to expect this link between market integration and pass-through are the following:

- A fully integrated money market – as it is now given for the countries of the Euro zone – implies a single level of volatility of money market rates. Furthermore, an integrated financial market fosters diversification of credit risk across corporate sector issuers of debt securities. As a consequence, also smaller companies will have access to direct finance. Therefore, with market rate volatility and availability of direct finance relevant determinants of pass-through speed are equalised (Mojon, 2000).
- Full integration of financial markets implies that consumers chose among credit offers without paying interest to the domicile of a bank. If integration has advanced that far different pass-through speeds are eliminated directly through debtors' arbitrage: In a time of falling market rates, potential debtors would shop around all over Europe and choose the credit offers of fastest adjusting banks. In times of rising rates a bank moving ahead with lending rate adjustment immediately loses attraction.

This relationship between integration and pass-through speed allows to use the concept originating from the monetary transmission literature for different analytical purposes in the context of integration economics.

First, national differences in pass-through speed can serve as an indicator of integration. This usefulness is derived from the fact that full integration of financial markets is a sufficient (but not necessary) condition for convergence of pass-through speed. The only paper known to the authors using the pass-through approach in this respect is Sander and Kleimeier (2001). Second, national differences in pass-through speed can lay the base for the calculation of indicators of integration benefits. This idea will be developed up to a first quantification in the empirical part of the paper.

The following consideration shows that consumers benefit from a convergence of interest rate adjustment speed. Debtors in countries with banks that – before integration – adjust slowly would gain from integration in periods of decreasing market rates since the credit rate would be lowered earlier than in fragmented markets. Of course, the same debtors might loose in periods of increasing market rates. However, as discussed above asymmetry in the stickiness of retail rates can be observed. The pass-through to credit rates is higher in periods of increasing money market rates than in periods of decreasing market rates. Thus, over the whole interest rate cycle, debtors in today's slow adjusting markets would gain from more integration. An analogous argument applies to creditors of bank deposits. These would gain from a faster correction of deposit rates.

The extent of benefits depends on the level to which adjustment speed converges. In the following, convergence to the top is assumed. It can be regarded as likely that the degree of competition in a unified EU financial market will exceed the present national levels of competitive pressure. One could therefore even assume that the adjustment speed will exceed the degree of today's fastest adjusters. In this sense the assumption of convergence to the top is conservative.

2.4 Methodological Consequences

The insights of the existing pass-through literature demands a careful specification of the quantitative analysis in regard to the asymmetry of adjustment and the possible long-run restriction.

Since banks react differently in times of increasing and falling interest rates this has to be taken into account for the regressions. As we focus on potential benefits of debtors in periods of falling market rates, the estimation of the pass-through process must also be based on a period of mainly falling rates. This is the reason why we restrict the estimation base to the second half of the nineties where we are in the comfortable position that interest rates more or less constantly fell over a period of some years.

Furthermore, we follow the more advanced studies and account for a possible long-run link between costs of funds and lending rates. This is also necessary since we link interest rate pass-through with financial market integration which clearly requires also a long-run perspective. Our starting point is the approach undertaken, for example, by Mojon (2000). First, the error correction model of equation (4) is estimated provided that the variable costs of funds and the retail bank rate are cointegrated. In the case that the series are not co-integrated the error correction term is dropped from the equation and we come back to the standard pass-through model of equation (1) that is estimated in differences to avoid spurious regression problems due to the non-stationarity of interest rates.

While these first steps are more or less standard, the specific integration focus demands qualifications to the approaches of the monetary transmission literature. One difference concerns the choice of the market interest rate. In the monetary literature, money market or central bank rates are always used as cost of funds variables – even if the pass-through to long-run fixed rate credits is studied. Thus, the analysed adjustment effectively mixes up two different reactions: first the term-structure reaction of long- to short-term interest rates and second the reaction of retail lending to market interest rates. This approach is legitimate for this strand of literature which is exclusively interested in the effects of monetary policy. This paper, however, with its interest shifted to financial market integration has to be more precise. It has to disentangle the term structure link from the intermediation link. For this purpose, market rates are chosen corresponding to the maturity of the interest rate agreement. For mortgage lending rates, long-term government bond yields are used instead of money market rates as a basis for the pass-through analysis.

The analysis then enters completely new terrain by developing integration benefit indicators based on the pass-through concept. To reach this objective, we simulate development of retail lending rates in different markets assuming these markets were characterised by the pass-through speed of a fast adjuster. Potential interest rate savings are calculated for the falling market rate period in the second half of the nineties.

3 Data and Descriptive Analysis

The analysis is based on monthly data from the ECB data base "National Retail Interest Rates".[4] The ECB regards the rates included as the "main indicators of retail financial market conditions in the Member State concerned" (ECB, 2001). National series are summarised under common headings but are not fully harmonised. This means that underlying credits might be different between member states in regard to average size, default risk and other characteristics. Therefore, differences in levels between member states cannot be directly interpreted – which is a less serious problem for this paper's approach since it exploits only the link between market and retail rates *within* a country. The descriptive analysis is based on three lending rates and two deposit rates: mortgage loans to households ("N2" in ECB data base), consumer loans to households ("N3"), short-term loans to enterprises ("N4"), time deposits ("N8") and savings accounts ("N9"). The econometric analysis will focus exclusively on credit rates due to lacking data availability for deposit rates.

As explained in the preceding section, market rates are chosen corresponding to the maturity of the credit and deposit products. The 3-months money market rates from IMF's International Financial Statistics are used for all variable interest rate credits and deposits. For fixed rate products (most of the mortgage interest rates in the ECB data base refer to fixed rates) government bond yields, again from IMF's International Financial Statistics, serve as the market reference rate.

A first descriptive approach should make a difference between periods of increasing and falling interest rates since an asymmetric pass-through is demonstrated by the well established empirical facts. Based on development of average

4 These data can be downloaded from www.ecb.int (Statistics).

market interest rates (Figure 1) the following periods are chosen for calculations of simple correlations (Tables 1-5): 1995:03-1999:01 as a period of declining bond yields, 1999:01-2000:01 as a period of increasing bond yields, 1995:03-1999:05 as a period of declining money market rates and 1999:05-2000:10 as a period of increasing money market rates.

Figure 1: Average money market rates and government bond yields

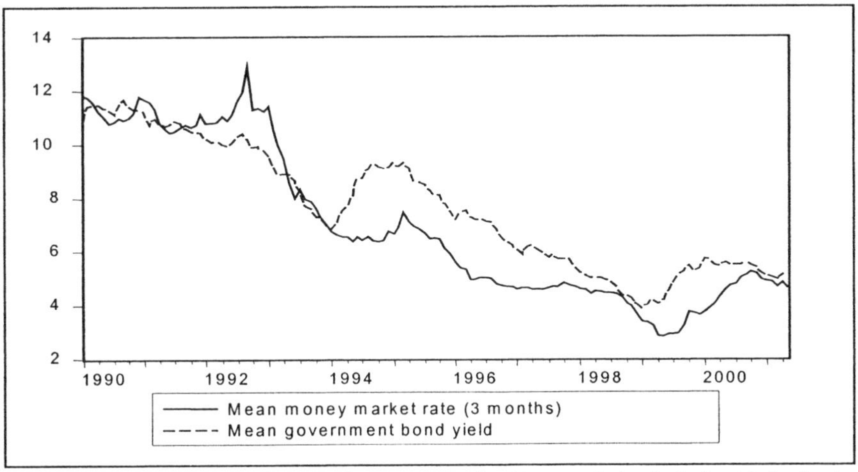

Unweighted average of: Belgium, Germany, Spain, France, Ireland, Italy, Netherlands, Austria, Portugal, Finland, UK.

Table 1: Correlation coefficients of mortgage loan rates and government bond yields

Country	95:03-99:01 decreasing bond yields	99:01-00:01 increasing bond yields
Belgium	0.882	0.923
Germany	0.987	0.988
Greece	-	-0.296
Spain	0.978	-0.200
Italy	0.928	-0.588
Netherlands	0.921	0.864
Austria	0.929	-0.091
Portugal	0.910	-0.524
Finland	0.926	0.308
UK	0.934	0.928
Ireland*	0.843	-0.702
Average	*0.924*	*0.146*

*Mortgage credits for Ireland included in the ECB data base are floating, therefore correlation with money market rate.

Table 2: Correlation coefficients of consumer loans and money market rates

Country	95:03-99:10 decreasing money market rates	99:10-00:10 increasing money market rates
Belgium	0.821	0.958
Germany	0.751	0.923
Greece	-0.108	0.897
Spain	0.981	0.913
Austria	0.798	0.976
Portugal	0.930	0.218
Finland	0.919	0.983
UK	0.130	0.266
Average	*0.653*	*0.767*

Table 3: Correlation coefficients short-term enterprise loans and money market rates

Country	95:01-99:07 decreasing money market rates	99:07-00:10 increasing money market rates
Belgium	0.980	0.993
Germany	0.861	0.958
Greece	0.406	0.966
Spain	0.990	0.921
France	0.704	0.941
Ireland	0.941	0.953
Italy	0.976	0.952
Netherlands	0.896	0.968
Austria	0.763	0.981
Portugal	0.984	0.710
Average	*0.850*	*0.934*

Table 4: Correlation coefficients time deposit rates and money market rates

Country	95:01-99:07 decreasing money market rates	99:07-00:10 increasing money market rates
Belgium	0.994	0.998
Germany	0.968	0.985
Greece	0.361	0.951
Spain	0.995	0.986
France	0.993	0.993
Italy	0.978	0.976
Netherlands	0.892	0.983
Austria	0.766	0.939
Portugal	0.991	0.951
Finland	0.829	-0.889
UK	0.928	0.873
Average	*0.881*	*0.795*

Table 5: Correlation coefficients of savings accounts rates and money market rates

Country	95:01-99:07 decreasing money market rates	99:07-00:10 increasing money market rates
Belgium	0.882	0.416
Germany	0.911	0.974
Greece	0.297	0.957
France	0.845	0.179
Ireland	0.840	0.938
UK	0.873	0.856
Average	*0.775*	*0.720*

Some of the correlation coefficients have to be treated with caution. This holds particularly for the period of increasing rates in 1999 which suffers from its short time-span and possible distortions through transitory EMU effects on the underlying interest rate series. Particularly the mortgage rate correlation coefficients for the increasing interest rate period seem to be affected resulting in implausible negative signs.

Nevertheless, the following stylised facts emerge: The pass-through of changing market rates to retail rates is relatively slow for consumer credits and savings accounts. The adjustment is faster for mortgages, short-term enterprise credits and time deposits. Average correlation coefficients support the asymmetry hypothesis for consumer loans, enterprise loans, time deposits and savings accounts: Here the adjustment is faster if it benefits the bank: for credits in times of increasing market rates and for deposits in times of falling market rates.[5]

As explained above the primary focus of this paper is on differences in pass-through speed between countries. Here the correlation coefficients give only a first rough but helpful insight – as can be demonstrated by one example: In the falling interest rate period the correlation analysis indicates for mortgages that Germany is a relatively fast and Portugal a slowly adjusting market. Figure 2 depicts the time series for these examples. It shows that market and retail rates in Germany move in a parallel way while the link is much less pronounced in the Portuguese case. In this falling market rate period this means that Portuguese debtors benefit less. In order to quantify these effects, a more precise approach will be employed in the following section.

Figure 2: Examples of a fast and a slow pass-through in the mortgage market

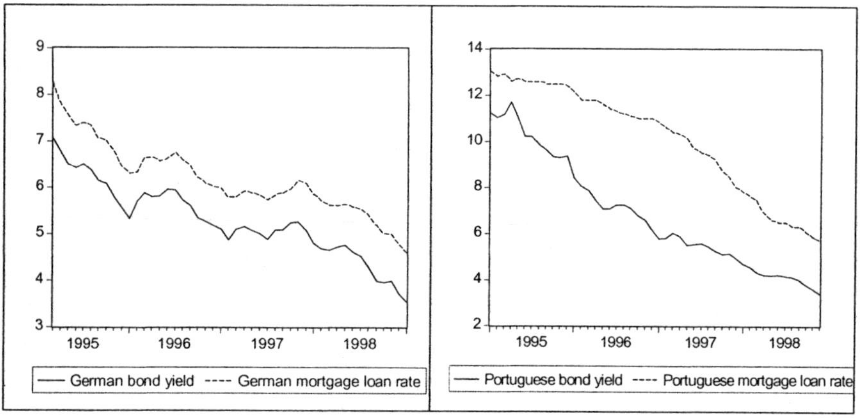

4 Adjustment Speed and Benefits of Integration

In order to quantify benefits of an accelerated interest rate pass-through our focus will be on the period of falling market rates between 1995 and 1999. We try to answer the following question: How much would debtors have saved in this period if all EU countries had been characterised by the adjustment speed of the fastest credit market?

---

5 Note, however, that for time deposits this result depends on the negative correlation coefficient for Finland.

In principle it is possible to pose a similar question for deposit markets and periods of rising market rates. Unfortunately, there was no period with increasing money market rates in the nineties lasting much more than a year. Thus, a data base for a similar analysis for deposit rates is lacking. Therefore, the following analysis is restricted to the markets for mortgage lending, consumer credits and short-term enterprise lending.

The econometric approach is based on the estimation of equation (4) and takes account of the possibility of cointegration between market and retail rates. The analysis proceeds in the following way: In a preparatory step (4.1), standard unit root and Johansen cointegration tests were executed in order to identify the level of integration of the time series and the existence of a cointegration relationship between market and retail interest rates. In a second step (4.2), the speed of pass-through is measured based on country-specific estimations of equation (4). In a third step (4.3), for each market the model of a fast adjusting market serves as a basis for the simulation of retail rates in other countries. This allows to calculate an indicator for integration benefits in terms of potential interest savings through a convergence in pass-through speed.

4.1 Preparatory Diagnosis

Standard unit root tests overwhelmingly indicate that market and retail interest rates included are first order integrated (results not reported). This finding is in line with well known time series characteristics of interest rates and allows to test for cointegration between market and retail interest rates. The Johansen procedure is applied using as many data points as available for each country retail market combination, the maximum range is from January 1980 to April 2001. One has to be aware that these long periods raise the possibility of structural breaks. This danger has to be traded off against the restricted meaning of cointegration tests for short periods since cointegration refers to a long-run relationship. Cointegration is accepted if the trace statistic indicates the existence of a cointegration relationship with a significance level of at least 5%. The Akaike information criterion is used to decide optimal lag length in the application of the cointegration test. These preparatory diagnostics lay the basis for the estimation of country-specific pass-through equations for the different retail rates.

4.2 Comparing the Adjustment Speed on the Basis of Country Specific Estimations

The estimation of equation (4) offers the basis for the measurement of adjustment speed. In the estimation the error correction term is included depending on whether the cointegration test has indicated a long-run relationship between market and retail interest rates or not. The length for the inclusion of lagged values of market and retail rates was again determined on the basis of the Akaike criterion.

Estimation period is identical to the periods with falling interest rates as used in the descriptive analysis. Although most time series are available starting with the early eighties the asymmetric nature of the pass-through forces to base the estimation on a restricted period. Thus for mortgage credit where the bond yield is the relevant cost of fund variable the estimation period is 1995:03-1999:01. For consumer and enterprise loans the estimation period is slightly longer (1995:03-1999:10).

Data availability allowed to estimate 23 pass-through equations indicating large country differences in the adjustment speed (estimation results are summarised in appendix 2).

In order to make results comparable the estimation results are used for simulating retail interest rate development for a common scenario – a decrease of market rates in period zero by one percentage point with no further fluctuations before and after that date.

For the assessment of reliability of these simulations, one has to be aware of the very different quality of the underlying regressions. As can be seen from appendix 2, results for mortgage markets are most satisfying in two respects: Goodness of fit is high and with one exception (Italy) the resulting pass-through processes are convergent. The results for consumer credit rates are far less satisfying. Goodness of fit is low and all processes are non-convergent, i.e. the resulting credit rate does not converge to a fixed value. The regressions for enterprise credit are again better apart from three country regressions with instable processes. Therefore, results for the mortgage market and the enterprise credit market should be taken more seriously than those for the consumer credit market.

Figure 3 depicts the pass-through to mortgage lending rates over a one year period. It shows that these retail-rates follow falling costs of funds only sluggishly. Even after six months the pass-through in two thirds of the countries is far from complete. Differences in speed between countries are most pronounced between two and four months. Judging on the basis of the 3-months adjustment, mortgage lenders benefit fast from falling market rates in Belgium, Germany and Netherlands. Consumers in the UK, Ireland, Italy and Spain have to be more patient. Adjustment is slowest in Austria and Portugal.

Table 6 summarises the results of the same analysis for all three credit markets based on the 3-months pass-through.

Figure 3: Pass-through speed for mortgage credit rates (in basis points)

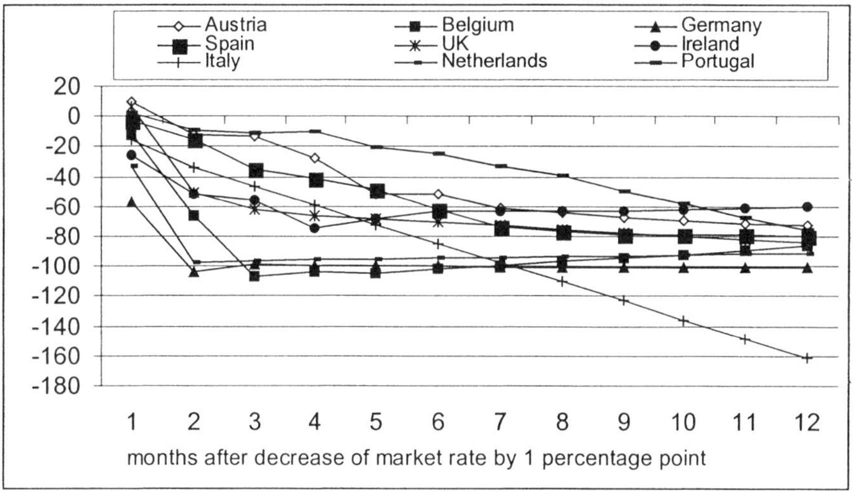

Table 6: 3-months decrease of retail rates after a one percentage point fall in market rates (in basis points)

Country	mortgage loans	consumer loans (short-term)	enterprise loans (short-term)
Austria	-14	-60	-44
Belgium	-107	-98	-83
France	-	-	-45
Germany	-99	23	-13
Ireland	-56	-	3
Italy	-47	-	-167
Netherlands	-97	-	-62
Portugal	-11	-32	-53
Spain	-35	-46	-75
UK	-62	-73	-

Simulated effect on retail interest rate of a 1 percentage point decrease in market rates (=government bond yields for most mortgage credit series and 3-months money market rate for all other series) given the estimation of equation (4). Estimation is based on the period of decreasing market rates 1995-1999 as explained in the text. Missings: No estimation and simulation possible due to data availability.

National differences in the adjustment speed for consumer loans are also substantial. While, again, Belgium is a fast adjuster where already after three months consumers get almost a hundred percent of the market rate decline adjustment is not noticeable at all in Germany and relatively slow in Portugal and Spain. For enterprise credits Italy is the fastest reacting country according to these results. A particularly slow pass-through occurs in Greece and Germany.

4.3 Benefits in Integration Scenarios

In the final step retail rates for EU countries are simulated assuming that the link between market and retail rates in each country would be as close as in a fast adjusting country. The choice of the reference country is based on the results of the 3-months pass-through section with some qualifications. Germany is chosen as a reference country for mortgage credits, although it is second to Belgium in terms of the 3-months adjustment. The reason is that the underlying regression has a much better fit for Germany than for Belgium and that the difference in 3-months adjustment speed is only of a minor magnitude (see Appendix 2). For consumer credits Belgium as the fastest adjuster is chosen as reference country. However, simulation results for consumer credits are less reliable than for mortgage due to the non-convergence of all estimated pass-through processes.

For short-run enterprise credits Italy appears to be the faster adjuster on the basis of the 3-months pass-through. The choice of Belgium instead of Italy is motivated by the fact that the underlying estimation of the pass-through process for Italy is exploding. This would pose serious difficulties for the simulation. The Belgian regression results indicate a convergent adjustment behaviour making it a better basis for the simulation.

Figure 4 depicts examples of the simulation results for mortgage credits for two polar cases: Belgium as a fast adjusting country and Portugal as a slow adjuster. The figure includes two series, the original and the simulated mortgage interest rate. Basis for the simulation is the country market rate and the pass-through equation of the reference country (which is Germany for mortgages).

As expected simulations come to different results for the relation between simulated and original series. Debtors in Belgium with its fast pass-through mortgage market would not benefit from the German link between market and retail rates. The simulated rate exceeds the original rate for about two thirds of the simulation period.

Figure 4: Simulation results mortgage rates – two polar examples (in %)

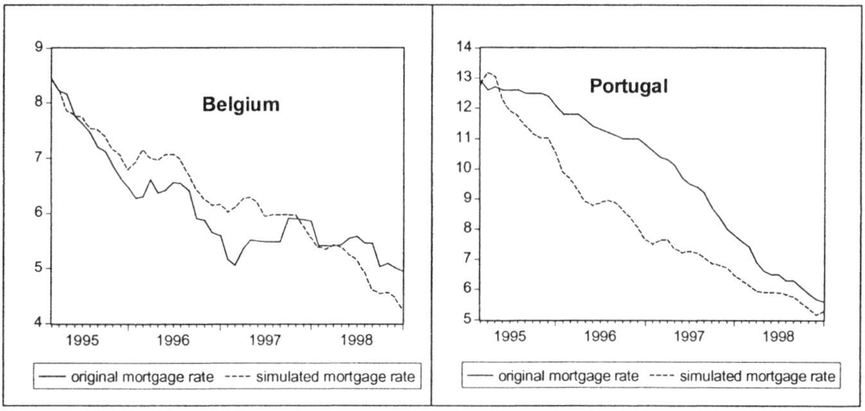

Simulation is based on country market rates and the German pass-through equation estimated on data from the declining interest rate period 1995:03-1999:01.

On average the simulated interest rates are 19 basis points higher than the actual values. The case is different for the slow pass-through market in Portugal. Here, consumers would have benefited to a large extent from German pass-through structures in the second half of the nineties. For most of the time the simulated rates are substantially below the actual series, on average the interest rate advantage amounts to 158 basis points for this period of declining market rates.

The same kind of analysis was executed for all three markets and all countries with sufficient data. Figures 5-7 summarise the outcomes of the simulations. Here, a negative (positive) value for the difference between the simulated and original series indicates that a country would benefit (lose) from the structures of the reference country.

Comparing the winner-loser pattern of these simulations corresponds in most cases with the results of the 3-months pass-through analysis. Relatively slowly adjusting countries tend to gain most.

Figure 5: Average mortgage credit interest rate 1995:03-1999:01 (in %)

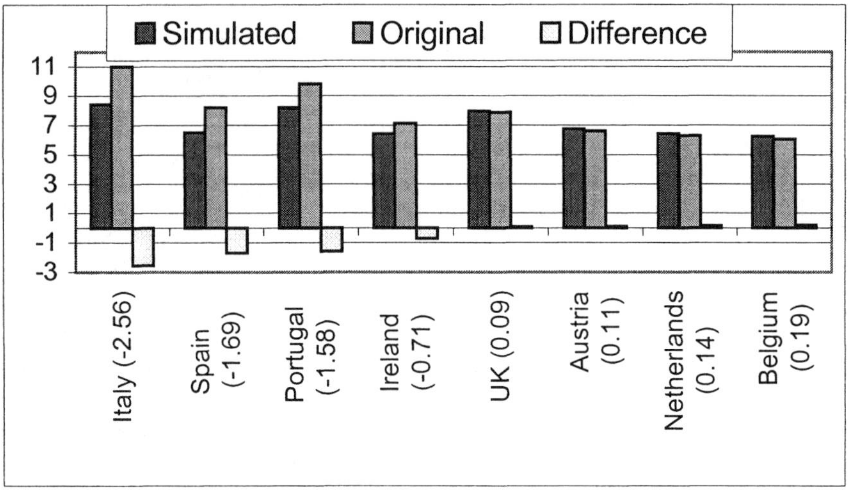

In brackets behind country name in figures 5-7: value of difference between mean original and simulated series. Reference country for the simulation is Germany.

Figure 6: Average consumer credit interest rate 1995:03-1999:10 (in %)

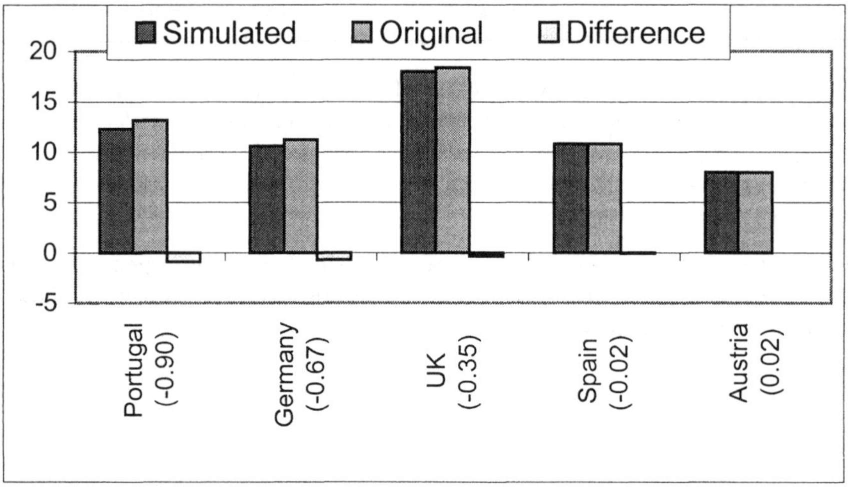

Reference country for the simulation is Belgium.

Figure 7: Average enterprise credit interest rate 1995:03-1999:10 (in %)

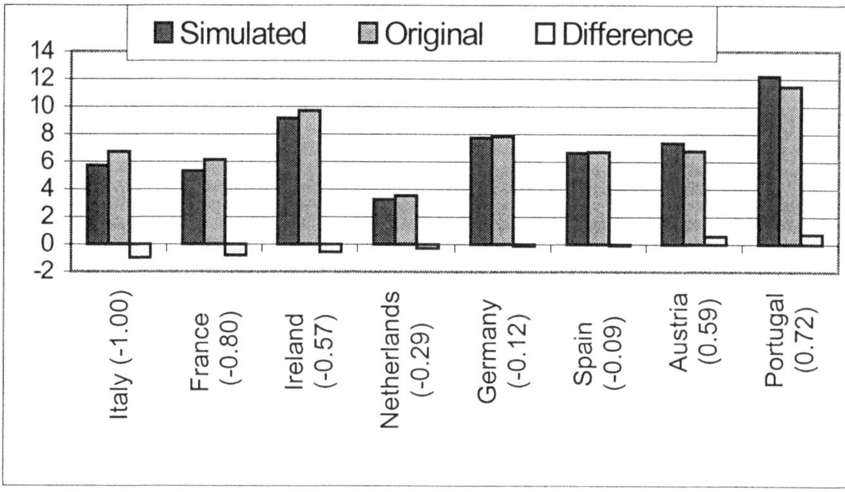

Reference country for the simulation is Belgium.

However, there are also contradictions between both approaches, the most striking concerns the Italian market for enterprise loans. Here Italy shows even an overcompensating 3-months adjustment. Nevertheless enterprise debtors in that country are identified as major winners from assuming the Belgian pass-through speed. Here the simulation can be regarded as dominating the 3-months pass-through result. As already explained above the Italian pass-through regression implies an instable process and thus has to be treated with caution. The simulation results for enterprise credit rates are not affected from this problem since they are only based on the regressions of the stable reference countries. Simulations for consumer credits are less reliable due to the fact of instable pass-through equations for all countries including the Belgian reference case.

For mortgage credits the simulations clearly split countries into two groups. For the UK, Austria, the Netherlands and Belgium on the one hand the pass-through structure of the German reference case would hardly make a difference. In Italy, Spain, Portugal and Ireland on the other hand, consumers would have gained much from the pass-through speed of the German market.

For consumer credits where data availability restricts the inclusion of countries and where the underlying regressions have less satisfying properties the picture is not as clear cut between Southern and Middle Europe. Now Portugal belongs together with Germany to the benefiting countries while Spain forms with Austria a group with no substantial differences from the Belgian reference case. The UK is in between.

On the enterprise credit market, creditors in Italy, France and Ireland would benefit most from a convergence of pass-through speed on the Belgian level. The

Netherlands, Germany and Spain are not very different from the reference case while Austria and Portugal would even lose.

5 Conclusion

The message of the pass-through related integration indicator is unambiguous. The substantial reaction differences of national bank retail rates to changes in costs of funds supports the view that retail credit markets in Europe are still far away from perfect integration. The pass-through indicator is a helpful corrective to the wholesale oriented integration indicators that regularly hint on high integration of EU financial markets.

The results show that incomplete integration is costly for bank customers – at least in some EU countries. In the falling interest rate period of the second half of the nineties, mortgage debtors in Italy, Spain and Portugal paid on average an excess interest rate of more than 150 basis points due to the particular slow pass-through in these markets. Because of the asymmetry of the pass-through these losses are not compensated by equally sized benefits in times of rising interest rates.

The insights in the determinants of pass-through speed show the way for reducing these customer disadvantages. The Euro and the resulting convergence of money markets and financial structure will work towards convergence of pass-through speed. A more reliable and probably faster mechanism would be activated if direct cross-border retail credits became more important. This kind of cross-border activity could set in motion an arbitrage mechanism that should force banks to speed up interest rate adjustments for the benefit of debtors and depositors.

Appendix 1
Results of the literature

Pass-through of a 1% change in the money market rates to the lending rate (the coefficients are not directly comparable since the underlying estimation periods differ).

Country	Study	Impact multiplier β_0	3-months interim multiplier	Long-run multiplier θ
Austria	CK			
	BF	0.40	0.78	0.86
	M			
	SK	-0.176		0.223
	DD			
Belgium	CK	0.21	0.67	0.87
	BF	0.61	0.99	1.27
	M		0.64	
	SK	0.771		0.940
	DD	0.27	0.44	-0.17
Finland	CK	0.13	0.23	0.28
	BF			
	M			
	SK	0.248		1.01
	DD			
France	CK			
	BF	0.43	0.45	0.74
	M		0.81	
	SK	0.073		0.509
	DD	0.11	0.35	0.45
Germany	CK	0.37	0.87	1.00
	BF	0.11	0.45	1.05
	M		0.67	
	SK	0.217		1.008
	DD	0.40	0.80	0.00
Ireland	CK	0.34	1.07	1.07
	BF			
	M			
	SK	0.668		0.911
	DD	0.11	0.34	0.03
Italy	CK	0.12	0.60	0.83
	BF	0.26	0.69	1.22
	M		0.54	
	SK	0.197		0.866
	DD	0.14	0.57	0.68

Appendix 1 – continued

Country	Study	Impact multiplier β_0	3-months interim multiplier	Long-run multiplier θ
The Netherlands	CK	0.52	0.82	0.82
	BF	1.08	0.96	1.08
	M		1.03	
	SK	0.115		0.983
	DD	0.71	0.97	0.24
Portugal	CK	0.47	0.95	0.95
	BF			
	M			
	SK	0.168		1.170
	DD	0.03	0.01	-0.41
Spain	CK	0.36	0.78	0.94
	BF	0.00	0.30	1.17
	M		0.51	
	SK	0.705		1.074
	DD	0.36	0.73	0.40
United Kingdom	CK	0.87	0.94	0.94
	BF	1.00	1.01	1.01
	M			
	SK	0.272		0.636
	DD			

Notes: CK=Cottarelli and Kourelis (1994), BF=Borio and Fritz (1995), M=Mojon (2000), SK=Sander and Kleimeier (2001), DD=Donney and Degryse (2001); for BF and DD the 1-month response is used as the impact multiplier; BF didn't calculate the 3-months multiplier but the response after 1 quarter, which is displayed instead; for DD the response after 60 months is taken as the long-run multiplier; for DD the short-run loans rate for enterprises is used.

Appendix 2
Summary of pass-through regressions

Country	Cointegration (inclusion of error correction term)	Optimal lag length (Akaike)	Adj. R^2	Convergent pass-through process
mortgage lending rate				
Austria	no	4	0.233	Yes
Belgium	no	2	0.362	Yes
Germany	no	1	0.858	Yes
UK	no	1	0.395	Yes
Ireland	no	3	0.527	Yes
Italy	no	1	-0.053	No
Netherlands	no	1	0.574	Yes
Portugal	yes	6	0.184	Yes
Spain	no	6	0.731	Yes
consumer short-term credit rate				
Austria	no	1	0.166	No
Belgium	no	1	0.043	No
Germany	yes	1	0.073	No
UK	no	1	0.063	No
Portugal	no	1	-0.006	No
Spain	yes	3	0.180	No
enterprise short-term credit rate				
Austria	yes	4	0.455	Yes
Belgium	no	1	0.595	Yes
France	no	1	0.315	Yes
Germany	yes	1	0.169	No
Netherlands	no	2	0.200	Yes
Portugal	no	1	0.164	No
Spain	no	3	0.555	Yes
Ireland	yes	1	0.503	Yes
Italy	yes	1	0.887	No

References

Borio, C. and W. Fritz (1995), *The Response of Short-Term Bank Lending Rates to Policy Rates: A Cross-Country Perspective*, BIS Working Paper No. 27, Basle.

Cottarelli, C. and A. Kourelis (1994), *Financial Structure, Bank Lending, and the Transmission Mechanism of Monetary Policy*, IMF Staff Papers, Vol. 41 (4), Washington.

Donney, M. and H. Degryse (2001), *Bank Lending Rate Pass-Through and Differences in the Transmission of a Single EMU Monetary Policy*, mimeo.

ECB (2001), *National Retail Rates, Methodological Notes*, Last update on 29 March 2001, download from www.ecb.int.

Hannan, T.H. and A.N. Berger (1991), The Rigidity of Prices: Evidence From the Banking Industry, *The American Economic Review* 81, 938-945.

Mester, L.J. and A. Saunders (1995), When Does the Prime Rate Change?, *Journal of Banking & Finance* 19, 743-764.

Moazzami, B. (1999), Lending Rate Stickiness and Monetary Transmission Mechanism: The Case of Canada and the United States, *Applied Financial Economics* 9, 533-538.

Mojon, B. (2000), *Financial Structure and the Interest Rate Channel of ECB Monetary Policy*, ECB Working Paper No. 40, Frankfurt.

Nabar, P.G., S.Y. Park and A. Saunders (1993), Prime Rate Changes: Is There an Advantage in Being First?, *Journal of Business* 66, 69-92.

Neumark, D. and S.A. Sharpe (1992), Market Structure and the Nature of Price Rigidity: Evidence From the Market for Consumer Deposits, *Quarterly Journal of Economics* 107, 657-680.

Sander, H. and S. Kleimeier (2001), Asymmetric Adjustment of Commercial Bank Interest Rates in the Euro Area: An Empirical Investigation Into Interest Rate Pass-Through, mimeo.

How Integrated Are the European Retail Financial Markets? A Cointegration Analysis

Martin Schüler and Friedrich Heinemann*

Centre for European Economic Research (ZEW), Mannheim, Germany

1 Motivation

There is a wide literature that tries to measure integration in financial markets. The results of these studies differ substantially. The predominant part of it is concerned with wholesale financial markets. Clearly, in the context of measuring integration the distinction between wholesale capital markets and retail financial markets becomes crucial. It appears that often this dichotomy between wholesale and retail financial markets is not sufficiently taken into account when assessing the degree of financial market integration.

In general, the existing evidence suggests that the wholesale financial markets such as the money market and the bond market are integrated to a high degree. Customers in these markets who are able to choose offers from different locations quit easily. With the introduction of a single European currency a single European money market emerged, too. However, in retail financial markets the physical distance to a certain bank still determines to a large extent the preference of the customer. Thus, integration in retail financial markets is lacking behind integration in wholesale markets.

In 1988, the Cecchini-Report (Commission of the European Communities, 1988) gave evidence of substantial fragmentation of the European financial services markets since it found substantial price differentials. In addition, potential benefits arising for the consumers with further integration were estimated. In order to realise some of these benefits the Second Banking Directive was implemented in 1993 and formally a single European banking market was established.

So far only a few studies have analysed the degree of integration in the European retail financial market coming to the result that retail markets are still to a large amount fragmented. Our study contributes to this discussion by extending the study by Sander and Kleimeier (2001). We examine four loans markets and two deposit markets using bivariate and multivariate cointegration techniques.

---

* Acknowledgement: The authors thank Michael Schröder and Herbert Buscher (both ZEW, Mannheim) for helpful comments.

The paper is organised as follows: Section 2 gives a systematisation of the existing literature for measuring financial market integration in general considering the distinction between wholesale and retail financial markets. In Section 3, the degree of integration in six financial retail markets is assessed. Finally, based on the results of the cointegration analyses obstacles to integration in the market for financial services are discussed.

2 Measuring Financial Market Integration – A Systematisation

Perfect financial integration is given if national borders do not play any role for cross-border financial transactions. Since the extreme cases of perfect integration and no integration are only of theoretical interest, the aim of the following analysis is to assess the degree to which financial markets are integrated.

Financial market integration can be measured directly or indirectly. Direct approaches target at the identification of regulatory and economic barriers to international capital mobility[1]. Indirect approaches relate to the observable consequences of existing barriers and are either quantity or price related.[2]

Table 1 gives a systematisation of the different approaches to measure financial market integration with regard to the distinction between wholesale and retail financial markets. The contrasting results of existing studies emphasise the importance of this distinction.

2.1 Quantity Concepts

The most widely known quantity measure proposed by Feldstein and Horioka (1980) involves looking at correlations between saving and investment.[3] This test is based on the following idea: In a world with fully integrated capital markets and a single world interest rate, domestic investment is independent of domestic sav-

---

1 The Annual Report on Exchange Arrangements and Exchange Restrictions of the IMF lists barriers to international capital flows for all IMF member countries. In addition to those official restrictions there are, of course, a lot of other barriers, such as differences in language and culture or information asymmetries. To know of such barriers is certainly important when talking about how integrated financial markets are. However, this information is not easily interpreted since the importance of specific barriers is not known (Goldstein and Mussa, 1993).

2 Schulze and Ursprung (1999) differentiate in that way when measuring globalisation.

3 For a good discussion of the Feldstein-Horioka-study see e.g. Heinemann and Stirböck (1999).

ing since it can be financed by foreign saving. If capital is perfectly mobile a shortfall in domestic saving in one country should not increase the domestic real interest rate or crowd out investment, since borrowing from abroad at the world interest rate is possible. Therefore, low (high) correlations indicate high (low) international capital mobility.

Another quantity approach looks at correlations between consumption across countries (Obstfeld, 1989).[4] When markets are fully integrated individuals are able to insure themselves against unexpected changes in their income streams stemming from regional shocks by diversifying their portfolio holdings. A high correlation between domestic and foreign consumption indicates a high degree of cross-border capital mobility and a high degree of financial market integration.[5]

By looking at correlations between saving and investment or between consumption across countries studies usually find evidence for relatively low degrees of capital mobility and subsequently low financial market integration. However, there are a number of studies (Tobin, 1983, Murphy, 1984, Obstfeld, 1985, Summers, 1988, Bayoumi, 1990, Taylor, 1994) that point out several shortcomings of the Feldstein/Horioka-test arguing that this criterion measures more than just financial capital mobility since high correlations between saving and investment do not necessarily contradict international capital mobility.[6] Thus, quantity measures à la Feldstein-Horioka do not seem very promising in assessing the degree of financial market integration.

2.2 Price Measures

The basic idea behind price measures is that in a perfectly integrated financial market arbitrage should safeguard that prices of identical assets traded in different markets are equal, i.e. the law of one price holds. Hence assessing the degree of financial market integration implies measuring the degree to which capital flows equalise expected returns on comparable assets traded in different countries and possibly denominated in different currencies (Eijffinger and Lemmen, 1995). According to Frankel (1992, 1993) and Lemmen and Eijffinger (1993) there are three different concepts of defining perfect capital mobility, that fit into the price approach.[7].

---

4 This approach also refers to the so-called "risk-sharing" hypothesis.

5 On the micro level there is numerous evidence that consumers clearly prefer shares and bonds issued in the home country. This lack of interregional risk diversification is widely know as the so-called home bias in investment portfolios (e.g. Tesar and Werner, 1992, Lewis, 1999, Hess and Shin, 2000).

6 For a useful survey of the criticism of the Feldstein-Horioka criterion see for example Lemmen and Eijffinger (1995).

7 A forth method of measuring capital mobility is the Feldstein-Horioka-criterion discussed above.

Table 1: Measuring financial market integration

	Direct approaches	Indirect approaches	
	I Identification of regulatory and economic barriers	**II Price measures**	**III Quantity measures**
A Integration of financial markets (focus on **whole-sale markets**)	Barriers relevant for transactions among professional financial market actors, such as existence of capital controls, regulatory impediments, information costs, transaction costs (IMF, The Annual Report on Exchange Arrangements and Exchange Restrictions)	Price equalisation for financial market assets (law of one price) - *Interest rate parity conditions* (Frankel, McArthur, 1988, Frankel, 1993, Lemmen and Eijffinger, 1993, Eijffinger and Lemmen, 1995, Lemmen and Eijffinger, 1995) - *Cointegration of interest rates* (Centeno and Mello, 1999) *Stock Market Integration* using *Uncovered interest parity* (Fratzschner, 2001) - *Arbitrage pricing theory* (Ferson and Harvey, 1991, Bekaert and Harvey, 1995, Dumas and Solnik, 1995, Hardouvelis et al., 1999) - *Distance between sets of stochastic discount factors* (Chen and Knez, 1995, Ayuso and Blanco, 2000)	*Saving-Investment-Correlations* (Feldstein and Horioka, 1980, Feldstein, 1982, Obstfeld, 1985, Summer, 1988, Sinn, 1992, Taylor, 1994, 1996, Lemmen and Eijffinger, 1995) *Consumption-Correlations* (Obstfeld, 1989, 1994 1995, Mace, 1991, Lemmen and Eijffinger, 1995, Bayoumi and MacDonald, 1995, Olivei, 2000)
B Integration of financial services markets (focus on **retail markets**)	Barriers relevant for transactions between financial enterprises and private consumers , such as existence of capital controls, regulatory impediments, information costs, transaction costs (IMF, The Annual Report on Exchange Arrangements and Exchange Restrictions)	Price equalisation for financial services (law of one price) Cecchini-Report - *Cointegration of interest rates* (Centeno and Mello, 1999, Kleimeier and Sander, 2000, Sander and Kleimeier, 2001) - *"Antitrust-Literature"* (Stigler and Sherwin, 1985, Keeley and Zimmerman, 1985, Berger and Hannan, 1989, Hannan, 1991, Hannan and Berger, 1991, Neumark and Sharpe, 1992, Jackson, 1992, Rhoades, 1992, Radecki, 1998, 1999, Heitfield, 1999)	*"Micro Home Bias Literature"* (Tesar and Werner, 1992, Lewis, 1999, Hess and Shin, 2000)

Those are well known as the interest parity conditions, namely covered nominal interest parity (CIP), ex ante uncovered interest parity (UIP), and ex ante real interest parity (RIP).[8] Obviously, the introduction of a single European currency has removed the existence of an exchange risk premium within the Euroland. As a result, tests for interest parity in order to assess the degree of financial market integration within EMU make no sense.

Usually, studies employing interest parity conditions focus on money market rates or other wholesale interest rates. Besides, there is a wide literature that tries to assess the degree of stock market integration. These studies use, for example, uncovered interest parity (e.g., Fratzschner, 2001) or some specification of the arbitrage pricing theory (APT) (e.g., Bekaert and Harvey, 1995, Dumas and Solnik, 1995, Ferson and Harvey, 1991, Hardouvelis et al., 1999).

2.3 Measuring Integration in Retail Financial Markets

Clearly, the above approaches aim on measuring integration in wholesale financial markets such as the money, the bond, or the stock market. Most of the studies considering wholesale financial prices lead to the conclusion that the degree of financial market integration is quite high. Obviously, since the introduction of a single currency on January 1, 1999, there is a single money market in the Euro zone and also the integration of other wholesale financial markets can be considered to be far advanced. However, the retail financial markets seem to remain quite fragmented in Europe and so far not much research work has been undertaken on this issue.

There are a number of studies that incorporate price data in order to measure integration in retail financial markets in the US.[9] These studies were often motivated from an antitrust point of view as they tried to quantify the regional extension of the market for financial services. If banking markets are non-local – i.e. "integrated" in our terminology – then local supply and demand conditions would not be relevant in the evaluation of the competitive effects of any given local merger (Rhoades, 1992).

However, there are only a few studies that try to measure integration in the European retail financial markets. In 1988 the Cecchini-Report (Commission of the European Communities, 1988) gave evidence of substantial fragmentation of the European financial services markets since it found substantial price differentials. Price differentials were based on the percentage differences in prices of standard financial service products for each country compared with the average price for the four lowest-priced countries. In a second step, Cecchini estimated potential

8 For a description of the interest parity concepts see for example Frankel (1992, 1993), Lemmen and Eijffinger (1995).

9 Table 1 refers to this strand of literature as the "Antitrust-Literature".

benefits arising for consumers from financial market integration, i.e. the gains in consumer surplus resulting from price reductions. The obvious problems with this kind of studies[10] are the big difficulties to find completely homogeneous financial products and the fact that absolute prices for not strictly homogeneous products are not comparable (Zimmerman, 1995).

Besides Cecchini, to our knowledge, only Centeno and Mello (1999), Kleimeier and Sander (2000) and Sander and Kleimeier (2001) focus on the European retail financial sector. All of them use cointegration techniques in order to measure financial market integration.

2.4 The Cointegration Approach

European retail financial markets are characterised by heterogeneity across countries that is caused by, for example, risk differences, cultural influences in bank-client relationship, country-specific strategic bank behaviour in order to cope with informational imperfections such as moral hazard or incentive effects (Sander and Kleimeier, 2001). Consequently, prices will not strictly equalise even in fully integrated markets. The law of one price, i.e. interest rate parity can hold solely for assets that are perfect substitutes across countries such as government bonds or money market instruments.

However, pricing in retail banking will be more closely tied together within an increasingly integrating region (Kleimeier and Sander, 2000). Thus, in integrated markets there should exist a certain long-run relationship between interest rates across countries. Certainly, this relationship does not require rates to equalise. And obviously, in the short-run retail rates will deviate from this long-run equilibrium but this existing long-run relationship limits divergence of rates in an integrated market. Therefore, the concept of cointegration can be employed to assess the degree of integration in retail financial markets. Cointegration means that there exists such a long-run relationship between two or more time series.

Centeno and Mello (1999) use cointegration techniques to test for financial market integration in six EU member states. They find money market rates to be closely linked across countries but the European bank loans market to be rather segmented.

Kleimeier and Sander (2000) also apply cointegration tests in order to assess the extent to which interest rate linkage in Europe might have become stronger over time. They apply the cointegration tests to lending rates, represented by the respective national prime rates, and to interest rate spreads, which they calculate by using the money market interest rate as a proxy for the deposit rate. They find

---

10 Gardener and Teppett (1995) replicate the microeconomic methodology of the Cecchini study and reveal other shortcomings.

prime rates and spreads not to be co-integrated for most of the European countries in the period between 1993 and 1997. This lack of cointegration could imply either that two markets are not linked at all or that convergence is under way since structural breaks in the standard cointegration tests can wrongly lead to the rejection of cointegration. Kleimeier and Sander (2000) infer an increase in the degree of financial market integration in the post-1993 period.

Using data from the ECB's National Retail Interest Rate Statistics, Sander and Kleimeier (2001) (SK from here on) perform cointegration tests for three retail rates: the mortgage loan rate charged to households (N2), the consumer loans rate charged to households (N3), and the short-term lending rate charged to the corporate sector (N4).[11] They find some tendencies for a more integrated corporate lending market, while consumer lending markets are still rather fragmented.

In this paper we choose a similar cointegration approach in order assess the degree of integration in the European retail financial market. We also use data from the ECB's National Retail Interest Rate Statistics but extend SK by an additional lending rate, namely the rate for medium and long-term loans to enterprises (N5) and two deposit rates, namely for time deposits (N8) and savings accounts (N9).

SK test for cointegration between the national retail rate and the average interest rate among the remaining Euroland countries. Using the average seems to be problematic because it imposes implicitly a severe restriction on the cointegration equation. Also, an interpretation seems to be difficult: What exactly does cointegration between one country and the EU average mean? Hence, we test for cointegration between every possible pair of national retail rates. By doing so, we try to get some kind of pattern of countries that are integrated for every retail rate. Additionally to this bivariate approach, we conduct multivariate cointegration tests.

Usually, in the cases where cointegration is found a vector error correction model is estimated. SK do so in order to assess the degree of market integration. Such an error-correction specification allows to estimate how fast retail rates are driven back to their long-run equilibrium. SK argue that the faster the adjustment process, the stronger is integration of the national market (with the average of the rest of the countries) which allows primarily for a comparison of the degree of integration across countries within one market. However, it seems to be more interesting to draw comparisons concerning the degree of integration among the different European retail markets. In this paper we test for bivariate cointegration between every possible pair of countries and take the relative number of cointegration relationships found in a certain retail market as an indication for the degree of integration. An additional estimation of the error correction model would not give any further information concerning the degree of integration – it would not make sense to compare the degree of integration between two pairs of countries. Consequently,

---

[11] N2, N3, N4, N5, N8 and N9 refer to the numbers of the series as reported by the ECB.

we do not estimate a vector error correction model and stop the analysis after having assessed integration by testing for bivariate and multivariate cointegration.

Furthermore, compared to SK we use a somewhat different definition of integration underlying the cointegration approach. SK do not differentiate between integration that is due to the single European currency and integration that is due to factors such as deregulation or technical progress since they use interest rate levels and do not adjust for exchange rate fluctuations before the introduction of the Euro. We regard this approach as problematic since the result of increasing integration in this type of analysis could simply be caused by the end of exchange rate volatility. This finding, however, does not say much about integration of retail markets. In order to allow for more meaningful results we instead adjust for exchange rate related interest differentials by using spreads between the national retail rate and the national money market rate. In the case of long-term lending rates, i.e. the mortgage rate, we subtract the bond yield.[12] Hence, the cointegration equation can be written as

$$S_{it} = a + bS_{jt} + u_t$$

where S_{it} and S_{jt} is the spread between the retail rate and the money market rate (or the bond yield) of country i and j at time t, respectively. u_t is an error term.

If cointegration between the interest rate spreads is found, this means that markets are tied together by a long-run relationship, i.e. markets are integrated. In the short-run, however, deviations from this relationship can occur. Such deviations should be corrected over time by cross-border lending or increasing international competition (Sander and Kleimeier, 2001): When banks shift their lending activities to countries where lending rates are the highest and consumers or firms borrow in countries where rates are lowest, this international arbitrage process leads to a correction of deviations from the long-run equilibrium. Furthermore, increasing international competition – or as to the theory of contestable markets, the threat of it – lead to similar pricing behaviour of banks. With an already fully integrated European money market this should lead to a harmonisation of retail prices, since banks should pass changes in the underlying cost of funds onto consumers in the same way across countries.[13]

---

12 These spreads can be interpreted as the bank margins. However, since the ECB statistic contains aggregated rates there may be differences in the term structure between lending rates and market rates that curtail this kind of interpretation. Consequently, spreads may also be negative over some periods – as Figures 1a and 1b beneath reveal.

13 However, so far interest rate pass-through in Europe is still heterogeneous (Heinemann and Schüler, 2002).

3 Integration in the European Retail Financial Market

3.1 The Data

As mentioned above we examine four lending rates and two deposit rates, that are taken from the ECB's National Retail Interest Rate Statistics. These are interest rates for mortgage loans to households (N2), consumer loans to households (N3), short-term loans to enterprises (N4), medium and long-term loans to enterprises (N5), time deposits (N8), and savings accounts (N9). Unfortunately, a problem of the database is that interest rates are not harmonised. However, as mentioned above, using cointegration analysis takes to some degree care of this problem since rates are not expected to fully equalise even when markets are fully integrated.

A second problem results from the fact that the introduction of the Euro may have led to a structural break in the cointegration relationship (e.g., Sander and Kleimeier, 2001). SK account for this structural break by dividing the data into a "pre-Euro period" and a "Euro period". However, cointegration analysis requires data over long periods of time. In addition, the time period for which data for all European countries is available simultaneously is limited. Therefore, we choose not to account for structural breaks explicitly. Possibly, using interest rate spreads instead of levels may weaken this disregard.

Another source for a structural break may have been the Second Banking Directive which was adopted in 1989 and implemented on January 1, 1993, and completed formally the single European banking market. Also, by the beginning of 1993 in all EU countries consumer interest rates were completely deregulated (Guardia, 2000). In order to account for this potential structural change, we use monthly data beginning in January 1993. For this period for almost all countries data are available and even in the rare cases where series start in 1995 cointegration results are comparable.[14]

In the following we use nominal rates because consumers and firms look at nominal rates when borrowing or investing money. Inflation in the foreign country, and thus, real interest rates do not matter to them.

Interest rate spreads are calculated by subtracting the long-term government bond yield from the mortgage rate. For all other lending rates the 3-months money market rate is used, both for the time and savings deposit rates. The bond yields and the money market rates are taken from the IMF's International Financial

14 All retail rates for Austria and the United Kingdom, as well as the mortgage rate and the time deposit rate for Italy are only available from 1995 on. For Germany the medium and long-term loans rate to enterprises starts in 1996.

Statistics. The study is conducted for Austria (AT), Belgium (BE), Finland (FI), France (FR), Germany (DE), Ireland (IE), Italy (IT), the Netherlands (NL), Portugal (PT), Spain (ES) and the United Kingdom (UK), although not all retail rates are available for every country.

The analysis proceeds as follows: Before testing for cointegration some descriptive statistics are presented. Then the spread series are tested for unit roots and in a first step we test for bivariate cointegration. Based on patterns obtained from this bivariate analysis, in a second step, multivariate cointegration tests are conducted.

3.2 Stylised Facts

Before testing for cointegration some simple descriptive statistics are presented. Figures 1a and 1b show exemplarily the evolution of the interest rate levels and the spreads for mortgage loans to households. Clearly, a convergence of the mortgage interest rates has occurred. However, the convergence of spreads is not as obvious, indicating that the convergence in levels may be largely due to the removal of exchange rate risk. This confirms our proceeding of using interest rate spreads instead of levels when testing for cointegration, since before 1999 the relationship between interest rate levels is biased due to exchange rates fluctuations. Basically the same holds true for the other retail interest rates, although convergence is not that obvious for all rates.

To get a first impression how strong interest rate spreads are linked correlation coefficients are calculated. Table 2 shows average correlations for the different countries for the six retail markets. The whole available sample period from January 1980 to Mai 2001 is divided into three sub-periods: the period before completion of the single banking market which was achieved by the Second Banking Directive in January 1993, the pre EMU period, and the EMU period.

Due to the lack of availability of data for a number of countries in the 1980s the coefficients for the period before the completion of a single banking market should not be taken too seriously. Comparing the coefficients for the periods before and after the introduction of the Euro shows that correlation for all countries has become stronger. In general, no consistent statement is possible concerning which market exhibits the higher correlations. Hence, Table 2 does not reveal which market may be more integrated. In the next section tests for cointegration are conducted in order to assess the degree of integration.

Figure 1a: Interest rates for mortgage loans

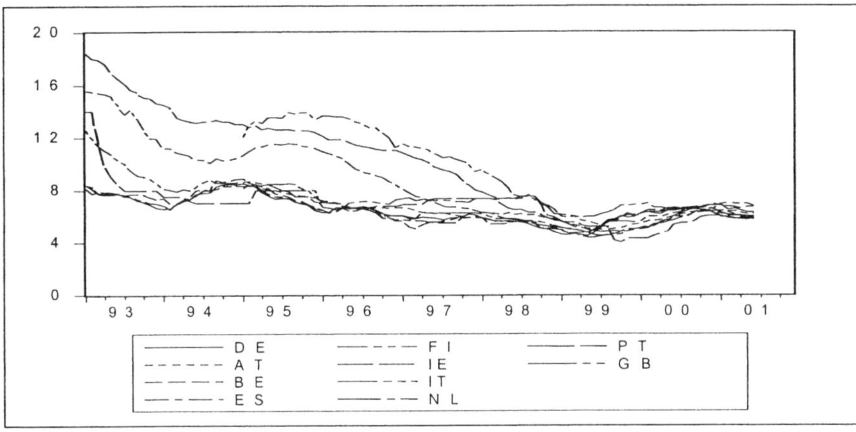

Figure 1b: Spreads between mortgage rate and the long-term government bond yield

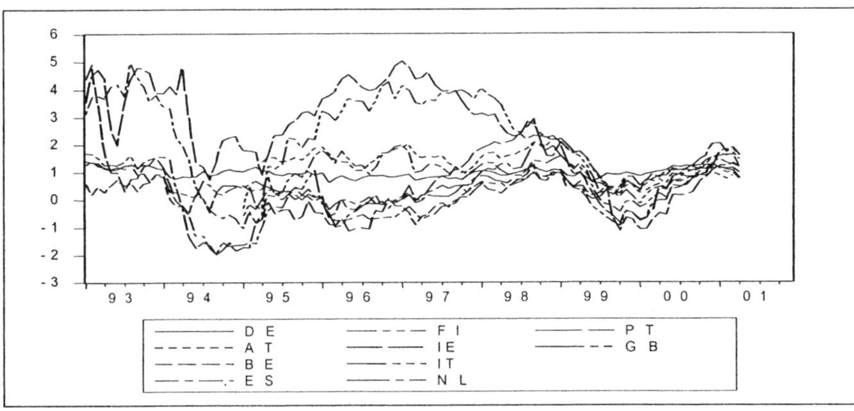

Table 2: Average correlation coefficients between national interest rate spreads

Period	DE	AT	BE	ES	FR	FI	IE	IT	NL	PT	UK	Total
Mortgage loans to households												
1980-2001	0.25	0.32	0.24	0.43	N.A.	0.54	0.43	0.14	0.25	0.20	0.34	0.31
1980-1992	0.42	N.A.	0.49	0.24	N.A.	N.A.	0.40	N.A.	0.38	0.53	N.A.	0.41
1993-1999	0.37	0.27	0.31	0.48	N.A.	0.57	0.52	0.10	0.43	0.07	0.43	0.35
1999-2001	0.45	0.66	0.59	0.76	N.A.	0.79	0.59	0.72	0.54	0.79	0.58	0.65
Consumer loans to households												
1980-2001	0.68	0.86	0.54	0.54	N.A.	0.61	N.A.	N.A.	N.A.	0.32	0.82	0.62
1980-1992	-0.18	N.A.	N.A.	-0.05	N.A.	0.10	N.A.	N.A.	N.A.	-0.39	N.A.	-0.13
1993-1999	0.69	0.75	0.42	0.48	N.A.	0.53	N.A.	N.A.	N.A.	0.38	0.73	0.57
1999-2001	0.68	0.86	0.54	0.54	N.A.	0.61	N.A.	N.A.	N.A.	0.32	0.82	0.62
Short-term loans to enterprises												
1980-2001	-0.06	0.14	-0.04	-0.05	0.12	N.A.	-0.10	0.01	-0.16	0.07	N.A.	-0.01
1980-1992	-0.10	N.A.	0.11	-0.08	0.15	N.A.	-0.03	0.10	-0.02	0.11	N.A.	0.03
1993-1999	0.09	0.19	-0.01	-0.03	0.17	N.A.	0.03	-0.08	-0.22	0.08	N.A.	0.02
1999-2001	0.66	0.67	0.28	0.47	0.50	N.A.	0.42	0.37	0.34	0.57	N.A.	0.47
Medium and long-term loans to enterprises												
1980-2001	0.39	N.A.	0.18	0.19	0.38	0.13	0.06	0.33	N.A.	N.A.	N.A.	0.24
1980-1992	N.A.	N.A.	0.00	0.21	0.23	-0.12	0.36	N.A.	N.A.	N.A.	N.A.	0.14
1993-1999	0.39	N.A.	0.17	0.22	0.49	0.25	0.00	0.30	N.A.	N.A.	N.A.	0.26
1999-2001	0.33	N.A.	0.20	0.53	0.45	0.14	0.52	0.58	N.A.	N.A.	N.A.	0.40
Time deposits												
1980-2001	0.30	0.45	0.26	0.20	0.10	0.34	N.A.	0.22	0.19	-0.11	-0.06	0.19
1980-1992	0.06	N.A.	0.21	0.12	0.17	0.24	N.A.	N.A.	0.22	0.18	N.A.	0.17
1993-1999	0.36	0.24	0.32	0.25	0.01	0.16	N.A.	0.30	0.27	0.22	-0.33	0.18
1999-2001	0.76	0.77	0.77	0.67	0.25	0.72	N.A.	0.76	0.43	0.77	0.38	0.63
Savings deposits												
1980-2001	0.50	N.A.	0.59	N.A.	0.43	N.A.	0.16	N.A.	N.A.	N.A.	0.04	0.34
1980-1992	0.03	N.A.	0.12	N.A.	0.00	N.A.	0.21	N.A.	N.A.	N.A.	N.A.	0.09
1993-1999	0.38	N.A.	0.45	N.A.	0.30	N.A.	0.27	N.A.	N.A.	N.A.	-0.30	0.22
1999-2001	0.87	N.A.	0.85	N.A.	0.88	N.A.	0.87	N.A.	N.A.	N.A.	0.56	0.81

Average of bilateral correlation coefficients of a country's retail rate with all other countries' retail rates.

3.3 Testing for Cointegration – The Bivariate Case

Before testing for cointegration, tests for the existence of a unit root in the time series of interest rate spreads were conducted. In the following, all series of spreads are treated as I(1) processes.[15] The results of the augmented Dickey-Fuller (ADF) and the Kwiatkowski, Phillips, Schmidt and Shin (KPSS) unit root tests are available upon request from the authors.

Cointegration is tested using the Johansen procedure. We use a model with an intercept in the cointegration equation but not in the vector autoregression part and with no deterministic trend as the data series exhibit such characteristics (first differences of the series fluctuate around zero). As for the lag structure in the model, an unrestricted vector autoregression model in first differences is estimated and the lag length is chosen according to the Akaike-criterion which makes sure that the residuals in each equation of the model are uncorrelated.

The results for the four lending rates and the two deposit rates are reported in Tables 3a to 3f. The tables display the lag length used for testing for bivariate cointegration and – according to the Trace statistic – if cointegration was found. One star indicates that cointegration was found at the 5% – two stars at the 1% significance level. More detailed results are available from the authors.

Table 3a: Results of bivariate cointegration tests: Existence of cointegration (optimal lag length in brackets): Mortgage loans to households (N2)

	AT	BE	ES	FI	IE	IT	NL	PT	UK
DE	no (2)	yes* (4)	yes* (3)	no (3)	no (5)	no (1)	yes** (1)	no (7)	no (5)
AT		no (2)	no (1)	no (1)	no (1)	no (1)	no (1)	no (1)	no (1)
BE			yes* (10)	no (3)	no (5)	no (1)	yes** (1)	yes* (8)	no (3)
ES				no (1)	no (10)	no (9)	no (4)	no (4)	no (4)
FI					no (1)	no (1)	yes* (3)	no (4)	no (4)
IE						no (1)	no (6)	no (10)	no (4)
IT							no (1)	no (1)	no (1)
NL								no (7)	no (3)
PT									no (1)

*/**: Trace statistic of Johansen test indicates cointegration with 5%/1% level of significance.

15 Only in the following cases we had problems to reject the null hypothesis of stationarity: for the mortgage rate and the short-term business lending rate for Ireland, for the time deposit rate for Belgium, Spain and France.

Table 3b: Consumer loans to households (N3)

	AT	BE	ES	FI	PT	UK
DE	yes** (10)	no (1)	no (2)	no (3)	no (4)	no (1)
AT		no (4)	no (1)	no (1)	no (1)	no (1)
BE			no (2)	no (5)	no (1)	no (1)
ES				no (10)	no (5)	no (1)
FI					no (9)	no (5)
PT						no (3)

Table 3c: Short-term loans to enterprises (N4)

	AT	BE	ES	FR	IE	IT	NL	PT
DE	no (1)	yes* (1)	yes* (1)	no (7)	yes** (8)	no (1)	no (1)	no (7)
AT		no (1)	no (5)	no (3)	no (1)	no (1)	no (1)	no (2)
BE			no (5)	no (10)	no (10)[16]	yes* (10)	no (1)	no (10)
ES				no (7)	yes** (8)	no (4)	no (1)	no (8)
FR					yes* (10)	yes* (9)	no (7)	no (9)
IE						yes** (5)	yes** (5)	yes** (10)
IT							no (1)	yes** (10)
NL								no (7)

Table 3d: Medium and long-term loans to enterprises (N5)

	BE	ES	FR	FI	IE	IT
DE	no (1)	yes** (6)	yes** (1)	no (2)	no (1)	yes** (1)
BE		yes** (10)	no (9)	no (5)	yes* (9)	no (1)
ES			no (10)	no (10)	yes** (10)	yes* (1)
FR				no (10)	yes** (10)	no (5)
FI					yes* (9)	yes* (2)
IE						no (1)

16 In this case two cointegration equations were found. When two cointegration equations are found in the bivariate case this indicates that the series are stationary. Indeed, we had problems to reject stationarity for Ireland whereas the Belgium series clearly is I(1).

Table 3e: Time deposits (N8)

	AT	BE	ES	FI	FR	NL	IT	PT2	UK
DE	no (3)	yes** (3)	yes** (10)	no (5)	yes** (9)	no (2)	no (1)	yes** (7)	no (2)
AT		no (1)	no (4)	no (2)	yes** (2)	no (1)	no (1)	no (2)	no (1)
BE			yes** (10)	yes** (10)	yes** (7)	yes** (3)	no (2)	yes** (8)	no (1)
ES				yes* (10)	yes** (10)	yes** (10)	yes** (2)	yes** (10)	no (2)
FI					yes** (7)	no (4)	no (2)	no (9)	no (1)
FR						yes** (9)	yes** (3)	yes** (10)	yes** (3)
NL							no (1)	no (8)	no (1)
IT								yes** (1)	yes* (2)
PT2									no (1)

Table 3f: Savings accounts (N9)

	BE	FR	IE	UK
DE	no (10)	yes** (3)	no (6)	no (1)
BE		yes** (10)	no (9)	no (1)
FR			yes* (10)	no (1)
IE				no (1)

Clearly, there are differences across the different markets. Looking at the relative numbers of cointegration relationships found, there is some evidence for integration in the market for short-term as well as for medium and long-term loans to enterprises, and also in the time deposits market. In the markets for mortgage loans and consumer loans to households as well as in the market for savings deposits only a few cointegration relationships are found, giving some indication that those markets are rather fragmented.

Looking in closer detail, in the market for *mortgage loans to households* in only 7 out of 21 possible combinations cointegration was found. Only the spreads for mortgage loans between Germany and the Netherlands, and the spreads between Belgium and the Netherlands were co-integrated at the 1% significance level. All in all there were 4 cointegration relationships found for Belgium, 3 for Germany and the Netherlands, 2 for Spain, and 1 for Finland and Portugal. No cointegration was found for Austria, Ireland, Italy and the United Kingdom. These numbers indicate that so far there exists no single European mortgage loans market although there is some evidence for integration in Belgium, Germany, the Netherlands and maybe Spain.

Figure 2 illustrates this pattern. The lines indicate that a bivariate cointegration relationship was found between the two countries, respectively.

Figure 2: Cointegration relationships in the mortgage market

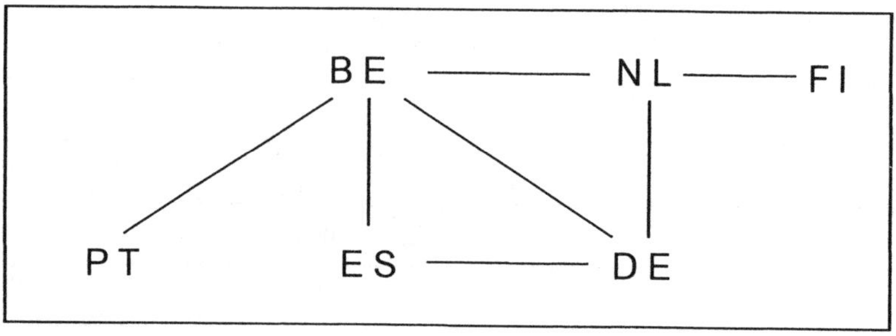

In the *consumer loans* market only one cointegration relationship was found, indicating that only the markets of Germany and Austria are integrated. This gives some evidence that there exist substantial obstacles to the integration of the European markets for consumer loans to households.

Hence, whereas the market for consumer loans does not show any sign of integration for the mortgage loans market there is at least some evidence for integration although there exists no single European mortgage market. This result seems to be plausible since in the mortgage market, for example, monitoring is a smaller problem than in the consumer loans market where also personal bank-customer-relationships probably play a major role.

The market for *short-term loans to enterprises seems to be more integrated.* In 11 out of 36 possible combinations cointegration was found. For Ireland 6 cointegration relationships were found, 4 for Italy, 3 for Germany, 2 for Belgium, Spain, France and Portugal, and 1 for the Netherlands. Only in the case of Austria no cointegration was found. Figure 3a illustrates the bivariate cointegration relationships in the case of short-term loans to enterprises. It seems that Ireland represents something like a centre that links a number of other national markets. However, we had problems with the rejection of stationarity for the spread series for Ireland which may be an explanation for the high numbers of cointegration relationships found for Ireland. When dropping Ireland from the sample, in 5 out of 28 possible combinations bivariate cointegration is found. Figure 3b illustrates this case which reveals some evidence for integration among Italy, Portugal, France, Belgium, Germany and Spain.

Figure 3a: Cointegration relationships in the market for short-term loans to enterprises

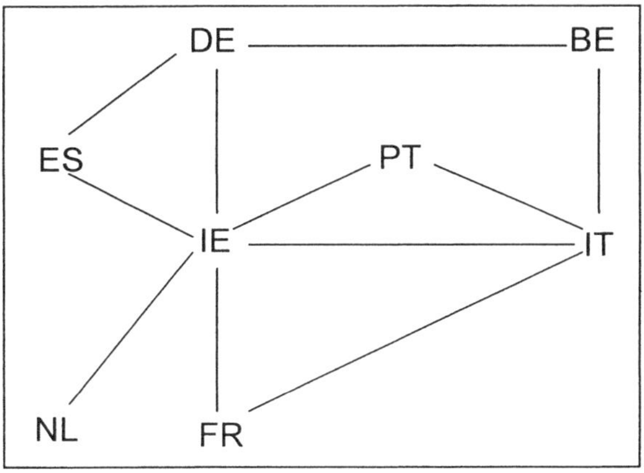

Figure 3b: Cointegration relationships in the market for short-term loans to enterprises when Ireland is dropped from the sample

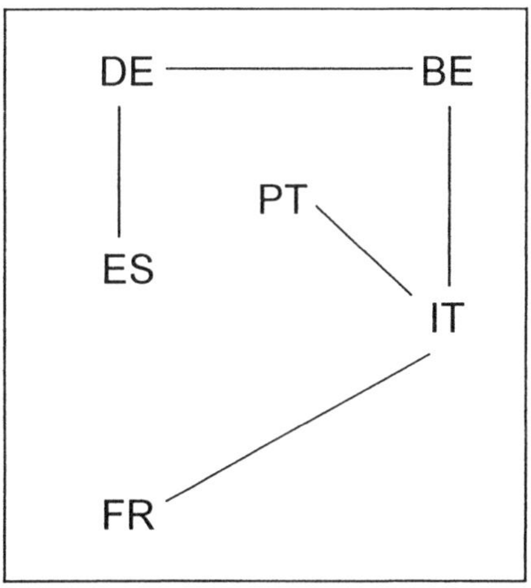

Also we get evidence that the European market for *medium and long-term loans to enterprises* is to some extent integrated since we found in almost every second case cointegration (10 out of 21). We found 4 cointegration relationships for Spain and Ireland, 3 for Germany and Italy, and 2 for Belgium, France and Finland. Figure 4 illustrates the bivariate cointegration relationships in the case of medium and long-term loans to enterprises.

Figure 4: Cointegration relationships in the market for medium and long-term loans to enterprises

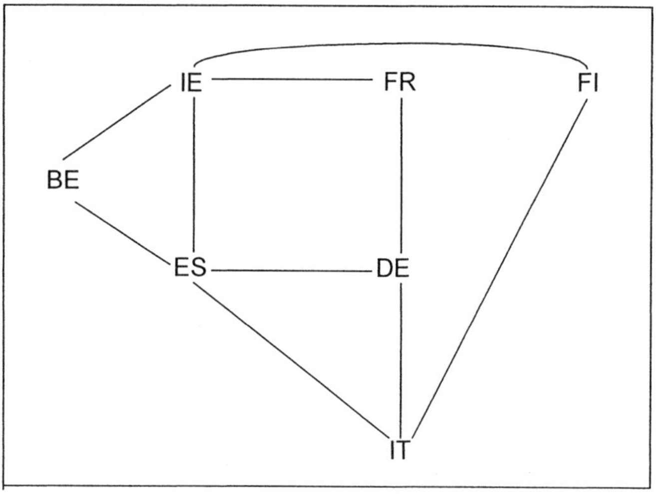

In general, it is enterprises rather than consumers that may borrow money from a bank abroad. Thus, cross-border competition in the markets for loans to enterprises probably is higher than in the markets for mortgage or consumer loans. This puts more pressure on banks in the enterprise loans market to pass a decrease in their cost of funds, i.e. the money market rate, to the lenders. In this way financial market integration is fostered and this explains our findings of lower integration in the mortgage and consumer loans market than in the loans markets for enterprises.[17]

In the *time deposits* market in 22 out of 45 possible combinations cointegration was found giving some evidence that the market is integrated to a large extent. This seems to be plausible since traditionally time deposits are strongly linked to the money market. With the introduction of a single currency a single European money market emerged which in the case of time deposits may have enforced integration. In addition, compared to, for example, savings deposits time deposits are predominantly made by wealthier or even institutional investors that may rather invest in a foreign country than a "normal saver". Thus, also higher cross-border competition may foster market integration. However, in this case we had

[17] Our finding that the firms loans market is more integrated than the households loans market is basically in line with Sander and Kleimeier (2001). However, they found evidence that the consumer loans market is somewhat more integrated than the market for mortgage loans market.

problems to reject stationarity for some spread series, namely for Belgium, Spain and France. Clearly, this limits interpretation.

There seems to be little evidence for integration in the European *savings deposit* market since we found only in 3 cases cointegration. It looks like France is integrated with Germany, Belgium and Ireland whereas no other cointegration relationships were found. A possible explanation for this lack of integration in the savings deposits market may be that savings deposits are usually made by savers that attach much importance to a personal customer-bank-relationship. Hence, cross-border competition is probably relatively low hindering integration in this market. Unfortunately, the number of countries for which interest rate data on savings deposits is available is small compared with the other markets so that comparisons have to be interpreted with caution.

To summarise, we find evidence that integration in the markets for mortgage and consumer loans to households is relatively low. The markets for short-term as well as medium and long-term loans to enterprises seem to be integrated at least to some extent. Concerning deposits, our results indicate that the time deposit market is to quite an amount integrated whereas the markets for savings deposits are rather fragmented.

3.4 The Multivariate Case

Based on the patterns obtained from the bivariate case (see Figures 2 to 4) we test for multivariate cointegration. The bivariate case ignores that there may exist integration of two markets through a third market, i.e. there may exist a long-run, cointegration relationship that ties several markets together whereas such a relationship is not found between two markets alone (Harris, 1995). So we look for samples of countries that exhibit one – and only one – cointegration equation. All countries in such a sample are tied to this one cointegration equation in the long-run which gives evidence for financial integration of these countries. When taking cointegration as evidence for market integration more than one co-integration equation economically does not make sense (Kremer, 1999). Therefore, when a sample of countries exhibits more than one cointegration equation we search for other samples that exactly have one cointegration equation.

Again, cointegration is tested using the Johansen procedure after choosing the lag length according to the Akaike criterion from a unrestricted vector autoregression model in first differences. The detailed test results can be obtained upon request. In the market for *mortgage loans to households* the sample of countries including Germany, Belgium, the Netherlands, and Spain exhibits exactly one cointegration equation. This confirms our findings from the bivariate cointegration tests illustrated in Figure 2. Although there exists no single European mortgage market there is some evidence that markets in Germany, Belgium, the Netherlands, and Spain are to some extent integrated.

In regard to the *consumer loans* market our finding from the bivariate case that there are no signs for integration are also confirmed in the multivariate case. The sample with all countries for which data is available reveals no cointegration. The same holds true when the United Kingdom as a non-Euroland country is dropped from the sample as well as for any other multivariate combination of countries.

For the *medium and long-term loans to enterprises* we find one cointegration equation for the sample including Spain, Germany, Italy, Ireland and Belgium. Looking at Figure 4 reveals that this finding confirms to some amount the results of the bivariate analysis. However, taking France and/or Finland into the sample one gets more than one cointegration relationships. This points to an integrated "core" of countries, namely Spain, Germany, Italy, Ireland and Belgium to which France and Finland have some link.

Concerning the *savings deposits* market we find one cointegration equation for the sample of all Euroland countries for which data is available, i.e. Germany, Belgium, France and Ireland indicating market integration for these countries. However, this evidence is rather weak since the Trace statistic allows only for a rejection of the null of no cointegration relationship at the 5% level and the max-eigenvalue test even indicates no cointegration among these countries. As mentioned above, bearing in mind that only for five countries data is available this result has to be interpreted with care anyway.

In regard to the European *time deposits* market we tested a number of possible combinations of countries for multivariate cointegration. We found for the sample including Germany, Belgium, Spain, France and Italy one cointegration equation. These countries were together with Portugal the countries for which the most bivariate cointegration relationships were found. Taking Portugal into the sample we found more than one cointegration equation. These findings indicate that there exists a "core" including the biggest European economies that have integrated markets for time deposits and that countries like Portugal, the Netherlands, Finland and Austria are linked through bivariate relationships to this "core". All in all the findings from the multivariate analysis – like the ones from the bivariate analysis – can be taken as evidence that the European time deposit market is to quite an amount integrated.

For the market for *short-term lending to enterprises* the results of the multivariate analysis are not presented as neither the results of the bivariate analysis are confirmed nor other reasonable patterns are obtained.

4 Obstacles to Integration in Retail Financial Markets

The analyses in the previous section give some evidence that although there are some signs for integration so far a single European retail financial market does not exist. This holds true especially for the loans markets to consumers, i.e. the mortgage and the consumer loans market, and for the savings deposit market. But also the loans market to enterprises seems to be not fully integrated. Thus, the question emerges of what are the reasons for this lack of integration, i.e. what are the obstacles to retail financial market integration.

In general, fragmentation in markets for financial services can either be due to policy-induced or to natural factors. Policy-induced obstacles are regulation and taxes, in particular, obstacles that can be reduced by policy-makers. As opposed to this, natural obstacles are independent of political actions at least in the short and medium-run. Such barriers to financial market integration are, for example, preferences and confidence of consumers, differences in culture and/or language, and distance.

SK cite Tommaso Padoa-Schioppa with the words "proximity is an intrinsic characteristic of the retail market with or without the emergence of a currency embracing a wider area" (Sander and Kleimeier, 2001: 1). In regard to loans to consumers the previous analyses somewhat confirm this assessment. In the mortgage market only between Germany and the Netherlands, and between Belgium and the Netherlands cointegration was found at a 1% significance level. In the consumer loans market only Germany and Austria were co-integrated. The closer links between neighbouring and common language countries indicate that for those markets distance and maybe also language may constitute natural obstacles to integration. However, this assessment is not confirmed for the other retail markets since there cointegration is found also for countries that are far away from each other. And even, when taking not just cointegration at the 1%-level distance seems to play no major role in the mortgage market.

In general, factors like distance, the presence of a common language, and a common legal system influence the information costs associated with bank lending. The presence of information costs hinders direct cross-border bank lending which means lower financial market integration (Buch, 2000). In particular, this should be essential for financial services that are not standardised and where monitoring plays a major role like with consumer loans or small business lending. Market segmentation that results from information costs can hardly be reduced by policy actions.

In addition to these natural obstacles to market integration there are policy induced obstacles – regulations in particular. Buch (2000) finds evidence that the EU's Single Market program and the Basle Capital Accord have had a positive impact on cross-border banking activity. On the other side, factors like the still high cost for cross-border transfers and lack of consumer protection may impair consumers in opening an account for time or savings deposits at a foreign bank. This includes issues such as cross-border redress and price transparency. Such obstacles should be addressed by policy makers and, to some extent, policy action has been taken or is underway.[18]

The revolution in information technology and in particular the internet is often said to overcome borders and in the context of financial retail markets to foster integration. Due to the technical advances, consumers are no longer bound to national or regional firms, they are able to shop around at all companies worldwide that provide services online. As a consequence, information costs are reduced and cross-border competition is enhanced which fosters financial market integration. However, due to factors like the preference of consumers for domestic suppliers overcoming fragmentation in retail financial markets remains hard to achieve (Schüler, 2002).

In summary, the cointegration analyses in the previous sections allows only for limited statements concerning the obstacles to integration of the European retail financial markets. For the loans markets to consumers there is some evidence that distance matters whereas for the loans markets to enterprises and the deposit markets this assessment is not confirmed. This seems to be quite plausible – firms rather than households may look for a cheaper credit at a foreign bank.

5 Conclusion

With the introduction of a single European currency a fully integrated European money market emerged and also other wholesale financial markets are generally regarded as highly integrated. In spite of this single wholesale financial market European retail financial markets still reveal substantial fragmentation. We analysed four lending markets and two deposit markets by testing for cointegration between national interest rate spreads. Comparing the markets in detail, we find evidence that the markets for loans to households are less integrated than the enterprise loans markets. In regard to lending to households we found more integration for mortgages than for consumer credit where almost no signs for integration were found at all. This may be explained by lower information costs for the mortgage credit since it is secured by real estate. We found evidence that the European time deposit market is to quite an amount integrated which is probably due to the fact that time deposits are traditionally strongly linked to the money

18 For a more detailed description of the policy action that has been taken to strengthen consumer protection in cross-border financial business see Schüler (2002).

market. For the savings deposit market the analyses showed a relatively low degree of integration.

Of course, the analyses in this paper can give just some evidence to the question of financial market integration since there remain problems with the data and also with the cointegration approach. For example, in periods of convergence cointegration tests may misleadingly reject cointegration (Kleimeier and Sander, 2000). However, as Section 2 has shown measuring financial market integration has been a difficult task – particularly for retail financial markets where the availability of useful data is strongly limited.

All in all the analyses have shown that retail financial markets seem to be far from being truly integrated. Thus, there is potential for further integration in retail financial markets. Clearly, a single European market for financial services would improve households' and firms' financing possibilities. However, considering the underlying obstacles to integration that are at least to some extent natural, in the short and medium-run national retail financial markets will remain segmented to a certain degree.

References

Ayuso, J. and R. Blanco (2000), *Has Financial Market Integration Increased During the 1990s?*, BIS Conference Papers No. 8, Basle.

Bayoumi, T. (1990), *Saving-Investment Correlations: Immobile Capital, Government Policy, or Endogenous Behavior?* IMF Staff Papers Vol. 37 (2), 360-387.

Bayoumi, T. and R. MacDonald (1995), *Consumption, Income, and International Capital Market Integration*, IMF Staff Papers Vol. 42 (3), 552-576.

Beckaert, G. and C.R. Harvey (1995), Time-Varying World Market Integration, *Journal of Finance* Vol. 50 (2), 403-444.

Berger, A. N. and T.H. Hannan (1998), The Price-Concentration Relationship in Banking, *The Review of Economics and Statistics* Vol. 71 (2), 291-299.

Buch, C. (2000), *Information or Regulation: What Is Driving the International Activities of Commercial Banks?*, Kiel Working Paper No. 1011, Kiel.

Chen, Z. and P.J. Knez (1995), Measurement of Market Integration and Arbitrage, *Review of Financial Studies* Vol. 8 (2), 287-325.

Centeno, M. and A.S. Mello (1999), How Integrated Are the Money Market and the Bank Loans Market Within the European Union?, *Journal of International Money and Finance* 18, 75-106.

Commission of the European Communities (1988), *European Economy: The Economies of 1992* (35), March, Brussels.

Dumas, B. and B. Solnik (1995), The World Price of Foreign Exchange Risk, *Journal of Finance* Vol. 50 (2), 445-479.

Guardia, N.D. (2000), *Consumer Credit in the European Union*, European Credit Research Institute, ECRI Research Report No.1, Brussels.

Eijffinger, S.C.W. and J.J.G. Lemmen (1995), Money Market Integration in Europe, *Swiss Journal of Economics and Statistic* 131 (1), 3-37.

Feldstein, M. and C. Horioka (1980), Domestic Saving and International Capital Flows, *The Economic Journal* 90, 314-329.

Feldstein, M. (1982), *Domestic Saving and International Capital Movements in the Long Run and the Short Run*, NBER Working Paper No. 947, Cambridge.

Ferson, W.E. and C.R. Harvey (1991), The Variation of Economic Risk Premiums, *The Journal of Political Economy* Vol. 99 (2), 385-415.

Frankel, J.A. (1992), Measuring International Capital Mobility: A Review, *The American Economic Review* 82 (2), 197-202.

Frankel, J.A. (1993), Quantifying International Capital Mobility in the 1980s, in: Bernheim, D. (Ed.), *National Saving and Economic Performance*, Chicago, 227-260.

Fratzscher, M. (2001), *Financial Market Integration in Europe: On the Effects of EMU on Stock Markets*, ECB Working Paper No. 48, Frankfurt.

Gardener, E.P.M. and J.L. Teppett (1995), A Select Replication of the Cecchini Microeconomic Methodology on the EFTA Financial Services Sectors: A Note and Critique, *The Service Industries Journal* 15, 74-89.

Goldstein, M. and M. Mussa (1993), *The Integration of World Capital Markets*, IMF Working Paper WP/93/95, Washington.

Hannan, T.H. (1991), Bank Commercial Loan Markets and the Role of Market Structure: Evidence From Surveys of Commercial Lending, *Journal of Banking and Finance* 15, 133-149.

Hannan, T.H. and A.N. Berger (1991), The Rigidity of Prices: Evidence from the Banking Industry, *The American Economic Review* 81 (4), 938-945.

Hardouvelis, G., D. Malliaropulos and R. Priestley (1999), *EMU and European Stock Market Integration*, CEPR Discussion Paper No. 2124, London.

Harris, R. (1995), *Using Cointegraion Analysis in Econometric Modelling*, London.

Heinemann, F. and M. Schüler (2002), *Interest Rate Pass-Through and Imperfect Integration of EU Markets for Financial Services*, ZEW Discussion Paper No. 02-26, Mannheim.

Heinemann, F. and C. Stirböck (1999), *Capital Mobility Within EMU*, ZEW Discussion Paper No. 99-19, Mannheim.

Heitfield, E.A. (1999), What Do Interest Rate Data Say About the Geography of Retail Banking Markets?, *The Antitrust Bulletin* (Summer), 333-347.

Hess, G.D. and K. Shin (2000), Risk Sharing by Households Within and Across Regions and Industries, *Journal of Monetary Economics* 45, 533-560.

International Monetary Fund (2000), *Annual Report on Exchange Arrangements and Exchange Restrictions 2000*, Washington.

Jackson III, W.E. (1992), Is the Market Well Defined in Bank Merger and Acquisition Analysis?, *The Review of Economics and Statistics* 74 (4), 665-661.

Keeley, M. C. and G.C. Zimmerman (1985), Determining Geographic Markets for Deposit Competition in Banking, *Economic Review – Federal Reserve Bank of San Francisco*, 25-45.

Kellermann, K. and C.-H. Schlag (1999), Eine Untersuchung der Ersparnis-Investitions-Korrelation in Deutschland, *Zeitschrift für Wirtschafts- und Sozialwissenschaften (ZWS)* 119, 99-119.

Kleimeier, S. and H. Sander (2000), Regionalisation Versus Globalisation in European Financial Market Integration: Evidence From Cointegration Analyses, *Journal of Banking and Finance* 24, 1005-1043.

Kremer, M. (1999), *Die Kapitalmarktzinsen in Deutschland und den USA: Wie eng ist der Zinsverbund? Eine Anwendung der multivariaten Kointegrationsanalyse*, Diskussionspapier 2/99, Volkswirtschaftliche Forschungsgruppe der Deutschen Bundesbank, Frankfurt.

Lapp, S. (1996), *The Feldstein-Horioka Paradox: A Selective Survey of the Literature*, Kiel Working Paper No. 752, Kiel.

Lemmen, J.J.G. and S.C.W. Eijffinger (1993), The Degree of Financial Integration in the European Community, *De Economist* 141 (2), 189-213.

Lemmen, J.J.G. and S.C.W. Eijffinger (1995), *Financial Integration in Europe: Evidence from Euler Equation Tests*, Working Paper, Tilburg University, Tilburg.

Lewis, K.K. (1999), Trying to Explain Home Bias in Equities and Consumption, *Journal of Economic Literature* 37, 571-608.

Mace, B.J. (1991), Full Insurance in the Presence of Aggregate Uncertainty, *The Journal of Political Economy* 99 (5), 928-956.

Murphy, R.G. (1984), Capital Mobility and the Relationship Between Saving and Investment Rates in OECD Countries, *Journal of International Money and Finance* (3), 327-342.

Neumark, D. and S.A. Sharpe (1992), Market Structure and the Nature of Price Rigidity: Evidence from the Market for Consumer Deposits, *Quarterly Journal of Economics* 107 (2), 657-680.

Obstfeld, M. (1985), *Capital Mobility in the World Economy: Theory and Measurement*, NBER Working Paper No. 1692, Cambridge.

Obstfeld, M. (1989), How Integrated Are World Capital Markets? Some New Tests, in: Calvo, G., R. Findlay, P. Kouri and J. Braga de Macedo (Eds.), *Debt, Stabilization and Development*, Oxford, 134-155.

Obstfeld, M. (1994), Are Industrial-Country Consumption Risks Globally Diversified?, in: Leiderman, L. and A. Razin (Eds.), *Capital Mobility: The Impact on Consumption, Investment and Growth*, Cambridge, 13-44.

Obstfeld, M. (1995), International Capital Mobility in the 1990s, in: Kenen, P.K., *Understanding Interdependence: The Macroeconomics of the Open Economy*, Princeton, 201-261.

Olivei, G.P. (2000), Consumption Risk-Sharing Across G-7 Countries, *New England Economic Review* (March/April), 3-14.

Radecki, L.J. (1998), The Expanding Geographic Reach of Retail Banking Markets, *FRBNY Economic Policy Review* (June), 15-34.

Radecki, L.J. (1999), Bank Restructuring and Financial Stability in the United States, *BIS Conference Papers* 7, Basle, 319-340.

Rhoades, S.A. (1992), *Evidence on the Size of Banking Markets from Mortgage Loan Rates in Twenty Cities*, Board of Governors of the Federal Reserve System Staff Studies No. 162, Washington.

Schulze, G.G. and H.W. Ursprung (1999), Globalisation of the Economy and the Nation State, *The World Economy* 22, 295-352.

Sander, H. and S. Kleimeier (2001), Towards a Single Retail Banking Market? New Evidence from Euroland, forthcoming in: *Australasian Journal of European Integration*.

Schüler, M. (2002), *Integration of the European Market for E-Finance – Evidence from Online Brokerage*, ZEW Discussion Paper No. 02-24, Mannheim.

Sinn, S. (1992), Saving-Investment Correlations and Capital Mobility: On the Evidence from Annual Data, *The Economic Journal* 102, 1162-1170.

Summers, L.H. (1988), Tax Policy and International Competitiveness, in: Frenkel, J. (Ed.), *International Aspects of Fiscal Policies*, Chicago, 349-386.

Stigler, G.J. and R.A. Sherwin (1985), The Extent of the Market, *Journal of Law & Economics* 28, 555-585.

Taylor, A.M. (1994), *Domestic Saving and International Capital Flows Reconsidered*, NBER Working Paper No. 4892, Cambridge.

Taylor, A.M. (1996), *International Capital Mobility in History: The Saving-Investment Relationship*, NBER Working Paper 5743, Cambridge.

Tesar, L.L. and I.M. Werner (1992), *Home Bias and the Globalization of Securities Markets*, NBER Working Paper No. 4218, Cambridge.

Tobin, J. (1983), Comments 'Domestic Saving and International Capital Movements in the Long Run and the Short Run' by M. Feldstein, *European Economic Review* 21, 153-156.

Zimmermann, G.C. (1995), Implementing the Single Banking Market in Europe, *Federal Reserve Bank of San Francisco Economic Review* (3), 35-51.

Integration of the European Market for E-Finance – Evidence from Online Brokerage

Martin Schüler*

Centre for European Economic Research (ZEW), Mannheim, Germany

"E-commerce may revolutionise the provision of financial services, especially cross-border within the Internal Market." (European Commission, Sept. 27, 2001)

1 Motivation

There are basically two factors that foster financial market integration. First, policy-induced deregulation both at a national and at an international level, and second, technological change, i.e. the revolution in information technologies (Buch, 2000).

The internet revolution has fuelled euphoric expectations of overcoming natural borders. The euphoric view can be summarised in the following way: Due to the technical advances, consumers are no longer bound to national or regional firms, they are able to shop around at all companies world-wide that provide services online. This holds true for quite a number of products and services in financial markets, such as online banking and brokerage but also mortgage loans and insurance policies, among others. Before actually purchasing a certain financial service online at a bank or insurance company, customers can compare mortgage, insurance, or lending products offered by different suppliers with the help of so-called aggregators[1] complementing the classic internet portals (Claessens et al., 2000: 10). On the one hand, the internet enables consumers to easily compare financial services and find the cheapest and for their needs best suitable supplier. On the other hand, the internet eliminates a number of processing steps and labour costs, and it avoids or at least reduces the fixed costs of branches and related mainte-

* Acknowledgement: The author is indebted to Friedrich Heinemann for helpful comments and discussion and to Niels Nauhauser for research assistance. I also like to thank Johannes Schmoeckel for comments on an earlier draft of the paper. All remaining errors are my own.

1 In Europe such aggregators are for example InsuranceCity and Interhyp in Germany.

nance. Thus new financial service providers can compete for customers more effectively and at a minimum of distribution cost.

However, this euphoric view might be erroneous. It overlooks the fact that the internet does not necessarily overcome all of the existing barriers to cross-border marketing of financial services. Obstacles like the consumer preference for domestic providers will still remain.

Therefore, what is required is a more balanced view. This analysis tries to contribute to it. With regard to a specific market, the market for online brokerage, it deals with the following question: To which extent does the internet allow for the existence of a truly European Market? The analysis is based on two data bases: (a) price data and (b) data drawn from a survey among European direct brokers.

The following section attempts to assess the extent to which the market for online brokerage in Europe is already integrated. Section 3 discusses the obstacles to further market integration in online brokerage and e-finance in general, Section 4 deals with the question of how these obstacles can be overcome and what the potential benefits for the consumer would be. Section 5 provides a conclusion.

2 Extent of Imperfect Integration on the Market for Online Brokerage in Europe

Online brokerage means purchasing and selling securities online, i.e. on the internet. It is one part of online banking, which includes bank transactions in general, such as credit transfers. In that sense online brokers or direct brokers are online banks offering security transactions, and apart from keeping an online account, they usually do not provide any other banking services. Studying the market for online brokerage more closely is facilitated by the fact that there is a homogeneous commodity, i.e. the purchase or sale of stocks for some amount of money. Thus, prices and conditions are comparable between different direct brokers within and also across countries.[2]

This section tries to assess the extent to which the European market for online brokerage is integrated. In this context, integration means that there are no barriers that prevent a consumer from purchasing securities using a foreign direct broker. And, that suppliers of financial services have access to foreign markets, which implies – in the market for online brokerage – that they can attend to foreign

2 Of course there may be differences in the provision such as offering consulting services or special investment products. However, in the following such „quality differences“ are disregarded. Rather we think of online brokerage as pure purchasing or selling of securities.

customers on their "domestic" homepage by simple translation into the language of their target group. Hence, if there was complete market integration, one would expect customers to switch to a foreign direct broker if this broker is more suitable to their needs or if this broker offers lower fees and commissions, provided that differences in quality are of minor importance here.

As a consequence, huge price differences between online brokers indicate incomplete integration. Of course, even in a fully integrated market, price differences remain due to different cost structures, quality differences, etc. However, if the differences in prices are significant, especially between direct brokers of different EU countries, this can be taken as some evidence for obstacles that remain powerful even in the internet age.

Price Differences in Europe

Figure 1 shows the leading European direct brokers by the number of accounts. Altogether these twelve providers account for over 70% of all European market online accounts.

Figure 1: Market shares of online brokers in Europe

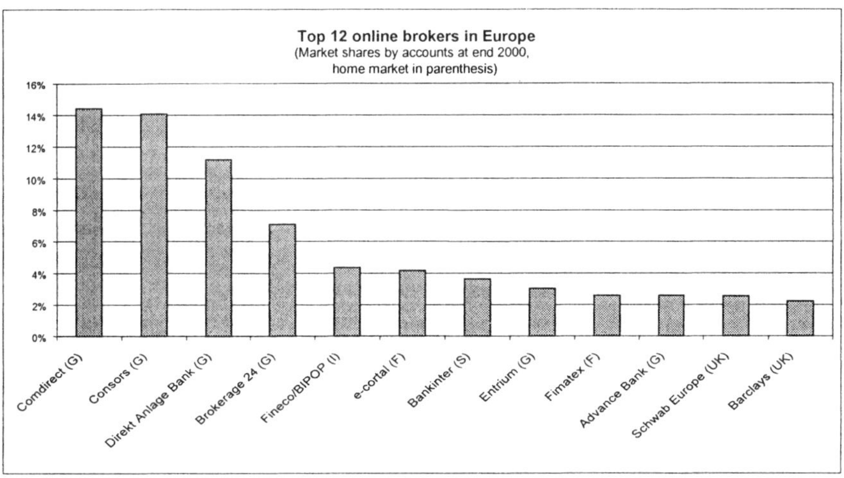

Source: JPMorgan (2001a).

With almost two million online accounts at the end of 2000, the German market for online brokerage is by far the largest in Europe, which explains that six (Comdirect, Consors, Direkt Anlage Bank, Brokerage 24, Entrium, Advance Bank) of those twelve leading online brokers are located in Germany.[3] E-cortal and Fimatex

3 According to a study by the Bundesverband deutscher Banken in the second quarter of 2001 8% of total population in Germany used the internet for brokerage services.

have France as their home market, the second largest market in Europe with about 415,000 accounts. Schwab Europe and Barclays primarily serve the British market which has about 280,000 accounts. Fineco/BIPOP is located in Italy and Bankinter in Spain. The Italian market has a total of about 230,000 accounts, the Spanish market of about 185,000 accounts.[4]

Figure 2 shows how much a purchase of stocks of an amount of 2,500 EUR and 6,000 EUR costs at each of the online brokers.[5] There are clear price differences ranging from as little as 4.75 EUR to as much as 27.40 EUR for the 2,500 EUR transaction and of between 11.40 EUR and 60.00 EUR for the 6,000 EUR transaction. For the 2,500 EUR transaction the mean over those twelve brokers is 13.11 EUR with a standard deviation of 5.81 EUR. For the 6,000 EUR transaction the mean is 21.13 EUR and the average deviation from the mean is 13.62 EUR. This comparison displays huge price differences among European online brokers.

Figure 2: Transaction costs in Europe

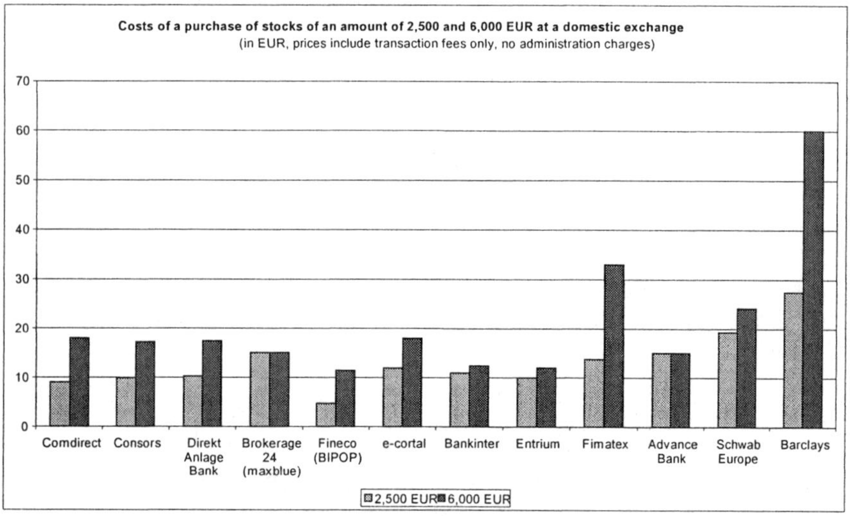

Source: Company data, own calculations; as of October 1, 2001.

---

4 Although being the third-largest market in Europe with about 410,00 accounts at end 2000, there is no Swedish online broker under the top 12. The market in the Netherlands has about 235,000 accounts, the Swiss market a good 100,000 accounts. Figures are taken from JP Morgan (2001a). In the following the focus is on the top 12 brokers in Europe since they serve the most important markets and since they are likely to be able to operate on a European scale.

5 All commissions and fees are taken from the online brokers' homepages. Considered are the costs for purchasing or selling of stocks at the domestic exchange. In the following price comparisons, additional fees for purchasing foreign stocks are disregarded. Those fees are usually low and thus the abstraction does not affect the line of reasoning. All prices are as of October 1, 2001.

However, the calculations of Figure 2 do not include any administration charges and do not allow for more sophisticated comparisons. Thus, five different customer groups are defined, namely the type “Student”, “Old Age Provision”, “Private Day Trader”, “Experienced Speculator”, and “Wealthy Investor”. Then the prices a consumer of each group would pay per year, including commission rates and fees for administration, are calculated. The characteristics of the different customer groups are shown in Table 1, the corresponding prices they pay in Figures 3 to 7.

Table 1: Defined characteristics of different customer groups

Customer group	*Characteristics*
“Student”	High risk of investment, small transaction volumes, small portfolio volume, medium number of trades p.a.
“Old age provision“	Low risk of investment, medium transaction volumes, medium portfolio volume, small number of trades p.a.
“Private Day Trader”	High risk of investment, medium transaction volumes, medium portfolio volume, large number of trades p.a.
“Experienced Speculator”	Medium risk of investment, medium transaction volumes, medium portfolio volume, small number of trades p.a.
“Wealthy Investor”	Low risk of investment, large transaction volumes, large portfolio volume, small number of trades p.a.

Figure 3: Annual costs for consumer type “Student”

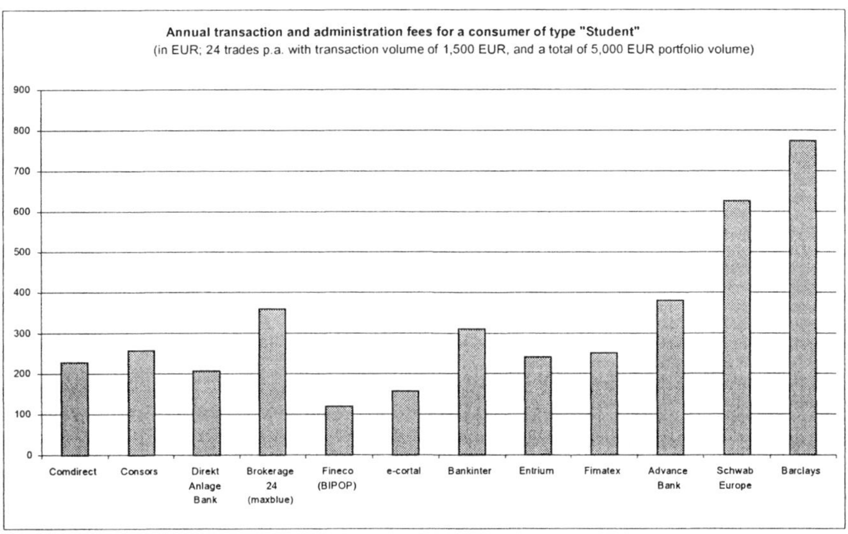

Source: Company data, own calculations; as of October 1, 2001.

Figure 4: Annual costs for consumer type "Old Age Provision"

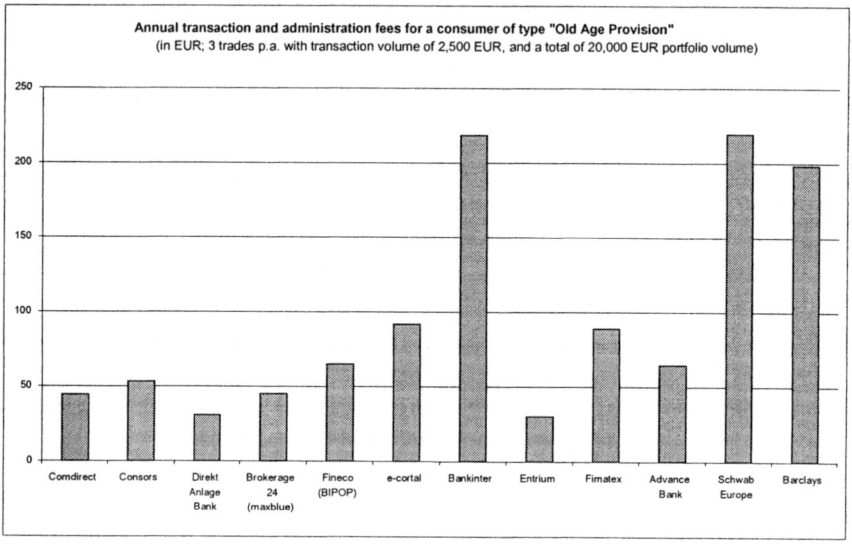

Source: Company data, own calculations; as of October 1, 2001.

Figure 5: Annual costs for consumer type "Private Day Trader"

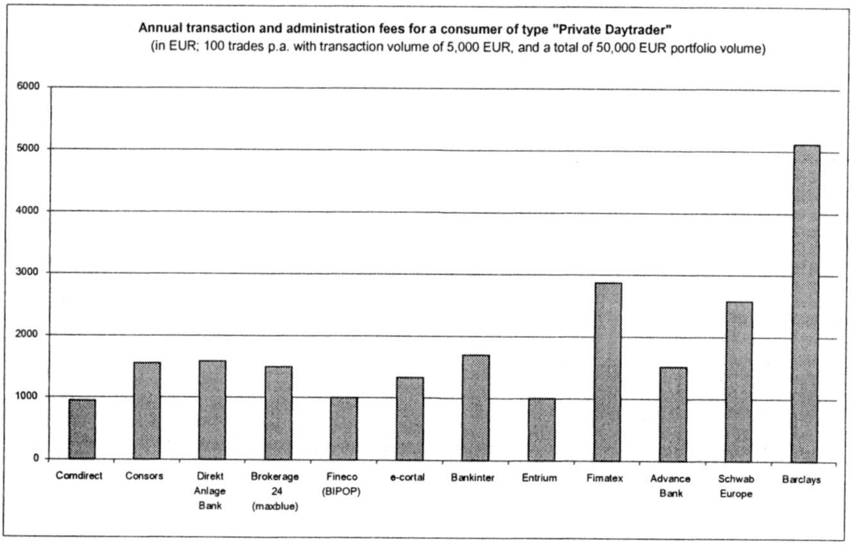

Source: Company data, own calculations; as of October 1, 2001.

Figure 6: Annual costs for consumer type "Experienced Speculator"

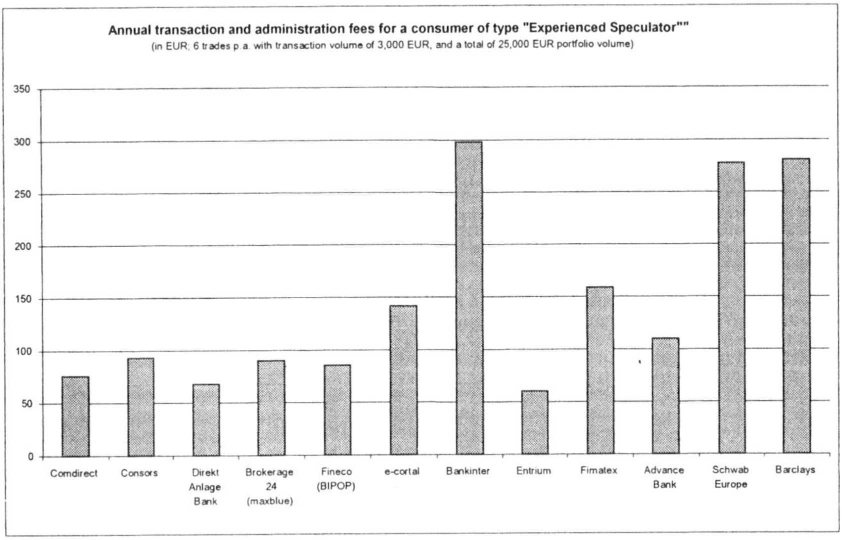

Source: Company data, own calculations; as of October 1, 2001.

Figure 7: Annual costs for consumer type "Wealthy Investor"

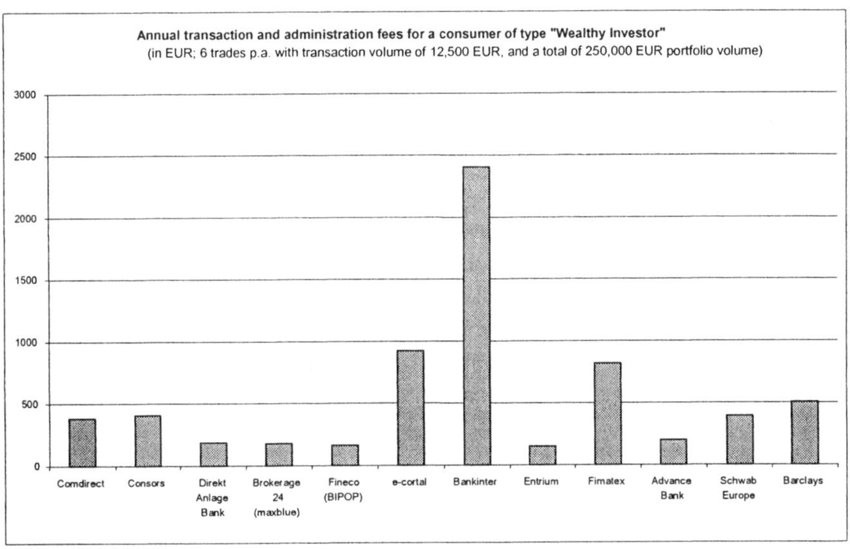

Source: Company data, own calculations; as of October 1, 2001.

Obviously, prices paid for online brokerage differ substantially for all customer groups. Even when eliminating the three most expensive brokers from the sample for each case, prices vary by quite an amount. For example, a consumer of type "Student" pays about three times as much when doing brokerage with Brokerage 24 in Germany as when using Fineco in Italy.

The important question in this context is whether there are any significant differences between countries and whether direct brokers within one country charge about the same prices. If this is the case, this would be at least some evidence for the observation that markets for online brokerage in Europe are not integrated. Thus "within" versus "between" price dispersions are compared. Indeed, the two French companies in the sample, e-cortal and Fimatex, which account for over 50% of the French market, have about the same price levels except for the consumer of type "Student" and "Old Age Provision". Also the German discount brokers show similar pricing behaviours. Usually, they are below the average in Europe. The two British online brokers, Schwab Europe and Barclays, which account for approx. 65% of the British market, are far above average except for the consumer type "Wealthy Investor". Bankinter, which has a market share of over 70% in Spain, is also far above average in most of the cases, only for the type "Student" and "Private Day Trader" is it slightly below the average in Europe. The Italian market leader Fineco/BIPOP with a market share of approx. 70% in Italy is below average for all customer groups.

Thus, taking into account that the companies in the sample are dominating their home markets, respectively, the above analysis shows that online brokers within one country are quite alike in their prices. As opposed to that, the differences in commissions and fees charged by online brokers between countries are considerable, indicating that the markets for online brokerage are rather fragmented in Europe.

Another point supports this assessment. Figures 8 to 11 show the prices charged by direct brokers and some of their foreign subsidiaries in comparison to the respective market leader. Consors has subsidiaries in France, Italy, Spain and Switzerland. The Direkt Anlage Bank serves France, Italy, Spain, and the UK through the online broker Selftrade. The two French direct brokers, e-cortal and Fimatex, have subsidiaries in Germany, the United Kingdom, and Spain.

Figure 8: Consors – comparison of transaction fees between parent company and subsidiaries

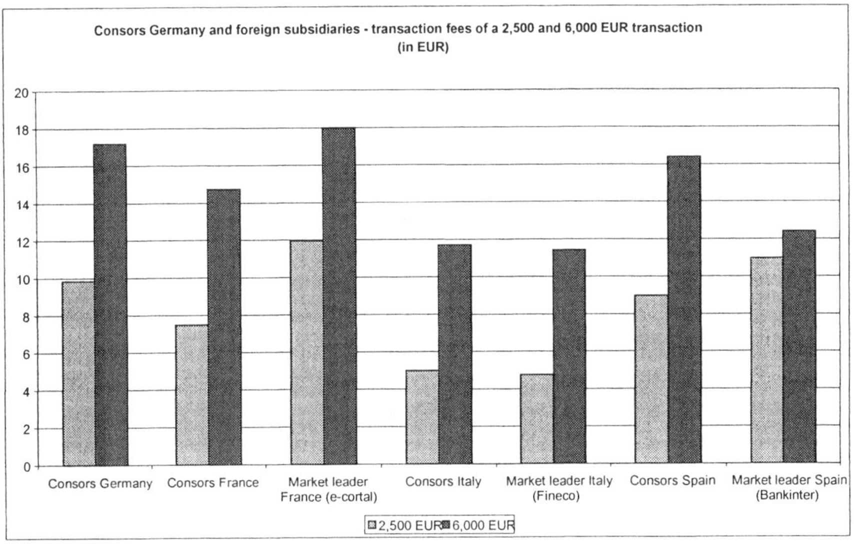

Source: Company data, own calculations; as of October 1, 2001.

Figure 9: DAB – comparison of transaction fees between parent company and subsidiaries

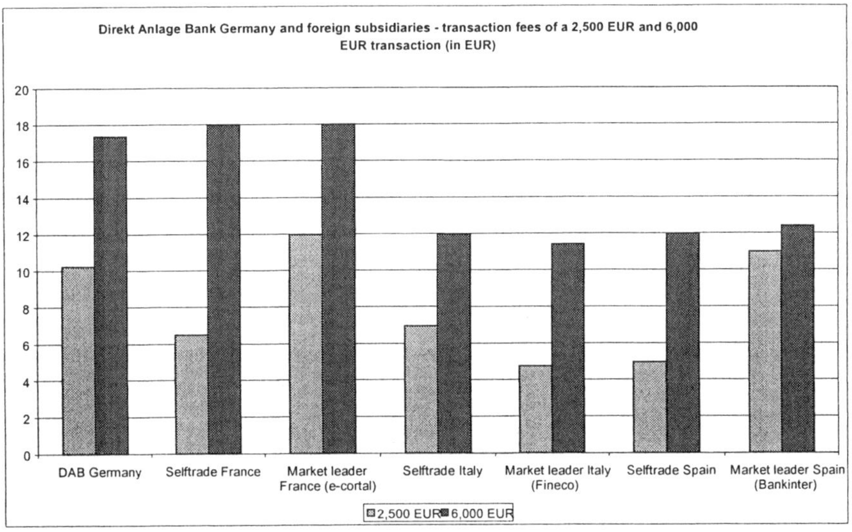

Source: Company data, own calculations; as of October 1, 2001.

Figure 10: e-cortal – comparison of transaction fees between parent company and subsidiaries

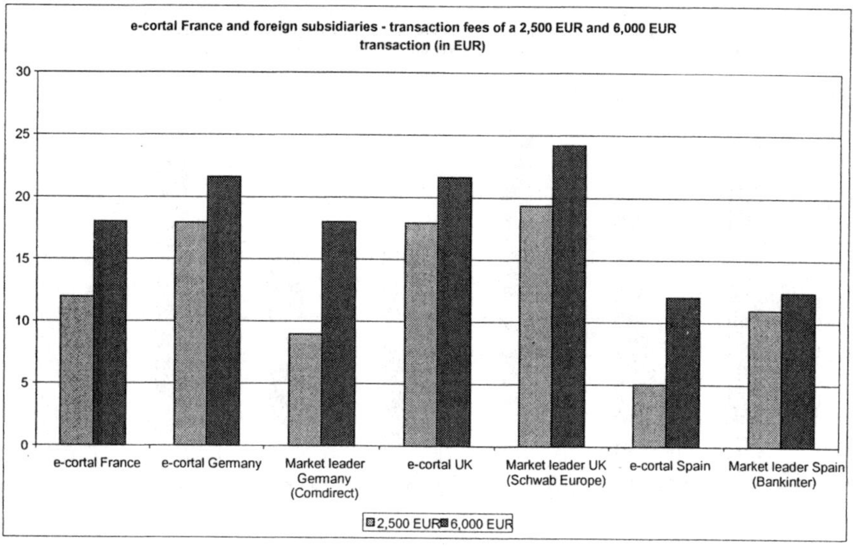

Source: Company data, own calculations; as of October 1, 2001.

Figure 11: Fimatex – comparison of transaction fees between parent company and subsidiaries

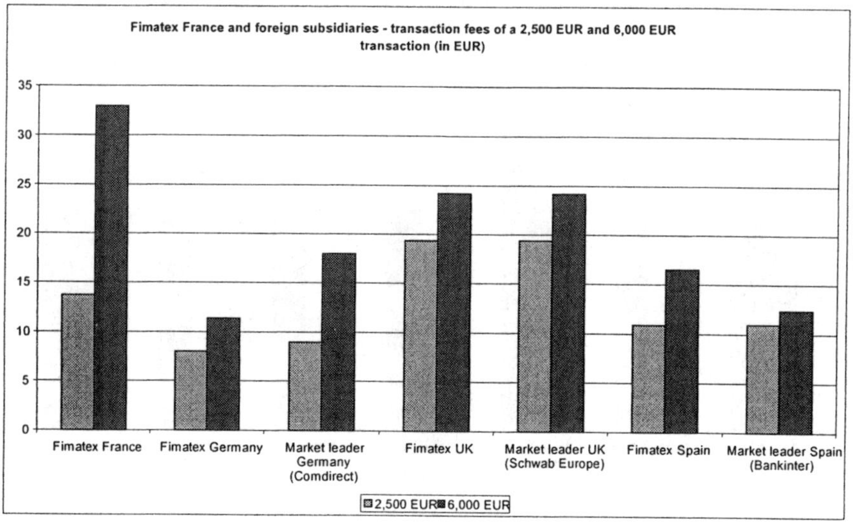

Source: Company data, own calculations; as of October 1, 2001.

Surprisingly, there are major differences in the prices charged by the parent company and the foreign subsidiaries. It looks like in some cases the foreign subsidiaries align with the respective market leader. This seems to be the case for Fimatex Germany (Figure 11), whose prices are clearly lower than those of its parent company in France. The same holds true for e-cortal Spain (Figure 10), Selftrade Italy (Figure 9) and Consors Italy (Figure 8).

To summarise, there are substantial differences in the pricing behaviour between direct brokers in different countries, even if they have the same parent company. Bearing in mind that we were to compare prices of a homogeneous commodity postulating that quality differences are of minor importance, the variety in prices indicates that the markets for online brokerage in Europe are rather fragmented than integrated.

The US as a Benchmark

Looking at the United States as a benchmark for an integrated market can help us interpret the above results. Figure 12 shows the costs of a 2,500 EUR and a 6,000 EUR purchase of stocks at the five leading US direct brokers that account for over 80% of the total US market.[6]

Figure 12: Transaction costs in the US

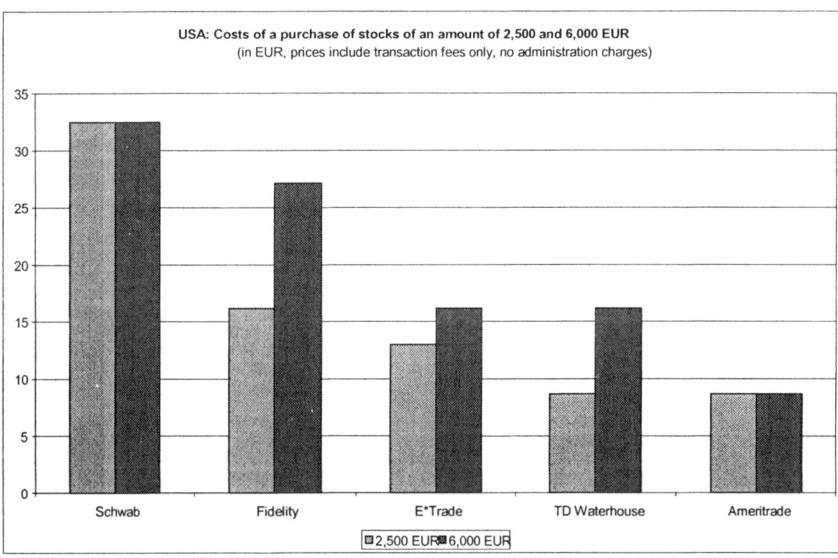

Source: Company data, own calculations; as of October 1, 2001.

6 Commissions and fees were converted to Euro equivalents at the exchange rate of 0.9216 USD/EUR.

Here the differences in prices are smaller than in Europe. Especially for a 6,000 EUR transaction, prices range from as low as 8.68 EUR to as high as 32.50 EUR in the US compared to as low as 11.40 EUR and as high as 60 EUR in Europe.

Of course, there are still differences in the commissions and fees charged due to differences in the structure and the aims of a given company or due to quality differences, such as offering consulting.[7] However, the smaller differences in the US seem to support the hypothesis that the market for online brokerage in Europe is not integrated yet.

Cross-Border Activities

Another indicator for financial market integration is the direct measure of cross-border activity. In online brokerage there are basically two types of cross-border activity. First, companies can get access to other markets by addressing the foreign client directly through the domestic homepage. Second, firms can establish a subsidiary, co-operate or merge with a company in the target country.

A survey (see box) among leading European online brokers showed that at the moment almost no broker has customers with place of residence outside their home market, when not accounting for customers that are attended to by foreign subsidiaries. Furthermore, a large part of the direct brokers do not expect any increase in the number of foreign customers within the next two or five years. In most of the cases they do not attach much importance to the strategy of attending to foreign customers through the domestic homepage, but prefer to enter new markets by co-operation with a provider in the target market or by undertaking mergers or acquisitions.

An exception to this are some Swiss banks, whose customers with foreign residence already account for about 5% on average, and who predict an increase for the next few years. It is highly important for this restricted number of brokers to serve customers in neighbouring countries like France and Germany directly through the domestic homepage, whereas they do not rely on subsidiaries, co-operation or mergers for gaining

> *Survey and Interviews*
>
> A survey among leading European online brokers was conducted by the Centre for European Economic Research (ZEW) in August/September 2001 as well as several interviews with selected direct brokers. The questionnaire included questions concerning the price differences on EU markets, strategies to gain access to other EU markets, the accessibility of EU markets and barriers to entry into foreign markets.
>
> The analyses in this paper are partially based on data gained from this survey and the outcome of the interviews.

7 Schwab, for example, clearly focuses on wealthier investors that usually also attach importance to consulting services. This is probably an explanation for Schwab's prices being above the US average.

access to foreign markets. However, the Swiss case clearly is an exception since in this case language problems are irrelevant. Furthermore, there may be a bias due to tax privilege issues. For almost all other online brokers surveyed, attending to their foreign clients on the domestic homepage is of minor or even no importance.

This result is quite surprising since the internet is said to make distance less important. Also one would expect that translating the domestic homepage is the most cost-effective way of addressing foreign customers. The fact that most direct brokers establish foreign subsidiaries or try to co-operate or merge with a foreign company indicates that some barriers or circumstances exist that make the strategy of attending to foreign customers on the domestic homepage the less successful one. Such circumstances are dealt with in Section 3.

3 Obstacles to Perfect Market Integration

Section 2 states that there are major differences in prices for online brokerage between direct brokers in different European countries and that almost no direct cross-border purchase takes place, i.e. online purchases of stocks are almost always done using a domestic direct broker. The question which suggests itself is why this is the case. What are the obstacles that cause this fragmentation of the markets for online brokerage in Europe? Due to the characteristics of the internet mentioned above, one would expect at least some Europeans to make use of the major price differences and open up an account for brokerage at a lower-cost, foreign direct broker.

In general, fragmentation in markets for financial services can either be due to policy-induced or to natural factors. Policy-induced obstacles are regulation and taxes, in particular, obstacles that can be reduced by policy-makers. As opposed to this, natural obstacles are independent of political actions at least in the short and medium run. Such barriers to financial market integration are, for example, preferences and confidence of consumers, differences in culture and/or language, technology and network cost.

Natural Obstacles

Related to e-finance, the obstacle question is of special importance. If it turns out that natural obstacles are the major reason for fragmentation, some sort of fragmentation will always remain and the market for e-finance will not become fully integrated – at least not in the short and medium run. Of course there is no question about the internet fostering market integration by giving consumers the possibility to purchase goods and services abroad more easily. However, the often praised quality of the internet to bust borders would lose relevance in this context.

In the past, i.e. for traditional distribution of financial services, sunk costs were important entry barriers (Claessens et al., 2000). Among them were, for example, branch networks, branding advantages involving large up-front advertising expenses, long-lasting customer relationships, substantial up-front investments in technology. With the internet, one would expect most of those barriers to have become obsolete.

Since e-finance obviously does not require the physical presence of the company, sunk costs arising from a branch network are losing relevance. The same holds true for up-front investment in technology. However, sunk costs like advertising expenses still play an important role since, according to some online brokers surveyed, a brand name is a prerequisite for acquiring new customers. Concerning long-lasting customer relationships the conclusion is not that clear-cut. On the one hand, one would expect customer-firm-relationships to continue to play an important role, especially when it comes to banking. On the other hand, customers doing online brokerage seem to be more open to switching providers in general.

In the survey among leading European direct brokers[8], almost all of them state that reaching the critical size for entering the market is very relevant as a barrier to entry as well as the fact that the respective market is already saturated. This is probably one reason why most of the online brokers aim at mergers and acquisitions or at establishing subsidiaries in the case of sufficient market growth in order to get access to new markets. This reveals continuing importance of sunk costs.

However, this does not per se rule out the strategy of acquiring new foreign customers directly through the domestic homepage, since in connection with this strategy the question of critical size is of no relevance (European Central Bank, 1999). Problems in this context are rather seen in language and other cultural differences or the lack of market experience. Obviously, those problems can hardly be solved from the home country by translating the web page alone. Instead, actual presence in the target market is required by establishing a subsidiary or merge with a local company in order to get the necessary know-how from local managers.

Furthermore the majority of the direct brokers surveyed stated the preference of the consumer for domestic companies to be a very important barrier for market entry. Also in this context, the restricted recognition of the trade mark was named as a reason why they find it difficult or do not even try to acquire foreign customers directly through their domestic homepage.

---

8 The online brokers were asked to assess the importance of various barriers to market entry in various European countries. Since the answers did not significantly differ between the European countries studied, the respective obstacles are regarded as barriers to entry for all European markets.

Policy-Induced Obstacles

The obstacles stated so far are all natural obstacles, i.e. barriers that cannot be removed by policy action, at least not in the short or medium run. Concerning policy-induced obstacles, companies surveyed valued regulation in general as irrelevant. However, a few stated that structural problems in the European payment system impair them in addressing foreign customers directly through the homepage. This is evident since investors do transfers between the online account at the direct broker and the current account that is usually kept at a bank located in the country of the consumer's place of work.

In this context the high cost for cross-border transfers play a major role. A study published by the European Commission in September 2001 (European Commission, 2001) shows that the average cost of a cross-border credit transfer of 100 EUR is still 24.09 EUR.[9] This compares to only about one Euro on average for a transfer within one country. The study was conducted in March 2001 by sending 1,480 cross-border transfers of 100 EUR in 15 EU Member Countries using 40 bank accounts. It was to verify the requirements of the Cross-Border Credit Transfers Directive (COM, 1997) adopted on January 27, 1997 that introduced provisions on transparency, performance and redress procedures concerning cross-border credit transfers. This directive was devised to ensure that funds could be transferred from one Member State to another rapidly, reliably and inexpensively. It was to be transposed into national law by August 14, 1999.

Figure 13 shows total transfer costs by sender country (European Commission, 2001). With an average of 47 EUR and 36 EUR, Greece and Ireland have the highest transfer costs. At the other end of the scale Belgium, Germany, and the Netherlands all have average costs of less than 15 EUR. Luxembourg has the lowest costs with an average of less than 10 EUR. Clearly, a cross-border transfer is much more expensive than a transfer within a country thus preventing customers from choosing a foreign direct broker and impairing cross-border business in general. This obstacle to financial market integration was addressed by the European Commission with a regulation that will be discussed in Section 4.

Another obstacle mentioned by the online brokers surveyed was identification of clients across borders. Unless a customer visits a branch in person, identification is frequently provided by local post offices which, according to a broker interviewed, often causes problems. However, another company stated that identification by the respective embassy or a notary is quite easy. Nevertheless, such a procedure may discourage consumers in choosing a foreign online broker.

---

9 Another survey on the cost of cross-border transfers published by the European Commission in July 2001 states that charges for cross-border transfer transactions of 100 EUR were 17.36 EUR. However, this survey is based on only 350 transfers carried out mainly in border areas.

Figure 13: Total cost for a cross-border credit transfer by sender country

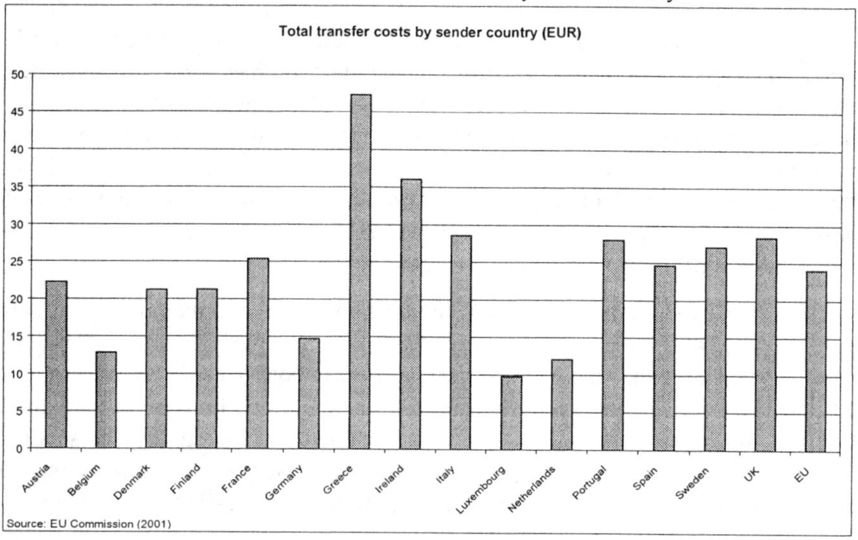

Source: EU Commission (2001).

Furthermore, the heterogeneity of the technical systems of stock exchanges was mentioned as an obstacle. Concerning the trading industry, increased integration between stock exchanges has taken place in the form of cross-border co-operation and mergers. However, the clearing and settlement infrastructure has remained relatively fragmented (European Central Bank, 2001a) As a consequence, some online brokers charge additional fees for purchasing and selling of stocks at foreign exchanges or do not even offer this service. This may also impair customers from choosing a supplier abroad.

Of course, the survey among online brokers states obstacles from the suppliers' point of view only. From a consumer perspective the question of consumer protection is of crucial importance when choosing a foreign supplier. This includes issues such as cross-border redress and price transparency. Also, common standards and protocols between countries are needed to assure desired privacy levels (Claessens et al., 2000: 5).

Table 2 summarises the barriers to integration in the market for online brokerage by natural and policy-induced obstacles. Most of the obstacles mentioned in the context of online brokerage should also be relevant for other online financial services such as mortgage loans or insurance policies, although other obstacles might arise like, for example, monitoring problems.

Table 2: Relevant obstacles to integration of the European markets for online brokerage

Natural obstacles	***Policy-induced obstacles***
Preference of the consumer for domestic online brokers	Structural problems in the transfer system; high cost of cross-border transactions
Language and other cultural differences	Cross-border identification
Sunk costs	Consumer protection
Critical size for entering the market is out of reach	Heterogeneity of trading, clearing, and settlement
Market is saturated	
Lack of market experience	
Lack of brand value	

4 Overcoming Fragmentation

The barriers mentioned by the online brokers surveyed, the saturation of almost all European markets, the failure to reach the critical size for entering the market, the lack of market experience and high up-front advertising expenses, are traditional entry barriers. These are the factors that impair suppliers of financial services and suppliers in general in the acquisition of foreign customers, thus representing obstacles to the integration of markets. These obstacles are natural and cannot – or should not – be addressed by policy makers with the exception of anti trust policy.

Then there are other natural obstacles like language and cultural differences that directly hamper market integration. The survey showed that those obstacles remaining at any rate are of quite an importance. Thus total market integration cannot be expected even if all policy-induced obstacles were removed.

Another very important obstacle to integration of online brokerage markets is the preference of consumers for domestic providers. Probably this holds true for e-finance in general. When it comes to investing or borrowing money or concluding an insurance the "handshake" is a very important prerequisite (Leamer and Storper, 2001). Since the internet does not allow for this "handshake", knowledge of the firm one is giving money to becomes essential. This is probably the main reason why consumers do not naturally switch to a foreign online broker even if they could save a lot of commission and administration fees. And this is why companies usually do not even try to acquire customers through their domestic homepage but rather secure themselves a brand name by co-operation, acquisition or merger with an established local company. Furthermore, this leads to developments where some online brokers get "offline" in the sense that they establish branches, so-called "investment centres", where people can literally get that "handshake".[10] In this context, consumer protection becomes an important issue, too.

Policy Actions

With cross-border transactions, the jurisdiction of the legislative or regulatory authority for investor protection must be clear-cut. This point is addressed by the Electronic Commerce Directive (COM, 2000) adopted on June 8, 2000 defining the place of establishment as the place where an operator actually pursues an economic activity through a fixed establishment, irrespective of where websites or servers are situated or where the operator may have a mail box.

But this implies that when a customer has some kind of problem with his foreign online broker he needs to know about the law of this foreign country. Consumers need to access cross-border redress easily. To ensure rapid, low-cost and effective cross-border out-of-court redress, the European Commission launched FIN-NET (COM, 1998a) on February 1, 2001, a European Union-wide network of financial services complaints bodies (see also box).

FIN-NET: Out-of-court complaint network for financial services in the European economic area

FIN-NET links more than 35 different national complaint bodies into an EU-wide complaint network. Thus the existing national infrastructure is used. The objective is to make out-of-court settlement of cross-border dispute accessible to the consumer when the consumer and the provider of the financial service do not come from the same Member State. This is achieved by mutual recognition of the national redress bodies and exchange of information.

In case of a dispute the consumer will be able to complain to a third party even if the supplier does not adhere to the complaint scheme in the consumer's country of residence. The complainant is put in touch with the redress body in the supplier's country of operation through the redress body in his own country of residence.

Except for very few cases, a consumer not satisfied with the outcome of the out-of-court settlement can still bring his case to court.

---

10 In particular, this physical presence becomes important when latent necessities have to be stimulated that, finally, are behind abstract goods like insurance coverage. Clemons and Hitt (2000: 27) note: "The industry adage, 'Insurance is a product that is sold, not bought, suggests that the agent may have a significant role in generating demand for insurance products."

Furthermore, a communication (COM, 2001) was released by the Commission in February 2001 that relates to the E-Commerce Directive and proposes several measures designed to enhance consumer protection and confidence. In order to increase people's confidence in foreign suppliers they need to get information that is of high quality and, above all, comparable information. Part of this problem is addressed with the harmonisation of key marketing rules in the proposed Distance Marketing Directive (COM, 1999) that aims at encouraging consumer confidence in retail financial services provided for example on the internet. This directive was proposed in July 1999 but has not been adopted yet. The Directive for the distance selling of financial services (COM, 1998b) was proposed in October 1998 and approved by the EU's Council of Ministers on September 27, 2001. Among other things it establishes several consumer rights such as a withdrawal-right and an obligation to provide consumers with comprehensive information before a contract is concluded. Therefore this directive certainly contributes to the strengthening of consumer protection.

Thus, concerning some of the above-mentioned policy-induced obstacles, policy action has been taken or is underway in order to provide suppliers with a clearly defined legal framework and to encourage consumer confidence. On the supply side this may actually lead to more internationally oriented strategies. However, it seems as if these directives and proposals are probably not effective enough to strengthen consumers' confidence in foreign suppliers of e-finance. One problem is that, very often, consumers have never heard of anything like FIN-NET. Beyond the above-mentioned policy actions, information and also comparisons of various suppliers could be provided, for example by consumer councils. So far such organisations as well as specific magazines and journals tend to compare national suppliers, only. Possibly, the consumers' confidence could be enhanced if they could read in magazines about the possibility of switching to a foreign direct broker and about the protection rules applicable. Furthermore, companies by themselves should step in when it comes to show the consumers the possibilities they have and what kind of consumer protection procedures, such as FIN-NET, already exist.[11]

Concerning the high costs for cross-border credit transfers discussed above, the EU Commission has proposed a regulation according to which charges for transactions in Euro in the internal market should be the same for cross-border payments as for domestic payments. Although it was discussed intensively and often criticised, among others by the ECB (Padoa-Schioppa, 2001) the European Parliament as well as the EU Ministers approved the proposal. Hence, the provision

---

11 There exists for example an initiative led by CEOs of more than 60 companies engaged in e-commerce globally, called Global Business Dialogue On Electronic Commerce (GBDe), that among other things, aims on fostering consumer confidence in the use of the internet world-wide.

will apply as of July 1, 2002 for card payment and cash dispensers and as of July 1, 2003 for bank transfers.

Bearing in mind that the Commission has been exhorting banks for more than 10 years to lower charges for cross-border transfers, price control looks like the only effective measure. However, this proposal has several problematic points. There are valid reasons why the costs for cross-border transactions are higher than for domestic transfers although this does not justify the current extreme amounts of fees. The main reason is that there is no common payment system for low-value transactions in the Euro zone yet, a fact which limits automated processing. Also, economies of scale are prevented since the volume of payments is not sufficiently large relative to national volumes. Obviously the creation of a common payment system would be the best solution. But this takes time, money and a kind of co-operation between financial institutions that does not exist so far. So if banks are forced to provide cross-border transfers below cost, this implies the risk that they seek compensation through an increase in domestic fees or that they stop providing that service altogether, which would certainly leave consumers worse off.

There is already an agreement among a number of banks to limit the price for a cross-border transfer to 3 EUR, namely the multilateral interchange fee (MIF) (Padoa-Schioppa, 2001; Financial Times, 2001). With such an agreement consumers would know when they pay too much and the barrier to cross-border transactions would at least be reduced. Furthermore, the banking industry made a voluntary commitment to lower prices substantially until they reach domestic levels by end of 2005. Nevertheless, at the end of the day a common payment infrastructure – also for low-value transactions – is necessary in order to remove this important obstacle to integration in the market for financial services. The recent proposal by the Eurosystem to either create a new automated clearing house or to link the existing domestic clearing houses seems to be promising (European Central Bank, 2001b).

To summarise, there are several policy actions underway that address most of the policy-induced obstacles. However, the proposed measures are very unlikely to encourage consumer confidence. The consumer's preference for the domestic supplier thus remains as a natural obstacle, as well as others that hinder integration in the European market for online brokerage and for e-finance in general.

Potential Benefits

The above analyses demonstrate that due to several obstacles the markets for online brokerage in Europe are to a large degree fragmented. Thus per se there seems to be potential for further market integration. Probably, progressive integration would lead to a greater diversity of online brokerage services provided and to more competition, unless major consolidation occurs. Prices for online brokerage services would converge and under normal circumstances decrease. Consumers in countries with online brokers that currently charge commissions and fees above the average would gain most, e.g. consumers in the United Kingdom and

Spain. Recalling that people in those countries often pay more than five times as much as investors in other EU countries, gains could be substantial. However, how much prices would move and consumers would gain is up to speculation.

Bearing in mind, however, that the most important obstacles seem to be natural and cannot be reduced by policy actions at least not in the short and medium run, the potential of further integration in the market for e-finance seems to be rather restricted. This corresponds with the results of some questions in the survey among online brokers. Only half of the online brokers surveyed estimate that prices for online brokerage on the most important European markets will converge in the next two years. About one third estimates that the average price level will decrease. Hence, also the potential benefits from a further integration of markets seem to be rather small in scale.

5 Conclusion

Comparing European countries, major differences in prices for online brokerage services can be observed, although the prices of direct brokers within one country are quite similar. Also, almost no direct cross-border transactions occur, i.e. almost all users of online brokerage have a domestic supplier. Usually, online brokers do not try to attend to foreign customers over their domestic homepage thus depriving themselves of utilising the advantages of the internet, i.e. cost savings, especially reducing fixed costs of branches and related maintenance. All this implies that there are various obstacles that cause markets to be rather fragmented than integrated.

The main reasons for this segregation of markets are natural obstacles such as the preference of consumers for domestic providers, or language and cultural differences. As long as consumers "think in borders and languages", full market integration is illusionary even with the internet that certainly helps consumers to get access to foreign suppliers.

This result may be somewhat frustrating, however, policy action is needed in order to reduce obstacles like the high cost of cross-border credit transfers or other policy-induced barriers. Some directives and proposals have been devised that address some of those obstacles. These policy actions may well lead to more internationally oriented strategies on the supply side since they provide suppliers with a legal framework. However, they will hardly strengthen consumers' confidence in foreign suppliers they just know from the internet.

The consumers' confidence not only in foreign online providers but also in the internet as a distribution channel in general is very important for fostering integration of the markets for financial services. As the above analyses have shown, cross-border activities of suppliers in the sense of establishing foreign subsidiaries alone do not really help to integrate markets and reduce price dispersion. A much faster way to achieve market integration is to dismantle the obstacles to direct cross-border activity.

References

Buch, C. (2000), *Financial Market Integration in the US: Lessons for Europe?*, Kiel Working Paper, No. 1004, Kiel.

Claessens, S., T. Glaessner and D. Klingebiel (2000), *Electronic Finance: Reshaping the Financial Landscape Around the World*, World Bank Financial Sector Discussion Paper, No. 4, Washington D.C.

Clemons, E.K. and L.M. Hitt (2000), *The Internet and the Future of Financial Services: Transparency, Differential Pricing and Disintermediation*, Wharton Financial Institutions Center Working Paper 00-35.

COM (1997), *Directive 97/5/EC of the European Parliament and of the Council of 27 January 1997 on cross-border credit transfers.*

COM (1998a), *Memorandum of Understanding on a Cross-Border Out-of-Court Complaints Network for Financial Services in the European Economic Area*, Brussels, 30.3.1998.

COM (1998b), *Proposal for a Directive of the European Parliament and the Council Concerning the Distance Marketing of Consumer Financial Services and Amending Council Directive 90/619/EEC and Directive 97/7/EC and 98/27/EC*; 98/0245(COD), Brussels, 14.10.1998.

COM (1999), *Amended Proposal for a European Parliament and Council Directive Concerning the Distance Marketing of Consumer Financial Services and Amending Directives 97/7/EC and 98/27/EC*; 98/0245 (COD), Brussels, 23.7.1999.

COM (2000), *Directive 2000/31/EC of the European Parliament and the Council of 8 June 2000 on Certain Legal Aspects of Information Society Services, in Particular Electronic Commerce, in the Internal Market ('Directive on Electronic Commerce').*

COM (2001), *Communication From the Commission to the Council and the European Parliament, E-commerce and Financial Services*, Brussels, 9.2.2001.

EU Commission (2001), *Study on the Verification of a Common and Coherent Application of Directive 97/5/EC on Cross-Border Credit Transfers in the 15 Member States*, London.

European Central Bank (1999), *The Effects of Technology on the EU Banking Systems*, July.

European Central Bank (2001a), *Blue Book – Payment and Securities Settlement Systems in the European Union*, June.

European Central Bank (2001b), *Towards an Integrated Infrastructure for Credit Transfers in Euro*, November.

Financial Times (2001), *Euro Transfers*, 25.07.2001.

JP Morgan (2001a), *Industry Update – European Online Investor*, London, February 21.

JP Morgan (2001b), *European Banking and Insurance – Asset Gathering in Europe*, London, May 17.

Leamer, E.E. and M. Storper (2001), *The Economic Geography of the Internet Age*, NBER Working Paper, No. 8450, Cambridge.

Padoa-Schioppa, T. (2001), *Toward a Single Payment Area*, Keynote address at the EU Commission conference "Payment in Euro in the Internal Market", Brussels, 24 September 2001.

Benefits of Diversification and Integration for International Equity and Bond Portfolios

Michael Schröder

Centre for European Economic Research (ZEW), Mannheim, Germany

1 Introduction

It is well known from portfolio theory that pure domestically invested asset portfolios are usually sub-optimal. If for example a private household in France invests only in French equities it will have a lower return-to-risk ratio than compared to a world-wide investment. As this is true in general for all types of investors, countries and assets, a better diversification should improve the performance of investments.

Capital market integration and diversification are connected in several ways. In a fully integrated capital market all risk factors trade at the same price. This means, for example, if the European capital markets were fully integrated then the business cycle risk or the inflation risk would have the same price in all European capital markets. Capital market integration means in other words that the law of one price is fully applicable to all traded assets. This per se should have a positive effect on the functioning of financial markets and indirectly on the performance of investments.

But integration of capital markets has also a more basic meaning: free access to foreign financial markets. Formally, all Europeans have full access to all other European and most of the non-European capital markets. But nevertheless only a small part of total assets of private households is invested in marketable assets such as equities and bonds. And there is also the well-known tendency to invest a very large position in the home country. One reason for this so-called home bias is that private as well as institutional investors prefer investments in equities and bonds denominated in the own currency. Since the introduction of the Euro this obstacle to foreign investments has been abolished. But nevertheless it will take some time until investors will change the composition of their investment portfolios.

Another possible cause of the home bias-phenomenon is information asymmetry. Usually investors are better informed and have lower information costs for domestic assets (equities as well as bonds). As the European Monetary Union will not change this information asymmetry, further activities are needed to overcome this problem. This is part of the Financial Services Action Plan (FSAP) which intends to harmonise e.g. accounting standards, listing requirements at the securities exchanges and other institutional arrangements. In addition, there are usually also higher transaction costs for trading foreign assets compared to domestic investments. In the opinion of private households these additional transaction costs might be too high to make foreign investments profitable. Better integrated European financial markets and an increase in competition across borders should diminish the differences between domestic and foreign investment costs. Thus, integration of financial markets in Europe could – at least to some extent – reduce the home bias of European investors.

2 Characteristics of International Stock and Bond Portfolios

More internationally diversified stock and bond portfolios should as a consequence shift the frontier of efficient portfolios upwards and therefore for each given risk the average portfolio return should increase. Thus, more integrated capital markets should lead to a larger portion of foreign stocks and bonds in the portfolios with the effect of better diversified investments. The following analysis tries to quantify the possible additional performance of stock and bond portfolios of European investors if the home bias is diminished in the future.

Tables 1 to 4 show the return/risk-relationships of different portfolios for German, French British and US investors. The return/risk relationships are shown both for portfolios without currency hedge and with fully hedged currency exposures. The performance of the equity portfolios is calculated using the market capitalisation weights and the country indices of Morgan Stanley (MSCI), whereas the bond portfolios refer to the capitalisation weights and country indices of Salomon. All figures of the Tables 1 to 6 have been calculated using monthly returns.

Table 1 shows for a German investor that world-wide and European-wide diversified equity and bond portfolios performed much better than portfolios restricted to only German assets. This can be seen from the so-called Sharpe ratios that are much higher when foreign assets are included in the portfolio. The Sharpe ratio is defined as the portfolio return minus a risk-free interest rate, divided by the standard deviation, which serves as the measure of risk. The Sharpe ratio therefore measures the premium which the investor earns for one unit of risk. The higher the Sharpe ratio the better is the performance of the portfolio.

The best performing stock and bond portfolios are those with a diversification amongst Europe-wide assets. The inclusion of other international assets is somewhat less profitable than using only European assets, which can be seen from the lower Sharpe ratios of the world portfolios. For a German investor holding foreign currencies resulted in additional diversification benefits. This is in contrast to the results for French, British and US investors who could significantly benefit from a full currency hedge in all portfolios shown in Tables 2 to 4. This is particularly true for British and US investors that could increase the Sharpe ratios of their portfolios by a very large amount due to avoiding the risk of foreign currencies.

Table 1: Return/risk relationships for a German investor
(Period: January 1978 - June 2001)

	Mean return (in %, p.m.)		Standard deviation (in %, p.m.)		Sharpe ratio	
	Unhedged	Hedged	Unhedged	Hedged	Unhedged	Hedged
Equities world	1.14	1.00	4.79	3.87	0.139	0.136
Equities Europe	1.16	1.05	4.57	4.43	0.149	0.133
Equities Germany	0.95	--	5.57	--	0.085	--
Bonds world	0.71	0.58	2.10	1.29	0.113	0.079
Bonds Europe	0.68	0.58	1.37	1.21	0.150	0.095
Bonds Germany	0.56	--	1.34	--	0.063	--

Table 2: Return/risk relationships for a French investor
(Period: January 1978 - June 2001)

	Mean return (in %, p.m.)		Standard deviation (in %, p.m.)		Sharpe ratio	
	Unhedged	Hedged	Unhedged	Hedged	Unhedged	Hedged
Equities world	1.28	1.25	4.70	3.90	0.119	0.134
Equities Europe	1.30	1.29	4.52	4.38	0.127	0.131
Equities France	1.40	--	6.03	--	0.112	--
Bonds world	0.86	0.83	2.08	1.34	0.064	0.076
Bonds Europe	0.82	0.83	1.49	1.20	0.067	0.089
Bonds France	0.79	--	1.56	--	0.042	--

Table 3: Return/risk relationships for a British investor (Period: January 1978 - June 2001)

	Mean return (in %, p.m.)		Standard deviation (in %, p.m.)		Sharpe ratio	
	Unhedged	Hedged	Unhedged	Hedged	Unhedged	Hedged
Equities world	1.22	1.30	4.55	3.88	0.095	0.132
Equities Europe	1.23	1.35	4.42	4.36	0.101	0.129
Equities UK	1.23	--	4.92	--	0.091	--
Bonds world	0.79	0.94	2.50	1.28	0.001	0.127
Bonds Europe	0.75	0.89	2.34	1.12	-0.012	0.094
Bonds UK	0.91	--	2.41	--	0.051	--

As for French and British investors, holding foreign currencies has not added value to the stock and bond portfolios of a US investor (Table 4). But unlike for other investors an international diversification of equities does not seem to create large benefits for a US-based investor.

In sum, there are large differences between the performance of asset portfolios of the four investors analysed in the Tables 1 to 4. The optimal decision concerning currency hedging depends largely on the domestic currency of the investor. Since the introduction of the Euro there should be only one optimal portfolio irrespective of the location of the investor. This not only concerns currency hedging but also the composition of stocks and bonds. The necessary degree of diversification (Europe-wide or world-wide) to create an optimal portfolio, although different across investors and assets in the past, has now the same solution for all investors located in Euroland.

Table 4: Return/risk relationships for a US investor (Period: January 1978 - June 2001)

	Mean return (in %, p.m.)		Standard deviation (in %, p.m.)		Sharpe ratio	
	Unhedged	Hedged	Unhedged	Hedged	Unhedged	Hedged
Equities world	1.11	1.13	4.02	3.91	0.119	0.130
Equities Europe	1.12	1.17	4.69	4.40	0.106	0.123
Equities USA	1.18	--	4.40	--	0.125	--
Bonds world	0.68	0.73	2.55	1.28	0.023	0.085
Bonds Europe	0.64	0.73	3.30	1.10	0.006	0.097
Bonds USA	0.66	--	2.49	--	0.015	

The analysis also shows that there is a clear answer to the question whether international diversification matters: Holding only domestic assets is only an inferior solution. The performance of the portfolios could be significantly improved by investing in international stocks and bonds. It is also interesting to note, that a Europe-wide diversification for stock and bond portfolios leads to the best results. A world-wide diversified stock portfolio could cause lower risk-adjusted returns to the investor than a Europe portfolio. This is a very promising result concerning the integration of European capital markets: A better diversification amongst European equity markets is the best a Europe-based investor can do.

3 Stability of Diversification Benefits and Possible Gains for Investors

Table 5 shows the stability of diversification benefits over time. The figures are calculated as the difference of the Sharpe ratios of the world or Europe portfolios to the fully locally invested portfolio. As all portfolios are calculated without currency hedge the figures slightly underestimate the true benefits of diversification for British, French and US investors. There are two results that can be derived from this table. First, the benefits of diversification change significantly over time. And second, except for the US investor, the benefits of diversification are always existent. Therefore, the investors could mostly increase the performance of their portfolios by investing in international assets.

Table 5: Stability of diversification benefits over time, difference of sharpe ratios of world and Europe portfolios relative to a purely local portfolio (unhedged currency returns)

	Jan. '78 - June '01	Jan. '89 - June '01	Jan. '95- June '01
Equities world			
British investor	0.004	0.009	0.012
French investor	0.007	0.014	0.012
German investor	0.054	0.031	0.071
US investor	-0.006	-0.071	-0.078
Equities Europe			
British investor	0.011	0.008	0.003
French investor	0.015	0.015	0.018
German investor	0.064	0.032	0.078
US investor	-0.019	-0.086	-0.093

In Table 6 the excess return of the optimal portfolio is compared to a purely locally invested stock portfolio for each investor. The excess return measures the average premium earned in excess of the risk-free interest rate. The excess return of the optimal portfolio is compared to (1) the return of a portfolio with 80% domestic stocks and 20% world-wide diversified stocks and (2) a portfolio that consists only of domestic stocks. To calculate the excess returns of columns 3 and 4 the risk is fixed to the standard deviation of the optimal portfolio. The composition of the optimal portfolio is given in column 2 in brackets (domestic:foreign).

The optimal portfolio of the German investors is simply the world portfolio, the French investor should hold 70% in French equities and 30% in the world portfolio and the optimal portfolio of the British investor consists of 10% of the domestic and 90% of the world portfolio. All three investors should therefore invest a relatively large part of their total investment in foreign assets. Only the US investors cannot significantly improve the portfolio performance by investing abroad: He should hold 100% in domestic equities.

Table 6: Mean excess return of risk adjusted portfolios (portfolio risk equal to standard deviation of optimal equity world portfolio), Period Jan. 1995-June 2001

	Optimal equity world portfolio[1] (Domestic:foreign)	80:20 portfolio	Local investment
British investor[2]	0.78% (10:90)	0.60%	0.52%
French investor[2]	1.069% (70:30)	1.066%	1.05%
German investor[3]	1.21% (0:100)	0.96%	0.86%
US investor[2]	0.96% (100:0)	0.94%	0.96%

Notes: [1]The optimisation has been done only with respect to the weights of the domestic equity portfolio. A full optimisation that includes all weights of the world portfolio should result in even higher excess returns for the optimal portfolio. [2]World portfolio is fully currency hedged, [3]world portfolio is not currency hedged.

Table 6 shows the additional excess return that can be gained by a better diversification of the portfolio. The 80:20 portfolio can serve as an approximation of the actual investment position of the investors.[1] The highest additional excess return could have been earned by a German investor: 0.25% per month = 3% per year = 82% in 20 years! Although the possible improvements in the portfolio return of the British investor are not that impressing, they are nevertheless significant: 0.18% per month = 2.2% per year = 54% in 20 years. For the French investor the additional earnings are rather small and for the US investor equal to zero.

To sum up, international diversification results in significant additional returns for the investors under consideration (except the US investor). Although these additional returns are time-varying and different according to the currency of the investor, a better international diversification improves the portfolio performance. A Europe-wide diversification leads to a significant increase in the Sharpe ratio, which is in most cases even higher than the improvement due to a world-wide diversification. Therefore, a further integration of European capital markets that diminishes the home bias should result in higher portfolio returns for European investors.

---

1 For example Brealey et al. (1999) show that in 1993 the different investors held the following investment positions in domestic equities: German – 78%, French – 92%, UK – 69%, US – 95%.

Reference

Brealey, R., I. Cooper and E. Kaplanis (1999), What Is the International Dimension of International Finance?, *European Finance Review* 3, 103-119.

Deepening European Financial Integration: Theoretical Considerations and Empirical Evaluation of Growth and Employment Benefits

Markus Neimke, Carsten Eppendorfer and Rainer Beckmann*

Ruhr-University Bochum, Germany

1 Introduction

This paper analyses the macroeconomic effects of further integration in the European markets for financial services. In particular we are interested in growth and unemployment benefits of the reduction and abolition of cross-border barriers impeding the entry into the market of banking and insurance products. Usually, it is argued that facilitating the entry of foreign financial firms into the local market intensifies competition, improves efficiency, and increases the quality of the financial infrastructure. As such, foreign firms can be seen as an important catalyst for the sort of financial development that promotes growth.

Our main research aim – evaluation of the change in the GDP growth rate and the change in the unemployment rate following deeper financial integration respectively – is analogous to the Cecchini Report in which the growth effects of the 1992 Single Market Programme were estimated. In particular the Cecchini Report predicted a bonus of 4.5% in terms of GDP growth, resulting from a free flow of consumer products, capital and labour. One third, or 1.5 percentage points of the growth bonus were attributed to the integration of financial markets in particular. Since 1992 the average growth rate of real GDP in Europe has not exceeded 2% per year. Hence the average growth rate equals the "equilibrium growth rate" or total factor productivity growth. Based on this observation we cannot exactly asses whether the expectation of the Cecchini Report was too optimistic, however we can strengthen the arguments for further financial integration with new empirical results. We argue that the creation of a functioning single market for financial services is a substantial prerequisite for generating higher growth rates and reducing unemployment, because the degree to which financial markets are inte-

* Acknowledgement: The authors have benefited from comments of Prof. Dieter Bender, Friedrich Heinemann, Claudia Buch and other seminar participants at the *ZEW*, Mannheim and the *Institut für Weltwirtschaft* (IfW, Kiel). We would also like to thank Inka Schöwe for technical assistance.

grated is a determinant of financial development which in turn causes economic growth.

The following Section 2 analyses the connection between financial development and economic growth from a theoretical view. The approach is in line with the increasing interest for the finance-growth nexus in recent publications (e.g. World Bank, 2001). It is argued that the level of financial development of an economy seems to be characterised mainly by its financial market's size, structure and efficiency and through these transmission channels influences economic growth. We implement this characterisation of the financial sector in a simple endogenous growth model. This model can be used to illustrate the influence of financial development on the overall growth rate of an economy as well as the growth effects of financial integration.

In Section 3, major steps towards an integrated financial market in Europe are summarised and confronted with the empirical evidence. This descriptive analysis of foreign market penetration in banking and insurance markets already reveals the existence of substantial obstacles to cross-border business. Some attempts to abolish these obstacles are implemented in the Financial Services Action Plan in which the European Commission formulates policy priorities for pushing financial integration. The elements of the Financial Services Action Plan are also briefly discussed.

In the econometric evaluation in Section 4, we try to assess the macroeconomic impact of an increased activity of foreign companies in domestic financial markets in Europe. The analysis of the EU member states follows a three-step approach.

In a first step, we estimate a growth equation with typical "growth determinants" – investment rate and population growth – and different indicators of financial market development on the right-hand side. The panel data estimation results of the first step reveal country-specific regression constants which can be interpreted as total factor productivity growth rates. Obviously, not all indicators are suitable to show the influence the financial sector has on the real economy. In consequence, we obtain the constants from the regression, which fits the data best. These constants – the country-specific growth rates of total factor productivity – are defined as dependent variables in the second estimation step.

To estimate the extent to which European financial integration has influenced total factor productivity growth we utilise a simple cross-country regression approach. Analogous to the first step, we estimate a number of equations with different financial integration indicators and control variables on the right-hand side. The regression results provide ambiguous evidence for a correlation between financial market integration and total factor productivity growth. However, it is possible to identify a weak influence of foreign market penetration in the sector for banking products. Hence, deeper financial integration generates a growth bonus. In the context of theoretical examinations this growth bonus does not only mean a more rapid convergence to the steady state ("neoclassical growth effect") but also a higher equilibrium growth rate in the long run ("endogenous growth effect").

In a third step, the analysis of the macroeconomic growth effects is supplemented with an analysis of the link between financial integration and unemployment. To asses the potential benefits of a fostered financial integration we estimate country-specific Okun-coefficients that provide information about the growth rate a country needs in order to reduce unemployment. We show that a convincing increase in financial market integration is required to generate a growth bonus that can substantially reduce unemployment in the EU member states.

Section 5 provides a conclusion and points to some aspects of the estimation results and their further interpretation that must be seen with considerable reservation.

2 Financial Development, Financial Integration and Economic Growth

This section outlines selective links between financial market development and the real economic sector. In particular it shows which transmission channels of the financial sector can be identified. The different approaches to finding causal combinations between the financial market development of an economy and its per-capita growth rate were motivated by two factors: the upcoming of the "new growth theory" and the detection of empirical phenomena such as the identification of specific convergence processes in the world economy.[1] The finance-growth nexus in a closed economy is discussed extensively in the literature. In contrast, theoretical approaches to determine the growth implications of financial market integration are rare. Our aim is not to remove this shortcoming but to give some intuitive indications on the basis of a simple growth model. We argue that the removal of obstacles to cross-border financial activities is a substantial prerequisite for generating higher growth rates because the degree to which financial markets are integrated is a determinant of financial development which in turn influences economic growth.

1 Influential theoretical contributions in the context of the new growth theory are Romer (1986, 1990), Lucas (1988) and Grossman and Helpman (1991). The empirical approaches of Barro and Sala-i-Martin (1992) and Mankiw, Romer and Weil (1992) should also be mentioned in this context. For an overview see Barro (1998).

2.1 Transmission Channels of the Financial Sector

In growth theory the evolution of the financial services sector as a whole represents only one determinant of country-specific differences in growth processes. Nevertheless, the financial sector appears to have special importance in two ways. First, the financial sector has the function to canalise savings into investment and innovation activities.[2] Second, it is possible to interpret the degree to which the financial sector is developed as a measure of something like *broad macroeconomic efficiency*. Thus financial development influences total factor productivity and the long-run growth rate.[3] These two characterisations of the financial sector as a determinant of economic growth already reflect the competing approaches of the *neoclassical* and the *endogenous growth theory*. In neoclassical growth theory only increases in the level of macroeconomic efficiency are responsible for a permanent growth of per capita income, which is attained by presuming an exogenous productivity growth rate. An increase, for example, of the savings rate induces a growth effect that is only *transitory*. Endogenous growth models, by contrast, permit also the possibility of a *permanent* increase in the growth rate of per capita income through an increase of the macroeconomic savings rate or through research and development activities. However, the endogenous growth approaches are not able to explain the convergence dynamics, that can be discovered empirically and constitute a special characterisation of neoclassical models.

In the following we will not attempt a discriminating analysis of the connection between financial development and economic growth within neoclassical and endogenous models.[4] The purpose of this section is rather to discuss the different *transmission channels*, identified in both neoclassical *and* endogenous growth models. These characteristics will also be implemented in a simple *integrated growth-model* in the next section. In both neoclassical and endogenous models the long-run economic development of per-capita income is basically driven by two factors: the *accumulation of input factors* and the change in the *macroeconomic efficiency* in allocating these input factors. The change in macroeconomic efficiency is often described as the growth of total factor productivity.

---

2 This view is based on the work of McKinnon (1973) and Shaw (1973). One of the first analyses of the finance-growth nexus is Goldsmith (1996).

3 See King and Levine (1993 a, b); Levine (1998); Rajan and Zingales (1998).

4 For an extensive summary of this discussion see Levine (1997).

Figure 1: Economic growth, financial development and financial integration

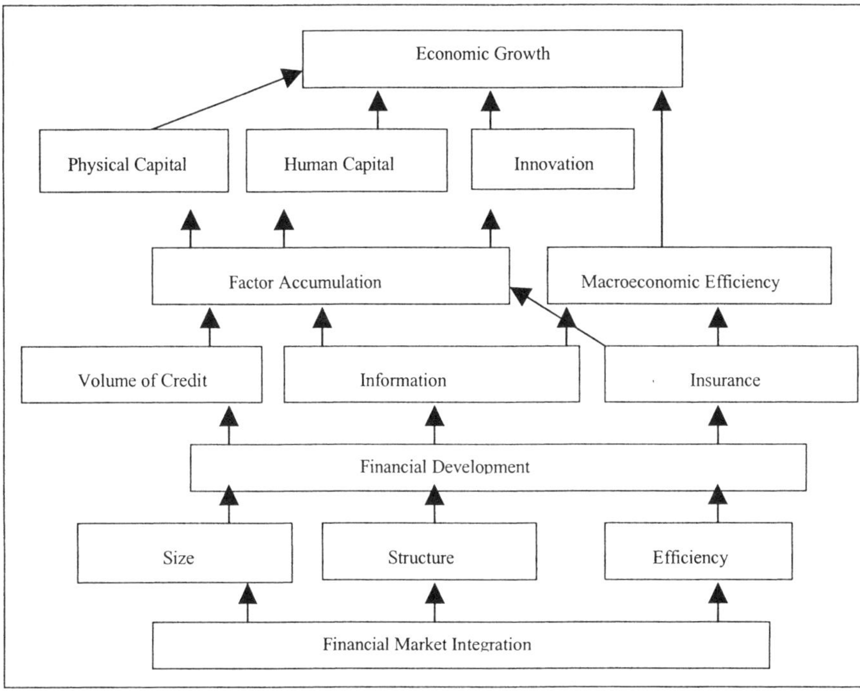

The degree of financial development can be measured in terms of different components, namely the *size*, the *structure* and the *efficiency* of the financial sector.[5] This characterisation is shown in Figure 1. Indicators that measure the size of the financial sector basically include information about the depth of financial intermediation. With the help of structural indicators we can obtain information about the allocation of resources and the relevance of an economy's different financial institutions, e.g. the impact of private and state-owned banks. Using efficiency indicators the level of transaction cost, the degree of information asymmetries and in particular the competition environment can be recorded. As Figure 1 reveals, each of the different measures of the degree to which the financial sector is developed can be influenced by financial market integration.

Following Figure 1, the financial sector affects both driving forces of growth, factor accumulation and efficiency of allocation. Literature has identified different channels making up the link between the financial sector and economic growth:

5 See King and Levine (1992) for this classification.

- *Supply of Credits for Investment*
  A developed, competitive financial sector ensures relatively small deviations between lending and deposit interest rates, which in turn enlarges that part of macroeconomic savings that can be transformed into credits for investment projects of the non-banking sector.[6] According to the analysis of McKinnon (1973) and Shaw (1973) a functioning financial sector ensures high private savings rates due to an attractive interest rate, high private savings facilitate investment activities of private firms, and it enables an economy to grow at a high speed. This savings rate effect is intensified when the growth dynamics are also driven by human capital accumulation. Hence, the financial sector can raise the formation of human capital through the provision of credit to private households which use such financial means for private education investments.[7]
- *Provision of Information*
  In economic theory the task of the financial sector should be, among other things, to channel savings into the most profitable investment projects. A developed financial sector facilitates this if banks and insurance companies monitor investment projects and provide information about potentially innovative enterprises to their customers.[8]
- *Insurance of Risks*
  Since more profitable investment projects are usually associated with higher risks, improving the possibilities to insure oneself against these risks can significantly increase investments financed by given savings (see Obstfeld, 1994). This insurance function is the more important the more economic growth is driven by technological innovations that are linked to high sunk costs (see Saint-Paul, 1992). Through spillover-effects R&D drives the technological knowledge stock of an economy which in turn increases total factor productivity.

To summarise, following economic theory the growth rate of a country is basically driven by factor accumulation and improvements in macroeconomic efficiency, i.e. growth of total factor productivity. A functioning financial sector is in part responsible for the accumulation of input factors as well as for the efficiency with which the input factors can be used. The degree of the financial sector's development can be measured in terms of its size, structure and efficiency. Each of these different financial measures can be influenced by financial market integration. Therefore, an increase in the degree of financial market integration that results in a rise in the financial sector's development level enables a shift in the growth rate of per-capita income.

---

6 See Pagano (1993); Berthélemy and Varoudakis (1996 a, b); Atje and Jovanovic (1993); King and Levine (1993 b) and Bencivenga and Smith (1991).

7 See De Gregorio (1996) and Jappelli and Pagano (1994).

8 See Greenwood and Jovanovic (1990); Holmström and Tirole (1997).

2.2 Endogenous Growth and Financial Intermediation

Endogenous growth models opposed to traditional neoclassical approaches have the advantage that they enable us to give a convincing explanation of the *direct* influence the financial market has on an economy's long-run growth rate. A major disadvantage of endogenous growth models is that they frequently imply parameter dependencies. This results in an immediate "jump" of economies on their equilibrium growth path which is incompatible with the empirical regularity of income convergence that takes a long time. In the model briefly outlined below the transmission channels of a functioning financial services sector can be merged to a theoretically consistent approach. Furthermore, the model seems to be capable of analysing the impact of increasing financial market integration. The approach chosen is based on a production technology that allows to represent characteristics of both endogenous and neoclassical growth models. First, it includes the empirically observed phenomenon of convergence within specific groups of countries (conditional convergence), derivable from neoclassical models. Second, it implements main characteristics of endogenous growth models with a long-term positive growth rate that are independent of exogenous technological processes. Under the assumptions of the model it is shown that the convergence behaviour as well as the equilibrium growth rate can be directly influenced by the development of the financial services sector market and its deeper integration respectively.

The underlying macroeconomic production function Y exhibits constant returns to scale and transitional declining marginal products of capital and labour in F(K,L):

$$Y = AK + F(K, L) \tag{2.1}$$

Y stands for macroeconomic output, K for capital stock and L for the labour force of the representative economy. A describes the level of technology or, in a more wider definition, macroeconomic efficiency.[9] In per capita terms we can write (2.1) as:

$$y = Ak + f(x) \tag{2.2}$$

with k standing for capital intensity K/L.

Although we assume decreasing marginal products for the neoclassical part of the macroeconomic production function – f(k) in (2.2) – the endogenous part Ak guarantees a long-run constancy of the marginal product of capital so that a permanently positive growth rate is generated.[10]

---

9 This kind of production function is based on Jones and Manuelli (1990). Time indices are suppressed.

10 Formally this follows from the violation of one of the Inada-conditions because here in the long-run $\lim_{k \to \infty} \delta y / \delta k = A > 0$.

Capital intensity k evolves depending on investment activity I, population growth rate n and depreciation of the existing capital stock δK according to:

$$\frac{\dot{k}}{k} := \hat{k} = \frac{\dot{K}}{K} - n = \frac{I - \delta K}{K} - n = \frac{I}{K} - (\delta + n) \tag{2.3}$$

Following Pagano (1993), the financial services sector determines which part of savings is channelled into investment, i.e. into accumulation of the economy's capital stock (Pagano, 1993). Only a fraction λ of overall savings is available for investment activity:

$$\lambda S = \lambda s Y = 1 \text{, with } 0 < \lambda < 1 \tag{2.4}$$

The other fraction of savings $(1-\lambda)$ "vanishes" in the financial services sector. According to Pagano (1993) the financial component in the growth model can be described, for example, by the spread between lending and deposit interest rate. Therefore, a reduction in the interest rate spread, e.g. due to an increase in competition pressure, leads to a rising fraction of macroeconomic savings being channelled into investment. For the evolution of capital intensity this means:

$$\hat{k} = \frac{\lambda s Y}{K} - (\delta + n) = \lambda s \left[A + \frac{f(k)}{k} \right] - (\delta + n) \tag{2.5}$$

The modification of (2.5) results in a fundamental equation of the evolution of the capital intensity:

$$\hat{k} = \underbrace{[\lambda s A - (n + \delta)]}_{\text{long-term component}} + \underbrace{\lambda s \frac{f(k)}{k}}_{\text{component of convergence}} \tag{2.6}$$

By means of equation (2.6) a positive dependence of the growth rate on capital intensity can be identified when looking at both the long-term component and the convergence component. The influence of the convergence component decreases in time with increasing capital accumulation due to the decrease in the marginal product of capital. Countries that are already at an advanced stage of development show smaller growth rates than countries whose capital intensity falls relatively far below their equilibrium value.[11] In the long-run (i.e. $k \to \infty$) approaches a permanently positive and exogenous value which is determined by the difference between $\lambda s A$ and $(\delta + n)$. Hence, as a condition for a positive growth rate in the long-run the validity of $\lambda s A > (\delta + n)$ must be guaranteed.

11 In the context of the convergence discussion it is clear that this means conditional convergence. As a consequence the considered countries that show income convergence exhibit similar characteristics of the other relevant growth determinants.

In the steady state all considered variables grow at the same rate. Accordingly, the dependence on a convergence component $\hat{y}^t(\lambda)$ and a long-run component $\hat{y}^*(\lambda)$ is also valid for the growth rate of per-capita income:

$$\hat{y} = [\underbrace{\lambda s A - (n+\delta)}_{\substack{\text{long-run} \\ \text{component } \hat{y}^*(\lambda)}}] + \underbrace{\lambda s \frac{f(k)}{k}}_{\substack{\text{component of} \\ \text{convergence } \hat{y}^t(\lambda)}} \tag{2.7}$$

To summarise, in this section we identified long-term and transitional links between financial markets and economic growth from a macroeconomic perspective in a very simple approach. Using an integrated growth model that highlights both neoclassical and endogenous growth characteristics therefore constitutes an extension of the analysis of Pagano (1993). This is an important aspect because, based on the convergence component, the entire macroeconomic effect that is generated by a shift in the degree of the financial services sector's development results in a greater total growth bonus.

2.3 Growth Bonus of Financial Market Integration

The theoretical formula in Section 2.2. demonstrates that financial markets influence both the long-term component of the evolution of per-capita income and the transitional component. The level of λ is determined crucially by the level of development of the financial services sector, which in turn can be influenced by a variation in its size, structure and efficiency. These different measures of the stage of development can be significantly altered by financial market integration. Despite the fundamental implications of the finance-growth nexus, the theoretical model is only of limited use for examinations concerning the impact of financial integration. A shift in parameter λ following enhanced financial market integration causes a rise in the equilibrium growth rate due to a higher growth rate of total factor productivity. This effect is similar to the efficiency function of the financial sector described above. Moreover, a catching-up process can be identified that results in a higher transitional growth rate on the way to a new steady state. This second effect is induced by the accumulation function of the financial sector which stimulates investment into the macroeconomic capital stock. However, the extent of this catching-up effect depends on the stage of economic development a country is experiencing at the respective moment. This means that only a conditional convergence effect can be generated.

Figure 2 represents this way of formulating the "financial integration growth nexus" graphically. Obviously, a shift in the degree of the financial sector's development resulting in an increase in the part of savings that are transformed into investment ($\lambda_1 > \lambda_0$) leads to a higher growth rate. The shift in development can be measured in terms of an increase in the financial sector's size or efficiency or, a change in its structure. Here the shift in financial development and the higher growth rate can be attributed to financial market integration. Hence, financial market integration induces a short-run acceleration of the growth rate of per capita income. Furthermore, the long-term growth rate can be raised as well. The first effect can be called the "short-run growth bonus", the second one the "long-run growth bonus" of financial market integration.

Figure 2: Long-run growth and convergence bonus of financial integration

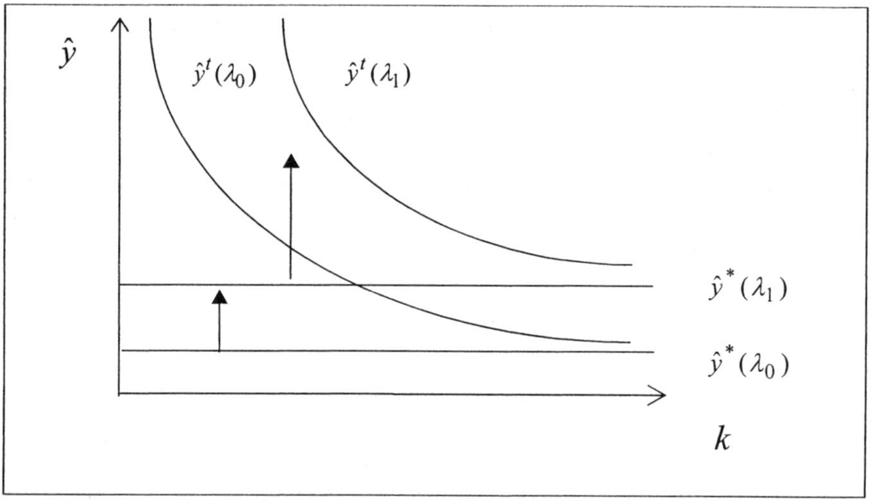

To summarise, financial market integration enhances an economy's growth possibilities through the following channels:

- Foreign banks and insurance companies improve the quality and availability of financial services in the domestic financial market by increasing competition.
- An increase in foreign bank penetration leads to lower profitability and overhead expenses (personal and other non-interest expenses) for banks, and this enhances economic growth by promoting domestic banking efficiency.
- Enhanced competition in connection with external economies of scale forces domestic institutions to apply more modern human skills and technology.
- The presence of foreign financial companies stimulates the development of the underlying legal framework, for example, banking supervision.
- Financial integration enhances a country's access to international capital.

The macroeconomic (static and dynamic) welfare gains over-compensate the decrease in banking profitability.[12] By way of example we could assume that a shift in the number of foreign retail banks will result in an increased competition in the domestic market for retail banking products and for this reason in a reduction of the spread between lending and deposit rate, which would improve investment possibilities for private and non-private firms as well as for private households. Consequently, in the context of the simple growth model developed above a promotion of the growth rate can be expected.

3 Financial Market Integration in Europe

This section outlines the extent to which the European markets for financial service products are currently integrated. In particular we are interested in the foreign activities of banking and insurance companies. It is worth mentioning that our analysis is not aimed at drawing a complete picture of all the competing definitions, determinants and political implications of the different indicators that measure financial integration.[13] We therefore concentrate on *macroeconomic* variables available over a relatively long time span which we use in our econometric estimations in the following section.

Historical evidence shows that several political attempts were made in the past to enhance the extent of European financial integration. Substantial obstacles to cross-border activities remain, however, resulting in potential growth and employment losses. In general, we can make a distinction between natural obstacles and policy-induced obstacles impeding cross-border activities. Natural obstacles are, for example, consumer preferences and cultural or language differences. In particular they are not changeable in the short-run by policy makers. However, policy-induced obstacles, which include taxes, national regulations and standards can be removed by policy makers. Since we are interested in the macroeconomic effects of financial market integration we do not analyse different obstacles that result in a fragmentation of the European financial markets in detail.[14] Rather, we point to some aspects of policy-induced obstacles as well as attempts to their removal. The main obstacles identified by the Lamfalussy report consist of the legal framework for cross-border activities and the degree to which existing Euro-

---

12 See Claessens et al. (1998), Demirgüç-Kunt et al. (1998) and Levine (1998). For an empirical assessment of the impact of foreign bank entry on the profitability in the banking sector and its welfare implications see Claessens et al. (1997).

13 For a comprehensive overview see e.g. Buch (2000); Lemmen (1998) and Danthine et al. (1999, 2000).

14 For an extensive analysis see Eppendorfer at al. (2002) for the banking sector and Beckmann et al. (2002) for the insurance sector.

pean laws are implemented in the EU member states.[15] Nevertheless, the Financial Services Action Plan, adopted by the European Commission, is an actual example that policy makers are aware of these problems and willing to tackle them.

3.1 The Legal Framework in a Historical Perspective

Figure 3 summarises the milestones of deregulation in the *banking products* sector. Policy-induced integration started in 1973 with directive 73/183 aiming at introducing the right of establishment and freedom to provide services for all financial professions. Other major steps towards an integrated market for banking products were incorporated in the banking directive of 1977 which included procedures for the co-ordination of national laws, administrative provisions relating to the taking-up and pursuit of the business of credit institutions. The main element of the Second Banking Directive 1989 was the introduction of a single banking licence allowing a branch of an institution authorised in another member state to be opened without authorisation from the host member state and without the need for separate endowment capital. This directive introduced the principle of "home-country control" for the first time in cross-border banking business. Later directives included the adoption of common solvency standards (1989) and the harmonisation of essential rules for supervising large exposures of credit institutions (1992). Minimum requirements needed to ensure an adequate level of customer information both before and after the execution of a cross-border credit transfer were implemented in 1997. One of the last major steps in spurring integration can be seen in the introduction of a technology-neutral legal framework in 2000 aiming at the implementation and the harmonisation of prudential supervision of electronic money institutions. It is expected that the New Basle Accord on banking supervision will be implemented in 2004.

Although deregulation steps were numerous they were often time-consuming. Figure 4 shows the time profile required for a directive to become community law with "period of implementation" standing for the period between the date of publication and the date of entry into force.

---

15 See Lamfalussy Report (2001).

Figure 3: Time line of EU financial services integration in banking markets

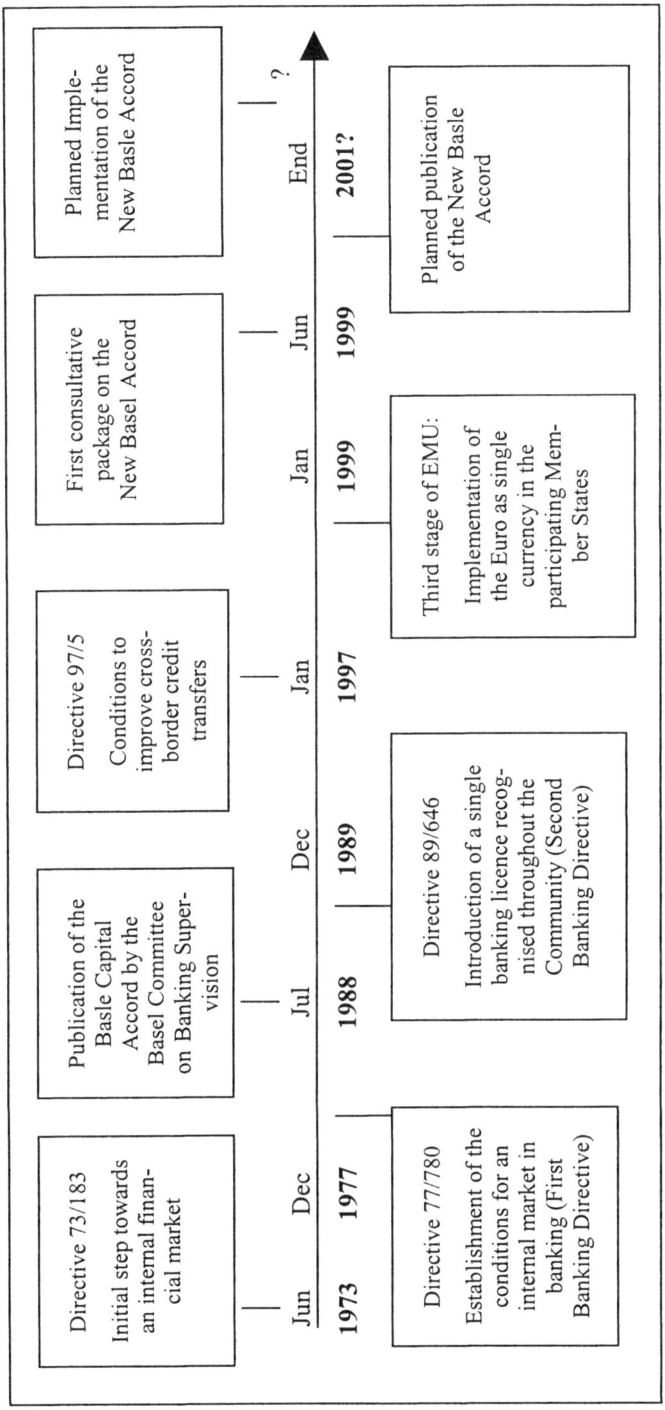

Source: EU (2001a,b).

Figure 4: Time profile required for a directive to become community law (banking)

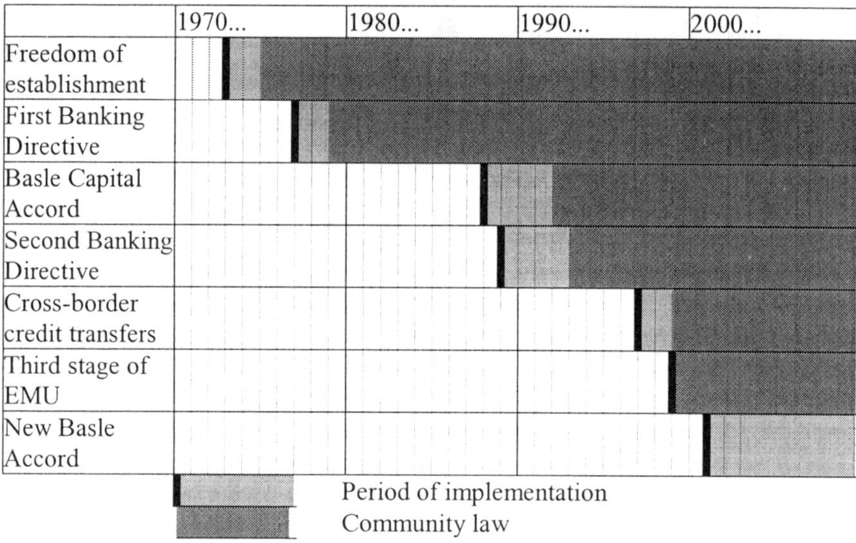

Source: EU (2001a,b).

In the insurance products sector integration started at the beginning of the 1970s as well. The time line of major integration steps is shown in Figure 5. Directive (72/166) in 1972 was aimed at the abolition of frontier controls of compulsory insurance for motor vehicles. The first non-life insurance directive of 1973 established an appropriate legal framework for exercising freedom of establishment in the Community in respect of non-life insurance. With the third non-life insurance directive in 1992 a single authorisation system was introduced. This implies that any insurance undertaking, whose head office is in one of the Community member states can establish branches in another member state and carry on business by way of providing cross-border services under the supervision of the member state where its head office is located. Hence, the principle of "home country control" was also established in the market for non-life insurance products. In the market for life insurance products major integration steps were implemented through the second life insurance directive which laid down two sets of arrangements with regard to the freedom to provide services: application of the principle of home country control, which covers those policy-holders not requiring specific protection due to the application of the rules of their member states of residence; application of the rules of, and supervision by, the member state in which the service is supplied (risk country control), this covers other policy-holders requiring such specific protection. The major objective of the third life-insurance directive was to complete the internal market in this form of insurance activity on the basis of the principles of a single administrative licence and supervision of the insurance undertaking's activities by the authorities in the member state in which that undertaking has its head office.

Figure 5: Time line of EU financial services directives in insurance markets

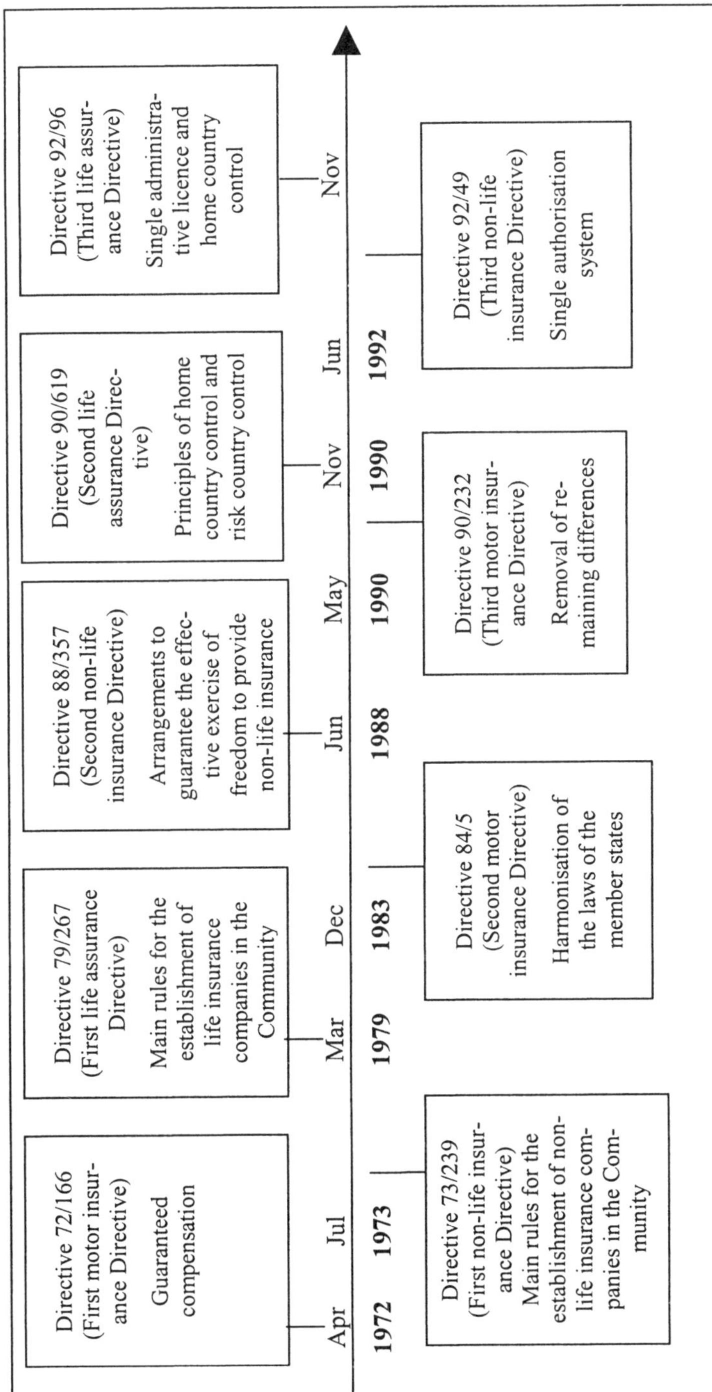

Source: EU (2001a,b).

Figure 6 shows the time profile required for an insurance directive to become Community law. As Figure 6 reveals, some directives took considerable time to become effective community law as can also be observed with the banking directives.

Figure 6: Time profile required for a directive to become community law (insurance)

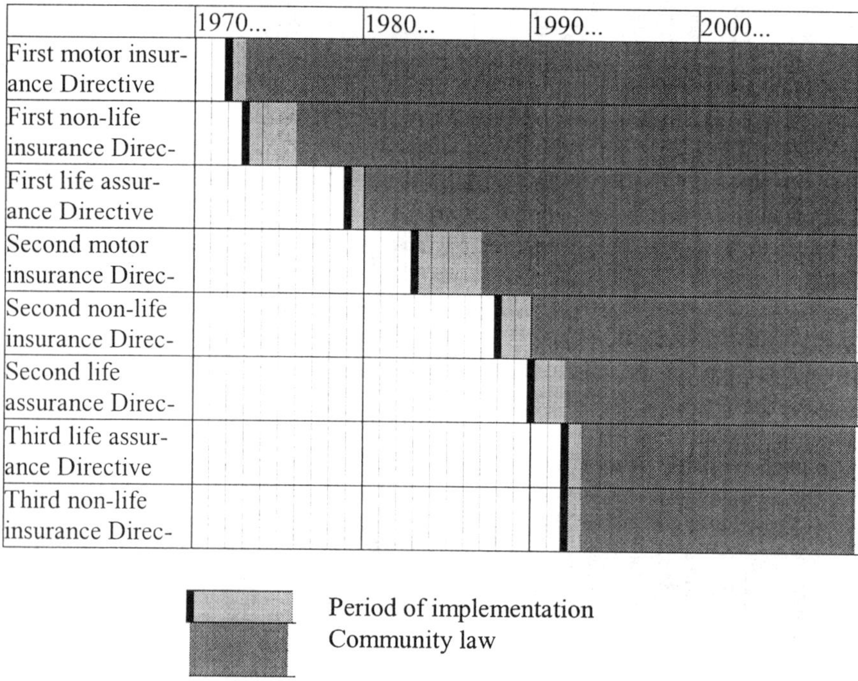

Source: EU (2001a,b).

To summarise, the Figures 3 to 6 show that in the past 30 years considerable attempts were made to enhance the degree of integration in the markets for financial service products. For instance, a significant degree of harmonisation has been achieved with the establishment of the banking and insurance directives. Furthermore, substantial obstacles impeding cross-border financial activities due to national regulations have been reduced. Nevertheless, this process moves forward very slowly as the figures for implementation periods reveal. Moreover, it can be suspected that substantial obstacles to financial services still remain, for instance in the field of international accounting standards, financial conglomerates, and cross-country mergers and acquisitions.

3.2 How Integrated Are European Financial Markets Actually?

In the previous section we outlined selective advances in establishing a sufficient legal framework to promote cross-border activities in the European financial services sector. Nevertheless we suspected that significant obstacles remain. Consequently, the following analysis tries to give an assessment of the extent to which the European financial markets are actually integrated. It is worth mentioning that macroeconomic data on cross-border activities of banking and insurance institutions are difficult to obtain. As we tried to use data that are available for a significant number of EU member states while capturing a relatively long time span, the analysis had to focus on foreign direct investment. Unfortunately, we thus had to neglect possible variables associated with "direct" cross-border business. However, as many banking and insurance institutions have become international since the implementation of the first directives in the relevant markets, this restriction does not change the results fundamentally. The following descriptive analysis shows to which degree banks and insurance companies have expanded abroad by establishing foreign subsidiaries and branches, or through mergers with and acquisitions of established foreign institutions, although we do not discriminate between these different strategies.

As a direct measure of integration in the European sector for *banking products* we display the *Foreign Bank Share* of selected European countries in terms of numbers (Figure 7) and foreign bank assets in total banking sector assets (Figure 8).[16] Both indicators of foreign banking penetration have been obtained from the database the World Bank has been published in 2001 as part of their "finance for growth" project.[17]

16 Due to missing data points Denmark, Finland, Ireland and Sweden have been ignored. See Eppendorfer et al. (2002) for a further analysis of foreign market penetration strategies in the banking industry.

17 See Beck et al. (1999). According to the definition of the World Bank (2001) and OECD (2000) a bank is called "foreign" if at least 50% of its equity is owned by foreigners.

Figure 7: Foreign bank share (ratio of domestic banks owned by foreigners)

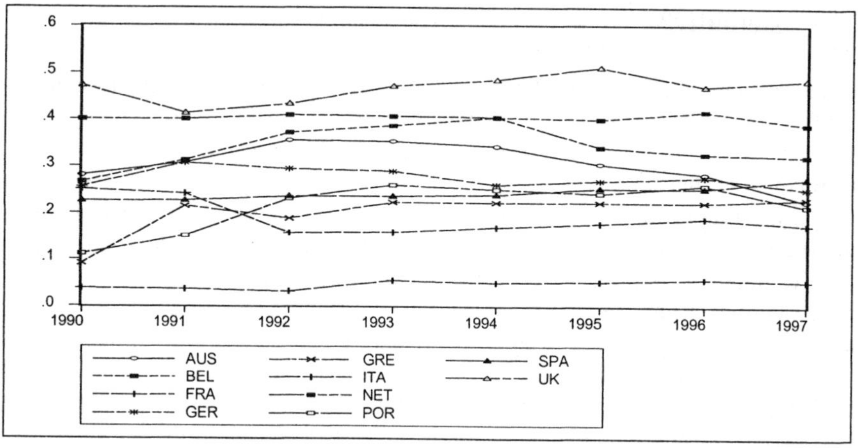

Source: Own calculations, data obtained from World Bank (2001).

Figure 7 shows substantial differences in the number of the foreign bank penetration measure. The banking sector of the United Kingdom, for instance, is characterised by a large number of foreign owned banks, whereas this banking integration indicator is nearly zero percent in Italy's banking market.[18] This picture is confirmed in Figure 8, with the volatility of this foreign penetration measure being even more pronounced.

Figure 8: Foreign bank share (ratio of domestic bank assets owned by foreigners)

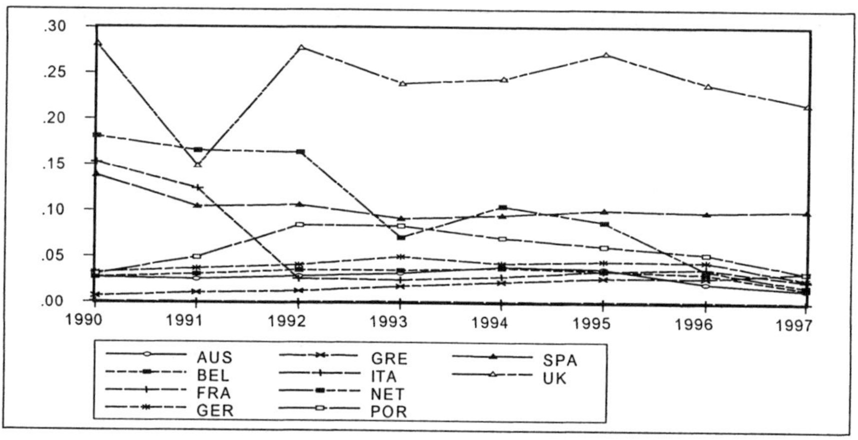

Source: Own calculations, data obtained form World Bank (2001).

18 The highest foreign bank share in numbers is ascertained for Ireland in 1997, with 65% of all banks belonging to foreign owners (not shown).

A comparison of Figure 7 with Figure 8 reveals that on average the foreign banks penetration indicator in pure numbers exceeds the indicator in terms of assets for most countries. This might reflect the empirical regularity that foreign banks tend to be smaller than domestic banks. Both measures of foreign penetration have not changed very much since the beginning of the 1990s, although we can even observe a fall in the ratio of foreign bank assets in total assets for some countries, e.g. the Netherlands.

Complementary to the time profile of the foreign bank share, another banking integration indicator is shown in Figure 9, which provides information about the attractiveness of a country for foreign investors in the banking sector. It is also calculated from World Bank (2001) data and is based on a survey that was sent to national bank regulatory and supervisory authorities in 1998.[19]

Figure 9 shows that there are substantial differences between the European countries concerning the ratio of foreign applications for banking licenses in percent to all banking applications in the domestic country. Nevertheless, the conclusion that countries with a low value of this integration indicator experience a low degree of foreign competition is misleading. On the one hand, 12 applications of foreign banks have been registered, for instance, in the Netherlands in 1998. But in the same year domestic institutes filed 30 applications for banking licenses. On the other hand, countries with a ratio of 100% of foreign applications like Belgium registered 24 foreign, but no domestic applications.

Figure 9: Ratio of foreign applications for banking licenses 1998 (in percent of total domestic applications)

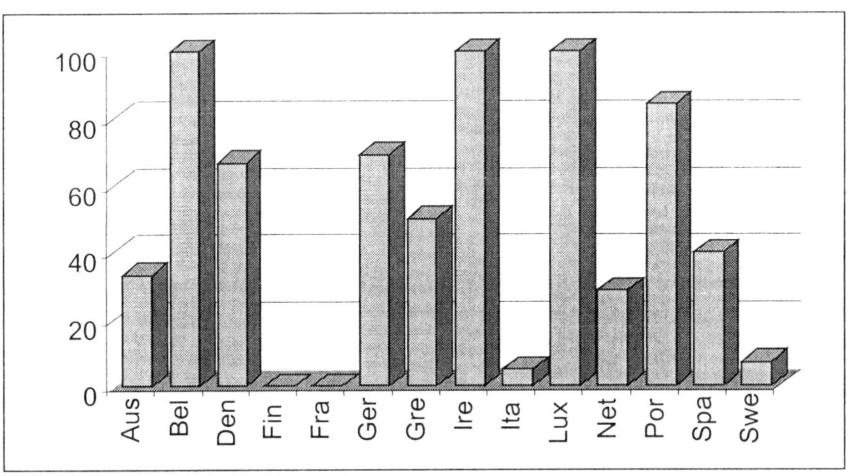

Source: Own calculations, data source is World Bank (2001).

19 See Barth, J. R. et al. (2001a,b).

The databases for a description of the integration progress in the insurance products sector are even more limited than for the banking sector. The World Bank (2001) database on finance and growth does not include insurance indicators comparable to the banking measures above. The most suitable database for our purposes is the *Insurance Statistics Yearbook*, published by the OECD.[20] But even this database raises serious problems, because due to the third insurance directive the composition of some indicators was changed in 1994.[21] Figure 10 shows the *Foreign Insurance Share (Life)* for the countries and the time span it is available for. This financial integration indicator represents a measure of foreign market penetration in the sector for life insurance products on a gross premium basis.

Figure 10 shows that, comparable to banking markets, substantial differences in the extent to which the European insurance markets are integrated can be observed in the sector for life insurance products. The picture of the time profile is also ambiguous. Austria, for instance, exhibits a relatively constant foreign life-insurance share, whereas this integration indicator is quite volatile in Spain. Hence, one cannot conclude from Figure 10 that any substantial integration advances were made in the European insurance markets over the last years.

Figure 10: Foreign insurance share (life) 1992-1999
(market share of foreign controlled companies on premium basis in percent)

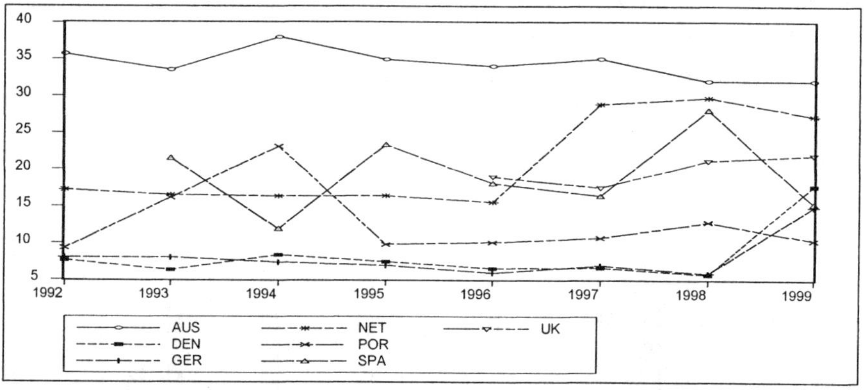

Source: Own calculations, data obtained from OECD, *Insurance Statistics Yearbook.*

20 See Beckmann et al. (2002) for a further analysis.

21 In consequence, we have to correct the former MK1 indicator, which includes foreign controlled companies as well as branches and agencies of foreign companies. Therefore, we simply calculate the difference between MK1 and MK2. The latter measures the market share of foreign branches and agencies, so that the resulting indicator includes solely the market share of foreign controlled companies. We do not control for the fact, that the OECD market share of foreign controlled companies includes countries that are not part of the EU. Apart form this, non-EU countries play a minor role in EU insurance business.

Figure 11: Foreign insurance share (non-life) 1992-1999
(market share of foreign controlled companies on premium basis in percent)

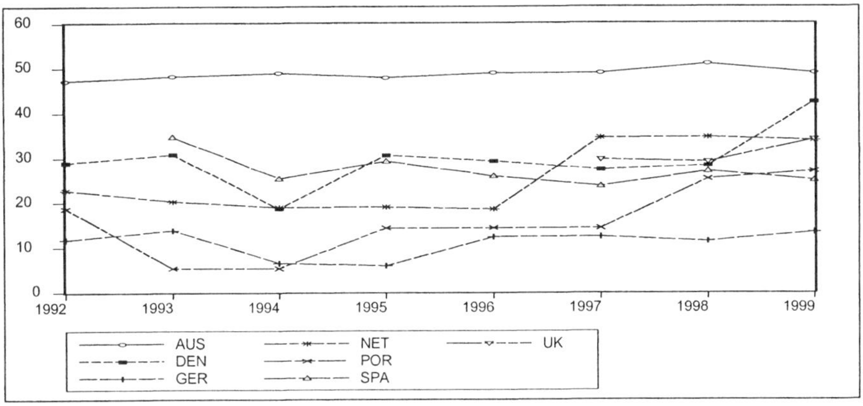

Source: Own calculations, data source is OECD, *Insurance Statistics Yearbook.*

Obviously, the foreign market share is higher in the sector for non-life insurance products than in the life-insurance markets. Perhaps this can be attributed to a lower degree of consumer sensitivity in this product category. Anyhow, the cross-country differences in the foreign market penetration in the sector for non-life insurance products are as distinctive as in life-insurance markets.

With regard to the varying foreign penetration shares we can summarise that the picture of integration in the European markets for financial services which can be drawn from indicators in the banking and insurance sectors is not very precise. Substantial differences can be observed for different countries and different integration indicators. Some countries like Austria show a substantially integrated insurance market, whereas the Austrian banking market can be considered as being almost closed. In contrast, Germany, which exhibits a relatively high ratio of foreign applications for banking licences in 1998, can be regarded as a relatively closed economy concerning its foreign insurance penetration ratio. Hence, despite substantial qualifications regarding the significance of the underlying data and the restriction to foreign penetration measures – which, for example, does not reflect the increasing relevance of e-banking or capture integration in the investment funds business - we can conclude that the extent to which financial markets in Europe are integrated is far away from reflecting a "Single Market for Financial Services".

3.3 The Financial Services Action Plan

The illustration of the development of the market share of foreign controlled companies has revealed substantial differences in the extent to which European economies are integrated. Furthermore, it was found that some countries may even be characterised as "closed economies" concerning their financial markets. Nevertheless, the potential loss of possible growth and employment benefits of a lagging European integration in the market for financial service products was widely recognised by the European authorities. The Final Report on the Regulation of European Securities Markets from the Committee of Wise Men chaired by Alexandre Lamfalussy is an essential contribution to necessary reforms of the regulatory framework for European financial markets. The Lamfalussy report (2001) identifies the legal framework for cross-border activities and the degree of implementation of existing European laws as main obstacles.[22] A series of policy objectives and specific measures to improve the framework for a functioning single market for financial services was outlined in the Financial Services Action Plan ratified by the European Council of Ministers in 1999 and adopted by the European Commission. In the following, selective elements of this important instrument to remove remaining policy induced obstacles to cross-border financial activities are briefly discussed.

In particular the Financial Services Action Plan suggests priorities and time-scales for legislative and other measures. Its primary aims lie in five imperatives: endowment of the EU with a legislative apparatus capable of responding to new regulatory challenges; elimination of any remaining capital market fragmentation; improvement of the possibilities for users and suppliers of financial services to exploit the opportunities offered by a single market, while simultaneously ensuring consumer protection; encouragement of a closer co-ordination of supervisory institutions; development of a European infrastructure to reduce the costs of retail and wholesale financial transactions.[23]

The Financial Services Action Plan consists mainly of three strategic objectives: ensuring a single market for wholesale financial services, open and secure retail markets and state-of-the-art prudential rules and supervision. The contents of these strategies are summarised in Table 1.

By establishing the Financial Services Action Plan the European Commission and the Council of Ministers have created a valuable instrument to demonstrate a further removal of cross-border barriers to European banking and insurance institutions by identifying main obstacles to the integration of financial markets and making serious suggestions as to how to overcome them. Hence, the Financial Services Action Plan can bee seen as a significant step towards faster and deeper European financial integration. Nevertheless, financial companies should be aware of time lags when implementing the strategic objectives into Community law.

---

22 The Committee was set up in a joint initiative of the French Presidency and the European Commission. For the full text see Lamfalussy Report (2001).

23 See European Commission (1999).

Table 1: Strategic objectives of the Financial Services Action Plan

Single EU wholesale market	- Single passport for recognised stock markets - Modernisation of admission to listing - Single prospectus for issuers - Adoption of international accounting standards - Adopting a Directive on Cross-border Use of Collaterals - Home country control for all wholesale markets - Definition of professional investors - Issuing a Commission Communication on Upgrading the Investment - Services Directive - Issuing a Commission Communication on the Application of Conduct of Business Rules Under Art. 11 of the ISD - Modernisation of investment rules for supplementary pension funds - Adopting the Directive on the Prudential Supervision of Supplementary Pension Funds - Adopting the two Directives on UCITS - Adopting the proposed Directive on Take Over Bids - Adopting the European Company Statute
Open, secure retail markets	- Issuing a Commission Communication on E-commerce Policy for Financial Services - Adopting the Directive on Distance Marketing of Financial Services
Sound prudential rules	- Creation of a Securities Committee - Adopting a Directive on Prudential Rules for Financial Conglomerates - Adopting a Directive Governing the Capital Framework for Banks and Investment Firms - Adopting a Directive on Market Manipulation - Adopting the Directive on the Reorganisation and Winding-up of Insurance Undertakings - Adopting the Directive on the Winding-up and Liquidation of Banks - Adopting the Amendments to the Money Laundering Directive

Source: European Commission (2000, 2001), own presentation.

The analysis of previous banking and insurance directives in the last section has shown that these time lags might be considerable. Furthermore, some major policy induced obstacles to cross-border financial activities are not included in the Financial Services Action Plan to a sufficient extent. For instance, the rising relevance of private pension funds in Europe requires a functioning legal framework that goes beyond the attempts shown in Table 1. There might be other serious problems such as differing principles of national supervisory authorities, accounting standards, European company law, consumer protection and personal bankruptcy law. We will not analyse these remaining obstacles and their determinants in detail. However, in the next section we will attempt to assess from a macroeconomic perspective to which extent the removal of cross-border barriers resulting in an increased foreign market penetration in banking and insurance markets affects growth paths and labour markets of the European economies.

4 Empirical Evaluation

In Section 2 we have shown in a simple endogenous growth model that financial development and financial integration undoubtedly enhances economic growth. Advances in deregulating the European financial services sectors were outlined in a historical perspective, supplemented with empirical evidence for the degree of effective integration in the banking and insurance markets in the last section. We then argued that the reduction of the remaining substantial obstacles to a functioning single market for financial services was extensively addressed in the Financial Services Action Plan of the European Commission. In this chapter the theoretical perceptions will be combined with the empirical evidence. We will attempt to give an assessment of the potential welfare gains in terms of a rise in growth rates and a reduction of unemployment rates the European economics will potentially experience when they implement an improved climate for cross-border activities in the financial sector.

4.1 Definition of Variables and Estimation Approach

The analysis of the EU member states is based on a three-step approach to quantify growth and employment benefits of financial integration. In a first step we try to control for the growth effects of financial development. To this end, we estimate a growth equation with typical "growth determinants" and different indicators of financial market development on the right hand side.[24] We employ a panel-data approach for the time series/cross-country data of the EU member states, with the exception of Luxembourg, for the years 1960 to 1999. A fixed and random effect technique is utilised to permit differences in the country-specific regression constants. Under the neoclassical growth theory these constants represent the rate of total factor productivity growth and include institutional characteristics. In the context of this paper we argue that these country characteristics capture the extent

24 In the first step we regress the growth rate on different indicators of financial market development for two reasons. First, it is necessary to control for monetary variables other than financial market integration. Second, in our approach we need to "produce" country-specific constants, which will be applied in the second estimation step. See Olson et al. (2000) for an equivalent approach.

to which financial markets are integrated as well as obstacles to financial integration due to national regulations.[25]

We refer to the growth of real per capita GDP and the unemployment rate respectively as welfare indicators. The indicators we use are primarily obtained from World Bank databases, namely from the *World Development Indicators* and from a new database, forming the basis of the World Bank project *Finance for Growth*, which comprises a considerable amount of valuable financial indicators. In the data pool all economies of the European Union except Luxembourg are included.

In the first step we follow a conventional econometric approach in which we define the yearly growth rate of real GDP per capita (GRWTH) as the dependent variable and test the explanatory power of some indicators of financial development. GDP per capita is based on purchasing power parities. The share of gross domestic investment in GDP (INVEST) is used as (traditional) control variable. Furthermore, the rate of population growth (POP) is included as an additional control variable.

In the first step the variable of interest is financial market development in terms of growth effects.[26] To control for the different transmission channels, the extent to which the financial market is developed is divided into the three sub-categories size, structure and efficiency. As defined above, size indicators include mainly information about the depth of financial intermediation. By applying structural indicators it is possible to obtain information about the allocation of resources and the relevance of different financial institutions of a country, e.g. the impact of private and state-owned banks. Efficiency indicators are used to record the level of transaction cost, the degree of information asymmetries and especially the competition environment. Every category of financial development is measured separately for the banking and insurance sector by applying one of the suitable indicators listed in Table 2.

The size of the banking sector is typically measured with the indicator *Deposit Money Bank Assets to GDP* (BANKS). The assets of deposit money banks include claims on the entire non-financial real sector relative to GDP. The size of the insurance sector can be measured with the indicator *Life Insurance Penetration* (LIP) which includes the volume of direct premiums of commercially active insurers written in the domestic life insurance sector relative to GDP. There is no distinction between the companies in state or private ownership and between

25 It is important to mention that we do not try to examine the growth model of chapter 2 literally. Although the main elements are implemented, we do not estimate the structural equation resulting from the theoretical analysis.

26 In the literature on finance and growth there is an extensive discussion whether the financial market development influences the real sector, i.e. the growth rate, or the other way around (see Levine, 1997). Even for the analysis here the direction of causality is not clear. The evidence of various tests for *Granger causality* with different indicators of financial development is not very clear-cut.

management by domestic or foreign insurers. LIP represents the relative importance of the insurance industry in the domestic economy.[27]

The structure of the banking sector is measured with *Private Credit by Deposit Money Banks to all Domestic Credit* (CREDIT) and, for the insurance sector, with the *Life Insurance Share* (LIS) indicator. CREDIT includes the ratio of claims on the private sector by deposit money banks opposed to all domestic credits which include also credits issued to governments and public enterprises.[28] LIS is defined as the ratio of gross life insurance premiums to total gross premiums of an economy. Hence, LIS reveals information about the relative importance of life insurance as compared to non-life insurance.[29]

Finally, efficiency in the financial sector is measured with the indicators *Concentration in the Banking Sector* (CONCEN) and *Direct Total Gross Premiums per Employees in the Insurance Sector* (PREMIUM).[30] The banking indicator reveals information about the competition environment in the banking market as it is defined as the ratio of the three largest banks' assets to total banking sector assets. The insurance indicator PREMIUM measures the relative efficiency of a national insurance industry. It is calculated by dividing the direct gross premiums by the number of employees in insurance companies. PREMIUM can be interpreted as a measure of efficiency as well as an indicator of competition in the insurance products sector.

After the estimation of the growth impact of financial market development, we can extract the country-specific regression constants to use them, in the second step, as dependent variable. To estimate the extent to which European financial integration has influenced total factor productivity growth we utilise a simple cross-country regression approach in this second step. Here we estimate, analogously to the first step, a number of equations with different financial integration indicators and control variables on the right-hand side. The integration of the banking products market is measured with *Foreign Bank Share* on the pure number and in terms of assets illustrated in chapter 3. The integration of the insurance products market is measured with *Foreign Insurance Share* for life and non-life business, both on the premium basis. Based on the regression results of the second step we are able to calculate the growth bonus that deeper European financial integration will generate analogously to the Cecchini Report.

In a third step the analysis of the macroeconomic growth effects is supplemented with an analysis of the link between financial integration and employment. To

27 Both indicators are taken from World Bank (2001).

28 CREDIT is obtained from IMF (2000), *International Financial Statistics*, series 32d/(series 32a,...,f).

29 LIS is obtained from various issues of the OECD *Insurance Statistics Yearbook*.

30 CONCEN is taken from World Bank (2001). PREMIUM is obtained from various issues of the OECD *Insurance Statistics Yearbook*.

assess the potential benefits of fostered financial integration we estimate country-specific Okun coefficients, which provide information about the growth rate a country needs to reduce unemployment.

Table 2: Indicators of financial development

Indicator	Banking Sector	Insurance Sector
Size	BANKS	LIP
Structure	CREDIT	LIS
Efficiency	CONCEN	PREMIUM

4.2 Estimation Results

4.2.1 Growth Bonus of Financial Market Integration

The results of ADF-Tests reveal that all financial development time series exhibit the property of one unit root, we thus use the growth rate of BANKS, CREDIT and CONCEN, and the growth rate of LIP, LIS and PREMIUM, respectively. Table 3 shows the estimation results for the different financial indicators and the two control variables .[31]

With regard to the traditional variables, only the share of investment in GDP is identified as a significant "determinant of economic growth". In all six regressions the coefficient of INVEST shows the expected sign at a high level of significance. The sign of the coefficient for population growth differs from the theoretical prediction in regression 1 and 2, albeit only insignificantly. In all the other regressions POP is significant and shows the expected negative sign.

There is no clear-cut empirical evidence for the financial indicators . In particular, the coefficient for the BANKS indicator and the penetration variable for insurance products (LIP) show an unexpected significant negative sign. CONCEN shows the expected negative sign but this is insignificant even at the 10% level. All the other financial variables are highly significant and show the expected sign. Therefore, a high growth of credits granted to the private sector relative to the growth of all domestic credit (CREDIT) generates a high growth rate of real GDP per capita. This result is also true for the growth of the ratio of life insurance premiums (LIS) and the growth of premiums per employee in the insurance sector (PREMIUM).

31 POP and INVEST are considered as usual in natural logarithms . We compute White heteroskedasticity-consistent standard errors and covariance and use cross section weights, i.e. cross section heteroskedasticity is also controlled for by using a GLS estimation technique.

The estimation results of Table 3 reveal a weak verification for theoretical approaches, which confirms that the structure of the financial sector is meaningful for the development in the real sector. The pure size of the financial sector cannot be called a "determinant of economic growth", here the indicators BANKS and LIP are even negative. For the efficiency of the financial sector a positive connection between both the insurance and banking indicator and the overall growth rate can be identified. In the banking sector an increase in competition (a reduction of CONCEN) corresponds to an increase in the growth rate of GDP per capita, albeit only insignificantly. An increase in PREMIUM corresponds to an increase in the GDP growth rate, a result that is counterintuitive when a rise in the premiums per employee in the insurance sector is interpreted as an indication of reduced competition in the insurance sector.[32] In contrast, the growth of the ratio of domestic credit to the private sector proportional to all domestic credits (CREDIT), which measures the structure of the financial sector, is connected with a positive growth rate. This positive influence of the financial structure, also holds true for the growth of the life insurance share (LIS).

However, the estimation results in Table 3 should not be read without considerable reservations. First, in *Reg1* the coefficient of BANKS does not show the correct sign. Second, the regressions for the insurance indicators (*Reg4*, *Reg5* and *Reg6*) cover only a very short time period due to data limitations. This restriction is also valid for *Reg3* using the concentration indicator in the banking sector as explanatory variable. Ultimately, only the second regression (*Reg2*) provides enough observations over a relatively long time span, a correct and significant sign of the financial indicator as well as an acceptable explanatory power to mirror the connection between financial development and economic growth.[33] Hence, we will use the result of this growth equation for the further analysis of the impact of financial integration.

But before we start with the empirical evaluation of the potential growth effects of a deeper European financial integration, we re-estimate *Reg2* with an alternative assumption for the country-specific effects to ensure our panel data results.

---

32 Due to data limitations UK is dropped from *Reg6*.

33 It is worth mentioning that the magnitude of CREDIT seems quite high: An increase in the growth rate of CREDIT of one percentage point would increase the growth rate of real per capita GDP by 8.6 percentage points. Nevertheless, this seems reasonable because the annual growth rate of the ratio of domestic credit to the private sector relative to all domestic credit amounts on average to 0.04% for the European economies.

Table 3: Estimation results for financial development and growth

	Reg1	*Reg2*	*Reg3*	*Reg4*	*Reg5*	*Reg6*
INVEST	0.06604***	0.05677***	0.05691***	0.05950***	0.11713***	0.09845**
	(9.70)	(7.97)	(2.96)	(4.49)	(4.88)	(2.33)
POP	0.00029	0.00096	-0.00922***	-0.00455**	-0.01290***	-0.01298***
	(0.24)	(0.79)	(-5.82)	(-2.50)	(-6.21)	(-6.04)
Banking						
BANKS	-0.03948***					
	(-2.92)					
CREDIT		0.08631***				
		(3.99)				
CONCEN			-0.00032			
			(-0.05)			
Insurance						
LIP				-0.01753*		
				(-1.86)		
LIS					0.03020**	
					(2.51)	
PREMIUM						0.02374**
						(2.21)
F-statstic	89.17***	87.69***	26.44***	23.30***	35.69***	25.20***
$\overline{R}^2$	0.26	0.26	0.28	0.21	0.40	0.38
Sample	1961-1997	1961-1997	1991-1997	1988-1996	1992-1997	1992-1997
Obs.	463	455	94	118	83	62

Note: Growth of real GDP per capita (GRWTH) is the dependent variable in all regressions.
t-statistics are displayed below the coefficients in parenthesis. Statistical significance at the 10%, 5% and 1% confidence level is indicated with *,**, and ***.

The assumption that the country-specific effects are fixed has some intuitive appeal because it implies that these effects are correlated with the other explanatory variables. However, the use of fixed effects becomes inappropriate when this assumption actually does not hold true. Particularly under these conditions the fixed-effect estimator is no longer efficient and a random coefficient model should be applied. We use the Durbin-Wu-Hausman-test to decide which alternative should be used.[34] The test is based on the null hypothesis that there is no difference between the random effects and the fixed effects estimator. Here the value of the test-statistic is -4.23. Compared with the critical value of the relevant chi-squared table with three degrees of freedom (7.81), it is clear that the null hypothesis that there is no difference between the two estimators cannot be revised at a significance level of 5%. Therefore, we use the specification of *Reg2* with country-specific random effects, which we define as dependent variable in the following analysis. According to neoclassical growth theory these country-specific effects measure the different growth rates of total factor productivity, which drives the income path of a country in the long-run. The country-specific effects are influenced by institutional infrastructure and other country characteristics, one of them being the degree of financial integration.

Since the country-specific effects of the first regression are defined as the dependent variable in the second step, a simple cross-section OLS-approach for the period 1990-97 is applied, which is the longest time span for which the relevant financial data is available. The indicators that measure the extent to which financial markets are integrated correspond to the descriptive view of Section 3. Table 4 shows the estimation results for different financial integration indicators, namely the Foreign Bank Share in terms of numbers (FBS_NUMBER) and in terms of assets (FBS_ASSETS). Furthermore, the Foreign Insurance Share for life insurance business (FIS_LIFE) and for non-life business (FIS_NONLIFE), both on a premium basis, are considered. Based on De Gregorio (1999) the average inflation rate (INFL) and the average annual sum of exports and imports of goods and services as percentage of GDP (TRADE), both for the period 1990-1997, are included as control variables.[35]

---

34 See Greene (2000: 576).

35 INFL is based on the average annual changes in consumer prices with the base year 1995 and is taken from IMF (2000), *International Financial Statistics*, series 64X. TRADE measures total trade in percent of GDP and is obtained from the World Bank (2000).

Table 4: Estimation results of financial integration and total factor productivity growth

	Reg7	*Reg8*	*Reg9*	*Reg10*
Const.	-0.00446	-0.00417*	0.00188	0.00124
	(-1.73)	(-1.93)	(1.056)	(0.65)
INFL	0.03234	0.03669	0.01192	0.01578
	(1.24)	(1.66)	(0.45)	(.556)
TRADE	0.00141	0.00209	-0.00685**	-0.00669**
	(0.45)	(0.92)	(-2.84)	(-2.63)
Banking				
FBS_NUMBER	0.00856			
	(1.35)			
FBS_ASSETS		0.01689**		
		(2.48)		
Insurance				
FIS_LIFE			0.00675	
			(1.71)	
FIS_NONLIFE				0.00543
				(1.61)
F-statistic	1.50	3.30*	3.14	2.75
$\overline{R}^2$	0.11	0.37	0.42	0.40
Obs.	13	13	10	9

Note: The country-specific effect of the re-estimated *Reg2* is the dependent variable in all regressions.
t-statistics are displayed below the coefficients in parenthesis. Statistical significance at the 10%, 5% and 1% confidence level is indicated with *,**, and *** respectively.

As the estimation results in Table 4 reveal, there is no clear evidence in favour of a link between insurance sector integration and growth. The indicator of the foreign market share in life insurance markets (FIS_LIFE) is insignificant as is the indicator of the foreign market share in non-life insurance markets (FIS_NONLIFE). Deeper integration in the banking sector has no significant influence on the country-specific effect when it is measured solely with the pure number of foreign banks (FBS_NUMBER). In contrast, a high foreign bank share is correlated with a high country-specific productivity effect, when these foreign banks have a significant weight in the domestic banking market. This weight of foreign market penetration can be measured in terms of the share of assets they own relative to the overall size of the domestic banking market (FBS_ASSETS).

Since the dependent variable reflects the country-specific growth rate of total factor productivity, which drives (additionally to investment in the capital stock and population growth) the growth rate of GDP per capita, it becomes clear that an increase in the foreign market penetration rises the overall growth rate. In particular, a one percent rise of the ratio of bank assets owned by foreign companies adds a "growth bonus" of 1.7 percentage points to the overall growth rate of the European economies. This growth bonus corresponds almost to the growth bonus the Cecchini Report attributed to financial market integration. It is worth mentioning that the magnitude of the growth bonus seems quite high. For some countries, however, a one percent increase of its foreign bank share already represents a fundamental alteration in the market structure. Italy, for example, exhibited between 1990 and 1997 an average foreign bank share of only 0.09% in terms of assets .[36] After all, the growth bonus should not be taken too literally, because due to a significant correlation between different integration indicators one can think of the growth bonus as a reaction more to a comprehensive rise in the presence of foreign financial companies than solely to an increase in the share of foreign bank assets.

Indeed, this is not the whole story, because country-specific growth rates of total factor productivity have been determined above. As a consequence, the growth bonus is conditional on differences in other institutional characteristics captured by the country-specific effects. Since all the considered countries show different long-run growth rates of total factor productivity, a positive effect of fostered financial integration alters the long-run growth rates for all economies in the same magnitude of 1.7%, but it cannot alter the long-run differences *between* the European economies. Every economy profits from a deeper European integration regarding GDP growth, but some will profit more than others due to a good institutional infrastructure and other country characteristics that are also included in

---

36 Obviously, the overall average of the foreign bank share 7.8% is dominated by high foreign bank shares in Ireland and the United Kingdom. The overall (unweighted) average growth rate of the foreign bank share in Europe between 1990 and 1997 amounts to 1.7%, which corresponds exactly to the growth bonus.

the country-specific effects.[37] One reason for these differences can be seen in differences in the ability to transform enhanced financial efficiency into broad macroeconomic efficiency due to variances in the degree of market regulations.

4.2.2 Employment Bonus of Financial Market Integration

Complementary to the welfare effects in terms of a shift in the real GDP growth rate we attempt to identify labour market effects of European financial integration. Hence, we will give an assessment of country-specific relationships between the output growth rate and changes in the unemployment rate in the following. The analysis is based on a modified version of the famous Okun´s law. This law can be interpreted in a way that an increase in the output growth rate that lies above an unemployment threshold ("normal" rate of production growth) reduces the unemployment rate.[38] We estimate country-specific equations of the yearly change in the unemployment rate ($\Delta \text{UNEMPL}_{it}$) with the GDP growth rate (GRWTH) of the former analysis as explanatory variable and c as the regression constant.[39] Formally the estimation approach can be written as:

$$\Delta \text{UNEMPL}_{it} = \text{UNEMPL}_{it} - \text{UNEMPL}_{i,t-1} = c + \beta_i \text{GRWTH}_{it} + \varepsilon_{it} \qquad (4.1)$$

The *country specific* coefficients of the growth rate β_i in (4.1) are assumed to be constant in time and expected to have a negative sign. The regression constants c_i are used to calculate the unemployment threshold under the assumption of no change in the unemployment rate as $(-c_i / \beta_i)$. Obviously, an economy must attain a GDP growth rate that lies above its normal rate to reduce the actual unemployment rate.[40] For the US the short-run "Okun coefficient" β has a magnitude of approximately -0.3, which means that a GDP growth rate that lies one percent-

---

37 The country-specific productivity growth rates *after* integration are specified in Table 6 together with the estimation results for the unemployment bonus.

38 The original work is based on Okun (1962). Here we do not undertake a serious analysis of the employment growth nexus, but understand it as a macroeconomic rule of thumb. For a recent survey and new econometric results see Döpke (2001). Further discussion and estimations for different country samples can be found in Lee (2000) and Padalino and Vivarelle (1997).

39 The unemployment rate UNEMPL measures the share of the labour force of a country that is without work, but available for and seeking employment. Definitions of labour force and unemployment differ by country. The data is taken from OECD (2000) *Statistical Compendium*, General Economic Problems, OECD Economic Outlook, country-specific series. GRWTH measures per capita GDP growth, defined as before. We use the growth rate of real GDP *per capita* as proxy for output growth, which implies a variation from approaches using the pure *output* growth rate. Since the growth rate of per capita GDP results from the difference between GDP growth and the growth rate of the population this will not be a serious problem.

40 For the normal rate it is assumed that it includes the sum of productivity growth and growth of the labour force.

age point above the normal rate reduces the unemployment rate in an order of 0.3 percentage points.

To control for positive autocorrelation in time (persistence of unemployment) we include the lagged endogenous variable as a further variable on the right-hand side of equation (4.1) (see Gordon, 1984 for this approach). This method has the additional advantage that it provides long-run Okun coefficients. The equation to be estimated can thus be written as:

$$\Delta \text{UNEMPL}_{it} = c + \beta_i \text{GRWTH}_t + \gamma_i (\Delta \text{UNEMPL}_{i,t-1}) + \varepsilon_{it} \tag{4.2}$$

The coefficient of the lagged endogenous variable can be used to calculate the long-run Okun-coefficients according to $\beta_i/(1-\gamma_i)$ (see Schalk and Untiedt, 2000).

Table 5: Estimation results for Okun´s law in the EU member states

	C	GRWTH	Δ(UNEMPL(-1))
Austria	0.29*** (3.99)	-0.07*** (-3.47)	0.14 (1.12)
Belgium	0.47*** (4.24)	-0.14*** (-4.78)	0.52*** (6.71)
Denmark	0.80*** (6.56)	-0.31*** (-9.29)	0.39*** (5.42)
Finland	0.98*** (8.07)	-0.29*** (-11.56)	0.41*** (7.58)
France	0.56*** (4.63)	-0.14*** (-3.68)	0.17 (1.49)
Germany	0.69*** (6.72)	-0.21*** (-7.32)	0.28*** (3.44)
Greece	0.20 (1.60)	-0.04* (-1.73)	0.57*** (5.00)
Ireland	0.94*** (3.89)	-0.22*** (-4.78)	0.13 (1.20)
Italy	0.37*** (3.32)	-0.10*** (-3.32)	0.58*** (4.96)
Netherlands	0.67*** (4.30)	-0.32*** (-5.38)	0.57*** (6.42)
Portugal	0.39** (2.38)	-0.09*** (-3.24)	0.52*** (4.75)
Spain	0.67*** (3.12)	-0.17*** (-3.86)	0.62*** (7.75)
Sweden	0.51*** (4.93)	-0.21*** (-6.68)	0.27*** (3.22)
United Kingdom	0.81*** (7.69)	-0.37*** (-10.24)	0.51*** (7.85)

Method: Seemingly Unrelated Regressions
Sample: 1962-1999; total panel (unbalanced) observations: 512
Adjusted R-squared: 0.59.

Note: $\Delta \text{UNEMPL}_{it}$ is the dependent variable. t-statistics are displayed below the coefficients in parenthesis. Statistical significance at the 10%, 5% and 1% confidence level is indicated with *,**, and ***.

The results of a SUR estimation of equation (4.2) are shown in Table 5.[41] With regard to the summary statistics the adjusted R^2 implies a satisfying explanatory power of the model. Except for Greece all short-run Okun-coefficients of the GDP growth rate (GRWTH) are highly significant and show the expected negative sign. Therefore, an increase in the GDP growth rate *above* the normal rate results in a reduction of the actual unemployment rate in comparison to the previous period.[42] The country-specific regression constants, which determine the unemployment threshold imply differences in the ability to transform GDP growth into a reduction of unemployment. All constants are statistically significant (except Greece), the normal rates of GDP growth can thus be calculated with the assumption $\Delta \mathrm{UNEMPL}_{it} = 0$. The lagged endogenous variables also show the expected positive sign and are all statistically significant with the exception of Austria, France and Ireland. Hence, this allows us to calculate the long-run Okun-coefficients for the EU member states .[43]

In Denmark, for instance, an increase in the growth rate above the normal rate of 2.6% of one percentage point leads to a decline of the unemployment rate in an order of 0.3 percentage points in the short-run an in an order of 0.5 percentage points in the long-run. The average dimension of the short-run "Okun coefficient" (0.19) is smaller than the coefficient for the US (0.3) which might be explained with relatively extensive labour market regulations in some EU member states.

Indeed, the estimation of the country-specific short-run and long-run Okun-coefficients serves only as a preliminary finding for the analysis of the employment impact of financial integration. With the Okun coefficients we have a useful indicator at hand to quantify the welfare gains of a further reduction of European cross-border financial barriers in terms of a reduction in the unemployment rate. With the use of the country-specific GDP growth effects that we have determined above, we can calculate the country-specific unemployment effects of further integration and quantify the *employment intensity* of the growth bonus.

In Table 6 we bring our main results together. First, the country-specific constants obtained from the most suitable growth regression (*Reg2*) are displayed. They denote the country-specific growth in total factor productivity and exhibit an

---

41 We use the method of Seemingly Unrelated Regressions (SUR) to take both cross-section heteroskedasticity and contemporaneous correlation into account. We can thus control for macroeconomic shocks that influence the unemployment rates of the European economies in a same manner.

42 We do not control for possible structural breaks due to oil price shocks, the unification shock in Germany etc. Furthermore, we do not include lagged values of the GDP growth rate as additional regressors. See Lüschow, Schalk and Untiedt (1997) for an alternative approach that includes these special features.

43 See Table 6 for the computation of the normal rates and the long-run Okun coefficients.

identical shift due to a change in the degree of financial market integration. In particular, all growth rates of total factor productivity include the overall growth bonus of 1.7 percentage points. As a consequence, the first column displays the differences in transforming the overall growth bonus into national shifts of the growth path. Second, the table includes the country-specific normal rates of growth as well as the short and long-run Okun-coefficients, which are all calculated on the basis of the estimation results obtained from Table 5. Third, we compute the country-specific short- and long-run unemployment bonus due to fostered financial market integration.

The results of Table 6 reveal a very differentiated picture of the changes in the EU economies due to deeper integration of financial markets. Although the overall growth bonus of an increased foreign bank share is of the same magnitude everywhere in Europe, some economies like Greece or Ireland are in a better position to transform it into a high national total factor productivity growth, because they would experience a positive long-run growth even without deeper financial integration. Other economies like Denmark or Portugal "need" the growth bonus to compensate for a negative growth rate of total factor productivity they would experience without further financial integration.

Concerning the benefits of financial integration in terms of a reduction in unemployment, we can observe substantial differences as well. There are considerable variances in the possibilities to reduce the unemployment rate. On the one hand, some economies like Austria will be able to benefit only to a small extent. In Austria a rise in the foreign bank share of one percentage point causes a short-run unemployment bonus of -0.12 percentage points. Even in the long-run there will be an unemployment bonus of only -0.14 percentage points. On the other hand, the United Kingdom exhibits an unemployment bonus of -0.62 percentage points in the short-run and of -1.26 percentage points in the long-run. These are substantial differences. Hence, differences in total factor productivity growth alone are not the only explanation. Rather, extensive variances in labour market conditions have to be considered as well.

Obviously, a one percent rise in the foreign bank share is not sufficient for any European country to reduce unemployment in the short- as well as in the long-run, unless it exhibits a growth rate *without integration* corresponding to its individual natural rates. This means, for instance, that Sweden will experience a reduction in the unemployment rate due to financial integration only if Sweden's growth bonus exceeds its natural rate, which is 2.4%.

Table 6: Growth and unemployment bonus of financial market integration

	Productivity Growth	Normal rate	Short-run Okun-coefficient	Long-run Okun-coefficient	Short-run Unemployment Bonus	Long-run Unemployment Bonus
Austria	1.54	4.20	-0.07	-0.08	-0.12	-0.14
Belgium	1.85	3.44	-0.14	-0.28	-0.23	-0.47
Denmark	1.42	2.58	-0.31	-0.51	-0.52	-0.86
Finland	1.46	3.34	-0.29	-0.50	-0.50	-0.84
France	1.62	4.10	-0.14	-0.17	-0.23	-0.28
Germany	1.57	3.32	-0.21	-0.29	-0.35	-0.49
Greece	1.96	4.69	-0.04	-0.10	-0.07	-0.17
Ireland	2.35	4.27	-0.22	-0.25	-0.37	-0.43
Italy	1.71	3.64	-0.10	-0.24	-0.17	-0.40
Netherlands	1.45	2.08	-0.32	-0.76	-0.54	-1.28
Portugal	1.44	4.22	-0.09	-0.19	-0.16	-0.33
Spain	1.90	3.98	-0.17	-0.44	-0.28	-0.74
Sweden	1.61	2.40	-0.21	-0.30	-0.36	-0.50
UK	1.75	2.20	-0.37	-0.75	-0.62	-1.26

Notes: Productivity growth includes the sum of the random effects of the re-estimated *Reg2* and the growth bonus. The normal rates are calculated dividing the constants by the GRWTH-coefficients obtained from Table 5. The short-run Okun-coefficients are equivalent to the GRWTH-coefficients in Table 5. The long-run Okun-coefficients are calculated according to $\beta_i /(1-\gamma_i)$). The country-specific short and long-run unemployment bonus is calculated by multiplying the relevant, country-specific Okun-coefficient with the growth bonus, which is 1.689 percentage points for every economy.

To summarise, in this section we tried to asses to which extent the European economies would gain from a deeper integration in the markets for financial services products. We were particularly interested in the growth and employment benefits resulting from an increase in the foreign market shares in the banking and the insurance sector. In a first step we identified a significant influence of the domestic financial structure to be responsible for the growth of GDP per capita. Since in the long-run economic growth is driven by the growth of total factor productivity, we analysed in a second step to which extent differences in this growth rate can be contributed to financial market integration. Indeed, we observed a growth bonus of fostered foreign market penetration in the banking sector. Furthermore, we showed that a growth bonus can be transformed into an employment bonus, but not without considering substantial country-specific differences due to varying productivity growth rates and labour market conditions. Although we were not able to verify an important contribution of foreign insurance companies, this does not mean that they play a minor role in the further European integration process. We attribute this expectation primary to measurement problems of foreign insurance companies.

Of course, the estimation results should not be read – as always – without reservations. In the first step only one of the six financial indicators was able to show a convincing correlation between the monetary and the real economic sector. In the second step, due to data limitations, financial market integration was only considered in a way that was strongly connected with foreign direct investment in the banking and insurance sector. Other strategies of financial integration were not analysed. For instance, we did not account for the increasing importance of e-banking, i.e. offering services on the Internet in different European economies, or for integration in the investment funds business. Furthermore, in the second step substantial econometric restrictions are required, because we only had a maximum of thirteen observations at hand in all four regressions.

5 Conclusions

The aim of this paper was to highlight some aspects of the growth and employment benefits the European economies will experience when integration in the markets for financial service products is spurred. We followed a theoretical as well as an empirical approach to make predictions about a growth and employment bonus.

In the growth model presented in Section 2 we demonstrated that enhanced cross-border activities of banking and insurance companies increase the overall growth rate unambiguously when the amount of savings channelled into investment increases. Hence, it should be clear that without a functioning domestic market for financial service products, deeper integration will not result in higher growth rates for per capita income.

In Section 3 major steps towards an integrated financial market in Europe were summarised and contrasted with the empirical evidence. On the one hand, it was shown that in the last 30 years substantial steps have been made to integrate the European financial markets. On the other hand, the descriptive analysis of foreign market penetration in banking and insurance markets already revealed the existence of remaining obstacles to cross-border businesses. The picture of integration in the European markets for financial services drawn from indicators of the banking and insurance sector was not very precise. Nevertheless, we concluded that the degree of integration in financial markets in Europe is far away from reflecting a "Single Market for Financial Services". Some attempts to abolish these obstacles are implemented in the Financial Services Action Plan adopted by the European Commission. This Action Plan outlines a series of policy objectives and specific measures to improve the framework for a functioning single market for financial services. In the Action Plan the European Commission formulates policy priorities and time-scales for legislative and other measures to push financial integration priorities. Therefore, the Financial Services Action Plan can bee seen as a significant step towards faster and deeper European financial integration. Nevertheless, financial companies should be aware of time lags concerning the implementation of the strategic objectives into community law. Furthermore, some major obstacles to cross-border financial activities are not sufficiently included in the Financial Services Action Plan.

In our empirical evaluation we estimated in a first step typical growth equations with different indicators of financial market development on the right hand side. The results from these regressions reveal a significant positive correlation between the overall growth rate and the extent to which the financial market is developed measured by its structure. The evidence provided by the regression results of a correlation between financial market integration and total factor productivity growth in the second step is ambiguous. However, we identified a weak influence of foreign market penetration in the sector for banking products. Hence, deeper financial integration generates a growth bonus. In the context of the theoretical examinations this growth bonus does not only mean a more rapid convergence speed towards the steady-state ("neoclassical growth effect") but also a higher equilibrium growth rate in the long run ("endogenous growth effect").

In contrast to the results of the influential Cecchini-Report we are able to distinguish between an "overall" growth bonus and country-specific differences to transform this growth bonus into a shift of total factor productivity growth. Hence, the long-run growth effect is conditional on differences in institutional characteristics captured by country-specific effects. As a possible explanation for these differences one might see remaining variances in the degree of national market regulations in the banking and insurance business. As a consequence, political activities should promote both the deregulation of national financial markets and the deregulation of cross-border financial activities to generate a positive growth bonus. The first recommendation aims at a deeper implementation of existing community laws into national legal frameworks. In addition, new European laws should be established on a supra-national level that abolish remaining obstacles to pan-European financial strategies and are better suited for enhanced world-wide competition in financial markets.

In a third step we supplemented the analysis of the macroeconomic growth effects with an analysis of the link between financial integration and unemployment. To assess the potential benefits of a fostered financial integration we estimate country-specific Okun-coefficients, which provide information about the growth rate a country needs to attain to reduce unemployment. We showed that the growth bonus can be transformed into an employment bonus, but not without considering significant country-specific differences. These differences are substantial. Hence, differences in total factor productivity growth alone are not the only explanation, rather extensive variances in labour market conditions have to be considered as well. We showed that there must be a convincing increase in financial market integration to generate a growth bonus that can substantially reduce unemployment in the EU member states.

References

Atje, R. and B. Jovanovic (1993), Stock Markets and Development, *European Economic Review* 37, 632-640.

Balestra, P. (1996), Introduction to Linear Models For Panel Data, in: Mátyás, L. and P. Sevestre (Eds.), *The Econometrics of Panel Data*, Dordrecht, 25-33.

Barro, R. J. and X Sala-i-Martin (1992a), Convergence, *Journal of Political Economy* 100 (2), 223-251.

Barro, R. J. (1998), *Determinants of Economic Growth – A Cross Country Empirical Study,* Cambridge.

Barth, J. R., G. Caprio Jr. and R. Levine (2001a), *Bank Regulation and Supervision: What Works Best?*, World Bank Working Paper, Washington D.C., forthcoming.

Barth, J. R., G. Caprio Jr. and R. Levine (2001b), *The Regulation and Supervision of Banks Around the World,* World Bank Working Paper No. 2588, Washington D.C.

Beck, T., A. Demirgüç-Kunt and R. Levine (1999), *A New Database on Financial Development and Structure*, World Bank Working Paper No. 2146, Washington D.C.

Beckmann, R., Eppendorfer, C. and Neimke, M. (2002), Financial Integration Within the European Union: Towards a Single Market for Insurance, published also in this study.

Bencivenga, V. R. and B. D. Smith (1991), Financial Intermediation and Endogenous Growth, *Review of Economic Studies* 58, 195-209.

Berthélemy, J. C. and A. Varoudakis (1996a), Economic Growth, Convergence Clubs, and the Role of Financial Development, *Oxford Economic Papers* 48, 300-328.

Berthélemy, J. C. and A. Varoudakis (1996b), Models of Financial Development and Growth. A Survey of Recent Literature, in: Hermes, N. and R. Lensink (Eds.), *Financial Development and Economic Growth*, London, 7-43.

Buch, C. M. (2000), *Financial Market Integration in the US: Lessons for Europe?*, Kiel Working Paper No. 1004, Kiel.

Claessens, S., A. Demirgüç-Kunt and H. Huizinga (1998), *How Does Foreign Entry Affect the Domestic Banking Market?*, World Bank Working Paper No. 1918, Washington D.C.

Danthine, J.-P., F. Giavazzi, X. Vives and E.-L. von Thadden (1999), *The Future of European Banking*, Centre for Economic Policy Research, London.

Danthine, J.-P., F. Giavazzi and E.-L. von Thadden (2000), *European Financial Markets After EMU: A First Assessment*, paper presented at the Bundesbank/BIS conference on "Recent Developments in Financial Systems and their Challenges for Economic Policy: a European Perspective", Frankfurt, 28/29 September.

De Gregorio, J. (1996), Borrowing Constraints, Human Capital Accumulation, and Growth, *Journal of Monetary Economics* 37, 49-71.

De Gregorio, J. (1999), Financial Integration, Financial Development and Economic Growth, *Estudios de Economia* 26 (2), 137-161.

Demirgüç-Kunt, A., R. Levine and H. G. Min (1998), *Opening to Foreign Banks: Issues of Stability, Efficency, and Growth*, World Bank, Washington D.C., mimeo.

Döpke, J. (2001), *The "Employment Intensity" of Growth in Europe*, Kiel Working Paper No. 1021, Kiel.

Eppendorfer, C., Beckmann, R. and Neimke, M. (2002), *Market Access Strategies in the EU Banking Sector – Obstacles and Benefits Towards an Integrated European Retail Market*, published also in this study.

EU (2001a), www.europa.eu.int/scadplus/leg/de/s08000.htm.

EU (2001b), www.europa.eu.int/eur-lex/de/lif/ind/de_analytical_index_06.htm.

European Commission (1999), *Financial Services: Implementing the Framework for Financial Markets: Action Plan*, Brussels, download: www.europa.eu.int/comm/internal_market/en/finances/general/actionen.pdf.

European Commission (2000), *Financial Services Priorities and Progress – Third Report*, Brussels, download: www.europa.eu.int/comm/internal_market/en/finances/actionplan/progress3en.pdf.

European Commission (2001), *Financial Services Political Challenges – Forth Report*, Brussels, download: http://europa.eu.int/comm/internal_market/en/finances/actionplan/progress4en.pdf.

Goldsmith, R. W. (1969), *Financial Structure and Development*, New Haven.

Gordon, R. J. (1984), Unemployment and Potential Output in the 1980s, *Brookings Papers of Economic Activity*, 537-564.

Greene, W. H. (2000), *Econometric Analysis*, Upper Saddle River, New Jersey.

Greenwood, J. and B. Jovanovic (1990), Financial Development, Growth, and the Distribution of Income, *Journal of Political Economy* 98, 1076-1107.

Grossman, G.M. and E. Helpman (1991), *Innovation and Growth in the Global Economy*, Cambridge.

Heinemann, F. and M. Jopp (2002), *The Benefits of a Working European Retail Market for Financial Services*, Ed.: Institut für Europäische Politik, Berlin und Zentrum für Europäische Wirtschaftsforschung, Mannheim, Europa Union Verlag: Bonn, downloadable from www.zew.de/erfstudyresults/ or www.iep-berlin.de/forschung/eu-market/.

Holmström, B. and J. Tirole (1997), Financial Intermediation, Loanable Funds, and the Real Sector, *Quarterly Journal of Economics* 112, 663-691.

IMF (2000), *International Financial Statistics*, Washington D.C.

Jappelli, T. and M. Pagano (1994), Saving, Growth, and Liquidity Constraints, *Quarterly Journal of Economics* 109, 83-109.

Jones, L. E. and R. E. Manuelli (1990), A Convex Model of Equilibrium Growth: Theory and Policy Implications, *Journal of Political Economy* 98 (5), 1008-1038.

King, R.G. and R. Levine (1992), *Financial Indicators and Growth in a Cross Section of Countries*, World Bank Working Paper No. 819, Washington D.C.

King, R.G. and R. Levine (1993a), Finance and Growth. Schumpeter Might Be Right, *Quarterly Journal of Economics* 108, 717-738.

King, R.G. and R. Levine (1993b), Finance, Entrepreneurship and Growth. Theory and Evidence, *Journal of Monetary Economics* 32, 513-542.

Lamfalussy Report (2001), *Final Report of the Committee of Wise Men on the Regulation of European Securities Markets*, Brussels, download: www.europa.eu.int/comm/internal_market/en/finances/general/lamfalussyen.pdf.

Lee, J. (2000), The Robustness of Okun's Law: Evidence from OECD Countries, *Journal of Macroeconomics* 22, 331–356.

Lemmen, J. (1998), *Integrating Financial Markets in the European Union*, Cheltenham.

Levine, R. (1996), Foreign Banks, Financial Development, and Economic Growth, in: C. E. Barfied (Ed.), *International Financial Markets*, Washington D.C.

Levine, R. (1997), Financial Development and Economic Growth: Views and Agenda, *Journal of Economic Literature* 35, 688-726.

Levine, R. (1998), The Legal Environment, Banks, and Long-Run Economic Growth, *Journal of Money, Credit, and Banking* 30, 597-620.

Lucas, R. E. (1988), On the Mechanics of Economic Development, *Journal of Monetary Economics* 22 (1), 3-42.

Lüschow, J., H. J. Schalk and G. Untiedt (1997), *Langfristige regionale Arbeitsmarktentwicklung*, Arbeitspapiere Bundesforschungsanstalt für Landeskunde und Raumordnung No. 4/97, Bonn.

Mankiw, N.G., P.M. Romer and D. Weil (1992), A Contribution to the Empirics of Economic Growth, *Quarterly Journal of Economics* 107 (2), 407-437.

McKinnon, R.I. (1973), *Money and Capital in Economic Development*, Washington D.C.

Moore,C. and J.M. Hill (1982), Interregional Arbitrage and the Supply of Loanable Funds, *Journal of Regional Science* 22, 499-512.

Obstfeld, M. (1994), Risk Taking, Global Diversification and Growth, *American Economic Review* 84 (5), 1310-1329.

OECD (2000), *Statistical Compendium*.

OECD, *Insurance Statistics Yearbook*, various issues.

Olson, M., N. Sarna and A. Swamy (2000), Governance and Growth: A Simple Hypothesis Explaining Cross-Country Differences in Productivity Growth, *Public Choice* 102, 34-364.

Okun, A. (1962), Potential GDP: Its Measurement and Significance, *American Statistical Association, Proceedings of the Business and Economic Statistics Section*, 98-103.

Pagano, M. (1993), Financial Markets and Growth. An Overview, *European Economic Review* 37, 613-622.

Padalino, S. and M. Vivarelli (1997), The Employment Intensity of Growth in the G-7 Countries, *International Labor Review* 136, 199–213.

Rajan, R. G. and L. Zingales (1998), Financial Dependence and Growth, *American Economic Review* 88, 559-586.

Romer, P.M. (1986), Increasing Returns and Long-Run Growth, *Journal of Political Economy* 94 (5), 1002-1037.

Romer, P.M. (1990), Endogenous Technological Change, *Journal of Political Economy*, 98 (5), 71-102.

Saint-Paul, G. (1992), Technological Choice, Financial Markets and Economic Development, *European Economic Review* 36, 763-781.

Schalk, H.J. and G. Untiedt (2000), *Wachstum und Arbeitslosigkeit*, Gutachten für die Friederich Ebert Stiftung, Bonn, download: www.gefra-muenster.de.

Shaw, E. S. (1973), *Financial Deepening in Economic Development*, New York.

World Bank (2000), *World Development Indicators*, Washington D.C.

World Bank (2001), Finance for Growth: Policy Choices in a Volatile World, Washington D.C.

Supervising the European Financial System

Karel Lannoo

Centre for European Policy Studies (CEPS)*, Brussels, Belgium

1 Introduction

The EU's financial sector has been undergoing an almost continuous wave of de- or re-regulation since the late 1980s. The single market programme with minimal harmonisation and home country control was implemented in successive periods for banking, insurance and the securities markets. By the end of the 1990s, however, under the impact of EMU, it was clear that this was not sufficient, and a Financial Services Action Programme set a schedule for the adoption of 42 directives to create a truly integrated financial market by 2005. Moreover, a Committee of Wise Men under the Chairmanship of Alexandre Lamfalussy made proposals to ease the adaptation of EU financial regulation to market developments.

In the meantime, a re-design of structure of financial supervision has been progressing. Traditionally designed along the different segments of the financial sector, a clear trend towards integration has emerged. At national level, the creation of the Financial Services Authority (FSA) in the UK was a clear signpost, which has been followed in the meantime in several other countries. At European level, a debate started with the creation of the European Central Bank (ECB), which has no powers in the area of financial supervision. This has given rise to the question whether home country control could continue to coincide with growing financial market integration, or whether a different structure will be needed at European level.

The debate has recently become more complex. While initiatives have been taken to strengthen co-operation between supervisors at European level, both within and across sectors, it has become clear that a solution for the European context will need to be specific and tailor-made. This is not only because of sensitivities with the member states towards too much centralisation, but also because supervision has been organised in different ways so far in the various member states, and the interests of different parties involved have to be accommodated. Moreover,

---

* Prepared for the European Roundtable of Financial Services (ERF). Based upon earlier work carried out in the context of a CEPS working party on "Challenges to the structure of financial supervision in the EU", July 2000.

Europe's financial markets remain fragmented and are in different stages of development.

The main actors in the debate are the national supervisory authorities, the European central bank and the European Commission, the financial institutions and the securities markets. The issues at stake are the role of the central banks, and the ECB, in financial supervision, integrated versus specialised financial supervision, the continuing relevance of the home country control principle and the adequacy of supervisory co-operation.

The purpose of this paper is to address the problems in reforming the structure of financial supervision in the EU and discuss the challenges, as seen from the point of view of supervisors as well as from the supervised. After reviewing the current models and structure of financial supervision, and the form of European regulatory and supervisory co-operation, we will address the shortcomings in view of continuing market integration and the possible remedies.

2 Financial Supervision: Current Models and Structure

Traditionally, the structure of financial supervision was based on the functional divisions in the financial services sector. Generally speaking, banks, insurance companies and securities markets had their own distinct supervisory authorities, under varying degrees of autonomy from the central government (see Table 1). The most homogeneously organised from a European perspective is insurance, which functions as a separate independent authority in most member states. The most heterogeneous is securities markets, where the powers are spread over single supervisory structures, combined with banking supervision or separately organised. Apart from that, aspects of securities markets supervision are often spread over different authorities, with important self-regulatory powers left to the stock exchange.[1] Banking supervision was until the early 1990s largely in the hands of the central bank, or executed in close co-operation with it.

In the meantime, the main change has been the gradual erosion of central banks' involvement in banking supervision. The predominant view is that central banking is about maintaining price stability, as was also laid down in the Maastricht Treaty. Involvement in banking supervision may create conflicts of interest with the price stability mandate of the central bank. Finance has also become more and

---

1 The control of brokers and investment funds, securities settlement systems, listing procedures and securities markets may, in the extreme case, be spread over different authorities, as was until very recently the case in Germany. See for an overview Lannoo (2001: 44).

more complex, and crossing the traditional sectoral borders of the industry, leading to the view that integrated financial services authorities may be better adapted. In these circumstances, the exercise of banking supervision under the roof of the central bank was seen as a barrier towards a more overall integrated supervision of the financial sector as a whole.

The first integrated financial supervisory authorities in Europe were created at the end of the 1980s in the Nordic countries. Norway integrated bank and insurance supervision in 1986, followed by Denmark in 1988 and Sweden in 1992. The most exemplified, however, was the creation of the UK Financial Services Authority (FSA) in May 1997, which regrouped 7 different financial sector supervisory authorities.[2] The German FSA, the Federal Agency for Financial Market Supervision, was proposed in January 2001 and formally started in May 2002, although some important exceptions remain, such as leaving the supervision of securities markets in the hands of the *Länder*. Moreover, the German structure will remain decentralised for some time to come, which raises question about its operational effectiveness. The FSA in Austria started to function in April 2002. In Belgium and Ireland, financial supervision will be integrated under the aegis of the central bank.

The advantages of an integrated financial supervisory authority, as compared to specialist supervisors, are not very clear-cut. Although it may seem obvious that integrated authorities are the most adapted to the evolutions in the financial sector, the first question that needs to be answered is: What is financial supervision about, and what structure fits best to meet these objectives?

Financial supervision is about protecting consumers and ensuring the stability of the financial system. At first sight, an integrated or specialist supervisory authority does not make much difference. It would be a matter of balancing the advantages of the different models in view of the policy priorities. A specialist authority can be better aware of and more specialised in the sector and products it supervises, whereas an integrated supervisory authority may ensure more streamlined supervision and better oversight of integrated financial groups. A schematic comparison of the main advantages of both models is given in Table 1.

An integrated authority is seen to generate economies of scale (and probably economies of scope) in supervision, as well as some practical and political advantages. It offers one-stop shopping for authorisations of conglomerate financial groups and eliminates any confusion over who executes lead supervision and final

2 The FSA has rule-making powers and is accountable to the government and Parliament. The Bank of England remains responsible for ensuring the overall stability of the financial system. The Bank would be the vehicle for lender-of-last-resort operations, if any, informing the Chancellor of the Exchequer, with the possibility then of an override by the Treasury. A Memorandum of Understanding between the Treasury, the Bank of England and the FSA sets out the respective responsibilities of the different bodies.

control. Expertise is pooled and co-operation between the different sectoral supervisors is guaranteed. Unnecessary overlaps are avoided and support services such as personnel, administration and documentation can be merged. An integrated authority should thus lead to lower supervisory fees, at least in these countries where the financial sector contributes directly to the cost of supervision, and to a lower cost of supervision in general.

An integrated supervisor will, however, only be effective in supervision if it is more than a combination of divisions, and if synergies can be exploited. It has been argued that the crucial thing is not whether all the functional supervisors are under a single roof, but whether they communicate with one another. This is certainly not a simple task, if one imagines that the British FSA employs about 2000 persons. If an integrated supervisor is no more than a combination of banking, insurance and investment business divisions, the full benefits of a single regulatory authority will not be achieved.

Table 1: Comparative advantages of the dominant models in financial supervision

Integrated financial supervisor	Specialist supervisor
– One-stop shopping for authorisations, and (possibly) a single rule book – Adapted to evolution in financial sector towards more complex financial products and financial conglomerates – Eases co-operation between sectoral supervisors; one lead supervisor or a single supervisory team for conglomerates – Can reduce regulatory arbitrage and deliver regulatory neutrality – Pooling of expertise and economies of scale (certain units could be merged, e.g. authorisations, support services) – Lower supervisory fees – More transparent to consumers	– Lower profile – Clearly defined mandate – Easier to manage – Better adapted to the differences in risk profiles and nature of the respective financial business (e.g. retail versus wholesale), clear focus on objectives and rationale of regulation – Closer to the business (but not necessarily) – Better knowledge of the business, more specialisation – Stimulates inter-agency competition

Financial supervision is also about avoiding to give the wrong signals. In this sense, an important argument against an integrated supervisor is its higher profile. A Leviathan supervisor could create the perception that the whole financial sector is secure. It may reduce the incentives for providers to prudently manage their business, and for users to carefully choose their financial services' provider, the so-called moral hazard. It could also be argued that the failure of one institution would have more widespread effects in a combined regime, because the effectiveness of supervision of the whole financial sector would be called into question.

The advantages of a specialist supervisor are its lower profile and a clearer focus on the sector and/or objective of supervision. It can allow for a greater proximity to smaller firms, on which a single regulator may be less inclined to focus, more specialisation, and better awareness of the problems of the sector. Two arguments stand out: a growing need for specialisation in supervision and inter-agency competition. Very distinct skills are required from supervisors, ranging from monitoring potentially dangerous exposures in increasingly globalised financial markets and validating statistical models in a bank's internal ratings models to supervising complex financial groups or tracking market behaviour of investment funds. It is an open question whether a single regulator can do this better than specialist supervisors.

The second argument, the advantage of inter-agency competition, is relevant, although it may, at first sight, seem difficult to advance in this context. Where several agencies work side by side, institutional competition can create incentives for each agency to work efficiently and concentrate, while reducing capture. An example is the US structure of banking supervision, where banks can be chartered at either state or national level. In the EU context, regulatory competition between states forms an integral part of the single market programme. Also financial supervision is part of this, and member states and financial centres are competing with different regulatory and supervisory models to attract business. This consideration has also played a role in the creation of the UK's FSA.

An outcome of the conglomeration trend, and of the undecided debate of single versus specialised supervisors, is that supervision may become more objective-driven. Since the functional divisions of the business will be increasingly difficult to make, authorities will look at another way to supervise the financial sector efficiently. One possible model calls for one agency to carry out surveillance separately for systemic stability reasons, a second for prudential motives and a third for conduct-of-business. Conduct-of-business supervision looks after transparency, disclosure, fair and honest practices, and equality of market participants. The "stability" agency should concentrate on macro-prudential problems, which affect the conduct of monetary policy or overall financial stability. And the prudential agency controls the solvency and soundness of individual financial institutions and enforces depositor and investor protection.

Table 2: Supervisors of banking, securities and insurance in Europe, Japan and the US (early 2002)

	Banking	Securities Markets	Insurance
B	BS	BS	I
DK	FSA	FSA	FSA
DE	FSA	FSA	FSA
EL	CB	S	I
E	CB	S	I
F	B/CB	S	I
I	CB	S	I
IRL	CB	CB	G
L	BS	BS	I
NL	CB	S	I
AU	FSA	FSA	FSA
P	CB	S	I
SF	BS	BS	I
SW	FSA	FSA	FSA
UK	FSA	FSA	FSA
CH	BS	BS	I
CZ	CB	SI	SI
H	FSA	FSA	FSA
N	FSA	FSA	FSA
PL	CB	S	I
SLOE	CB	S	G
USA	B/CB	S	I
J	FSA	FSA	FSA

Note: CB = Central Bank, BS = banking and securities supervisor, FSA = single financial supervisory authority, B = specialised banking supervisor, S = specialised securities supervisor, I = specialised insurance supervisor, SI = specialised securities and insurance supervisor, G = government department. The supervision of securities markets is a generalisation of the most prevalent model in a certain state; it does not take the spread of the elements of supervision over different authorities into account.

Such a horizontal supervisory structure was instituted in Australia, further to the Wallis Committee of Inquiry in 1997. The Australian Prudential Regulatory Authority (APRA) supervises financial institutions on prudential grounds; the Reserve Bank of Australia looks after systemic stability and provides liquidity assistance, if needed; and the Australian Securities and Investment Commission (ASIC) controls market integrity and conduct-of-business rules. Several EU countries have elements of an objective-driven system of supervision, mainly as far as the relationship between the banking and the securities supervisor is concerned. In Italy, for example, banks and securities houses are controlled by the Banca d'Italia on financial stability and prudential grounds and by CONSOB with respect to conduct-of-business. A similar model is to be introduced in the Netherlands in the course of 2002, where conduct of business supervision for the whole financial sector will come under a newly created Authority for Financial Markets. At prudential level, the central bank and the insurance supervisor will integrate supervision for cross-sector activities (see Jonk et al., 2001).

An objective-driven approach points to interesting routes for adaptation of the European structure of supervision. Rather than emulating one or another sectoral model at European level, an objective-driven approach may be better adapted to the economic and political circumstances of European integration. But we will first discuss the current structure of European supervisory co-operation.

3 European Regulatory and Supervisory Co-Operation

European regulatory and supervisory co-operation is more elaborate than one would think at first sight. All EU single passport directives for the financial sector also provide for a structure of co-operation among national *regulators*. Moreover, a structure is also in place to discuss cross-border *supervisory* issues. Two questions need to be addressed in view of growing financial market integration: 1) the appropriateness of the home country control principle, and 2) the relevance of the current structure of European regulatory and supervisory co-operation.

3.1 The Home Country Control Principle

The home country control principle is part of the minimal harmonisation approach of the single market, whereby only essential elements are harmonised to allow markets to integrate. Additional rules should under mutual recognition adjust in a competitive process between jurisdictions. This raises the issue of regulatory competition, and the degree of competition that is permissible in an EU context.

So far, the home country control principle has functioned fairly well. In response to growing market integration, a process of further harmonisation can be expected as a result of pressures from the market and authorities at national and European level. This will be required to reduce remaining powers of the host country in each of the sectors (e.g. the notification procedure and the general good principle in all the single licence directives, liquidity control of branches in the Second Banking Directive, etc.) or to expand harmonisation where it was insufficient (securities markets). Some of these issues have already been addressed in the Commission's Financial Services Action Plan.

But will the home country remain relevant in an EU context? Big players in the European market will increasingly have a range of home markets, so could the EU as a whole become the home market? Some large financial groups have thus argued for a single European regulator for some time. In the eyes of one of the most important proponents, "there is a marked trend towards a single European regulator. Following EMU and the single financial market, the decentralised regulatory model, although by all means successful in the past, is now weakening the efficiency of supervision and placing its competitive neutrality at risk. A united European approach would also carry greater weight in international negotiations on regulatory issues" (Deutsche Bank, 2000). Others have suggested that the single financial market could follow the two-tier US system of state and federally chartered banks. Large European banks could thus choose to be federally chartered and be allowed to regard Europe as a whole as their "home" country (Schoenmaker, 1995).

The discussion above about single versus specialised financial authorities has indicated that the answer is not so easy, however. From a supervisory perspective, a European FSA would exacerbate the disadvantages of a single regulator at national level, as discussed above. From a regulatory point of view, it would be difficult to reconcile with the basic principles of the single market, whereby only essential rules are harmonised, and the rest is left to adjust in a competitive process between jurisdictions. In this sense, it is certainly not proven that a single authority would improve supervisory efficiency, as it would eliminate this competitive process. Moreover, a single EU supervisor would lead to important legal problems for areas that have not been fully harmonised at EU level. Would a European supervised group fall under the single regulator for some aspects of its business, whereas others would fall under national law?

Also politically, it would be difficult to argue for a single supervisory authority, as it would have to be proven that financial supervision can be better executed at federal than at national level, leading in a second step to a Treaty change to create such a body.[3] Moreover, financial supervision implies accountability and tax powers for eventual bail-outs. While the former could be dealt with, the latter would be much more difficult, and would entail explicit agreements between member states for burden-sharing or bail-outs. Finally, smaller banks (and member states) may see a single regulator, and even more a dual framework, as a competitive distortion.

---

3 As would be required for a European Securities and Exchange Commission (SEC), a single banking regulator or a European FSA. It has been suggested that the ECB might assume the role of single banking regulator without a Treaty change, but it should be noted that Art. 105.6 of the EU Treaty reads: "The Council may (...) confer upon the ECB specific tasks concerning policies relating to the prudential supervision of credit institutions and other financial institutions with the exception of insurance undertakings", only refers to "specific tasks concerning policies", not to day-to-day supervision, in which case a Treaty change would also be required.

3.2 European Supervisory Co-operation

If home country control is to remain the basis of financial supervision in the EU, supervisors will need to ensure that bilateral and European co-operation works. Memoranda of Understanding provide the underpinning for supervisory co-operation at the bilateral level. At European level, several committees are in place to ensure co-ordination between regulators and supervisors.

A Memorandum of Understanding (MoU) is a form of agreement between supervisors, which has no legal force, but sets out the respective tasks and obligations of both parties. In principle, the EU directives make formal agreements between supervisory authorities of the member states superfluous, since they make co-operation a legal obligation. In practice, supervisors have continued to conclude MoUs to clarify what is involved in the supervision of financial institutions and markets, such as information exchange and mutual assistance, establishment procedures and on-site examinations. In banking, some 90 bilateral MoUs had been signed between EEA banking supervisors by the end of 1999, while there is a multilateral Protocol to the Insurance Directives which serves as an MoU, and the EEA securities commissions have, in the context of FESCO, also signed a multilateral MoU in relation to exchange of information for market surveillance purposes.

MoUs raise the question of supervisory methods and the content of information exchange. If the information which is demanded from financial institutions differs from member state to member state, the information exchange will be of little use. This will be even more so if it concerns a financial institution that is active in several member states. From the perspective of a financial institution, it will not be very attractive either, as they will need to report in different ways in the EU. The European Commission and national authorities have recently stepped up their activity in this area, and a study is expected to be published soon by the European Commission on the subject, as a first step to more harmonisation of supervisory practices.

Information exchange is even more important in crisis situations. However, EU directives do not impose an obligation for information sharing in times of crisis. A recent report of the EU's Economic and Financial Committee (2001) thus recommended that MoUs should be further developed to make them more concrete with respect to crisis management. The report suggested that this can best be done in the context of the several committees that exist at European level.

Several committees have been in place at EU level to promote co-operation between regulatory and supervisory authorities. Most of them were created with the start of European integration in the area. Their principal tasks are to:

1. Provide a forum for the exchange of views and to act as a sounding board for the Commission on any proposals for supplements or amendments to legislation;
2. Discuss and adopt technical adaptations to the directives within the perimeters foreseen in the directives (the "comitology" procedure); and
3. Discuss and compare issues of supervisory technique and to facilitate the exchange of information and co-operation with respect to problems with individual institutions.

This is, however, a general characterisation, which varies between the sectors of financial services. The committees are most developed in banking. The highest number of committees exists for securities markets, but with the least powers, at least until the Lamfalussy report was adopted. A schematic overview is given in Table 3, where we distinguish between Committees dealing with regulatory, supervisory and financial stability matters. This distinction is to a certain extent arbitrary, since the tasks of the different Committees are often not as clear-cut.

In banking, three committees are in place. The *Banking Advisory Committee* (BAC) principally advises the European Commission with regard to policy issues in the formulation and implementation of EC legislation for the banking sector. It can also, if foreseen by the directives, agree on technical adaptations to the directives. In order to do this, it brings together senior supervisory and finance ministry officials. The *Groupe de Contact*, which consists only of banking supervisors of the European Economic Area (EEA), has dealt for nearly 30 years with issues of bank supervisory policy and practice including the carrying out of comparative studies, arranging the exchange of information and handling co-operation with respect to issues arising from individual institutions. The *Banking Supervisory Committee* of the *ECB* brings together the banking supervisors to discuss macro-prudential and financial stability issues of all the EU countries, thus not only the Euro zone. It also assists the ECB in the preparation of the ECB's advice on draft EU and national banking legislation (within euro area countries) as laid down in Art. 105(4) of the EU Treaty and Art. 25(1) of the ESCB/ECB Statute.

In response to criticism on the lack of macro-prudential oversight in the EU, the ECB's has recently explicitly indicated that its Banking Supervisory Committee will also perform that role (Meister, 2000, EFC, 2001: 7). During the Russian crisis in 1998, it had appeared that European banks had large exposures to emerging markets, whereas no body was monitoring this from a European perspective. Such a situation could be systemic at Euro zone level, as financial crisis would rapidly spill-over from one market to another via the inter-bank market. It was therefore proposed to create a European Observatory of Systemic Risk (ESFRC, 1998).

In insurance, the BAC is broadly paralleled by the *Insurance Committee* and the Groupe de Contact by the *Conference of Insurance Supervisors*.

In the securities field, there was, strictly speaking, until recently no parallel structure to the legislative committees existing in the banking and insurance field. There were some committees, but they had only a consultative function, and lacked seniority. A first reaction was the creation of FESCO in 1997, but this happened outside the EU framework, as an intergovernmental consultative body. The Lamfalussy Committee (February 2001) discussed this situation at length, in the context of the need to adapt legislation rapidly to changing market circumstances. It proposed a four level approach as model for securities market legislation, which could also be applied to financial services legislation in general, consisting of:

4. framework legislation, which may be directives or regulations under EU law, and is limited to setting the general principles of legislation;
5. a new EU Securities Committee with broad implementing powers, i.e. large interpretative powers for those elements of the directives where it has a mandate;
6. strengthened co-operation between national regulators in the Committee of European Securities Regulators (CESR). This Committee replaced the FESCO (Forum of European Securities Commissions) structure, and gave it a formal mandate in the EU context;
7. stronger enforcement through more co-operation between national regulators and higher use of infringement procedures by the European Commission.

The Charter of *Committee of European Securities Regulators (CESR)* was formally adopted on 11 September 2001. It states that CESR will improve co-ordination among European securities regulators and advise the European Securities Committee on implementing measures, while remaining independent from the European Commission. The creation of the *European Securities Committee*, on the other hand, gave rise to lengthy discussions with the European Parliament (EP) on the degree of implementing powers of an unaccountable Committee. The EP requested a call-back on decisions taken by the Securities Committee, which the European Commission was unwilling to give for constitutional reasons. The EP finally agreed with the Securities Committee on 5 February 2002 (almost one year after the adoption of the Lamfalussy report) at the condition that it would be fully informed about the decisions taken by the Committee and that it would have sufficient time to make its wishes heard. Parliaments agreement also depends on and expires with a satisfactory solution being found to the "comitology" issue in the context of the 2004 Intergovernmental Conference.

From a sectoral perspective, the framework for regulatory and supervisory co-operation in the financial services sector could be considered as complete since the adoption of the Lamfalussy report. The structure has also become more complete as regards cross-sectoral matters. In 1999, *a Mixed Technical Group on Financial Conglomerates* was created to discuss cross-sectoral regulatory matters. In response to the recommendations of the Brouwer report (European Commission, 2000), a *Cross-Sectoral Roundtable of Regulators* was set up to promote exchange of information among supervisors. For conglomerates specifically, a new draft directive on financial conglomerates (April 2001) provides for mandatory appointment of one or more supervisory co-ordinators for any conglomerate that falls within the scope of the directive. The draft directive lays down the specific tasks of the co-ordinator of each financial conglomerate, such as the assessment of the financial situation of the group, its structure, organisation and internal control systems (Art. 7).[4]

Regulators have also taken initiatives to cover specific areas in the financial sector. In April 2001, the ECB announced the conclusion of an MoU between payment systems overseers and banking supervisors in the Euro zone, because of the financial stability dimension (ECB, 2001c). In October, the ECB also announced joint work with CESR on issues of common interest in the field of securities clearing and settlement systems, with the intention of establishing common standards. In a statement on the consolidation of central counterparty clearing (September 2001), the ECB insisted on the role of the Eurosystem in setting risk management standards of such systems, because of the systemic dimension. The ECB also indicated that, for the same reasons, any "domestic" market infrastructure for securities and derivatives denominated in euro should be located in the euro area.

This overview would be incomplete without a brief mention of the *Financial Services Policy Group* (FSPG) and the *Economic and Financial Committee* (EFC), although they are strictly speaking not part of the fora for financial supervision. The FSPG was set up by Commissioner Monti in 1998 as part of the effort to re-launch the internal market for financial services in the FSAP. Its main purpose is to set strategic directions for EU financial services regulation. It brings together finance ministry officials and other high-level civil servants. The EFC has discussed general macro-prudential and specific financial market issues in ad-hoc committees, and has made policy recommendations. There is thus clearly no lack of multilateral fora for regular consultation among the respective authorities of the EU member states.

---

4 Proposal for a directive on the supplementary supervision of credit institutions, insurance undertakings and investment firms in a financial conglomerate, COM(2001)213 of 24.4.01.

Table 3: The current structure of European supervisory and regulatory co-operation

Objective/ sector	Banking	Insurance	Securities markets	Cross-sector and horizontal matters
Regulatory	Banking Advisory Committee (BAC)	Insurance Committee (IC)	Securities Committee	Financial Services Policy Group (FSPG) Mixed Technical Group on Financial Conglomerates
Supervisory	Groupe de Contact	Conference of Insurance Supervisors	Committee of European Securities Regulators (CESR, formerly FESCO)	Cross-Sectoral Roundtable of Regulators
Financial stability	ECB's Banking Supervision Committee (ESCB plus EU non-central bank supervisors)			Economic and Financial Committee (EFC) ECB's BSC

4 Challenges to Adequate Regulation and Supervision

Most of the challenges to adequate regulation and supervision in the EU have been on the policy agendas since the start of EMU, or even earlier, but have not become less pressing in the meantime. They concern better enforcement of rules, the need to open-up retail financial markets and the problem of crisis management in the EU. Some new issues have emerged: They concern the functioning of the new "post-Lamfalussy" committee structure, the implementation of Basle II and the adequate regulation of securities markets.

4.1 Better Enforcement of Rules

Enforcement of EU regulation is known to be a problem since a long time, but was brought even more to the foreground by the Lamfalussy report. The latter recommended a fairly complex structure to improve enforcement of rules in securities markets, a structure that could also be transposed to the other sectors. It consists of the need to split legislation into framework principles and implementing measures, broader powers for a Committee to interpret and adapt legislation, the strengthening of co-operation between national regulatory authorities, and greater reliance upon judicial procedures.

Although the proposals contained in the Lamfalussy report can certainly be welcomed, the experience acquired to date is not sufficient to be conclusive. The first "Lamfalussy type" proposals have shown how difficult the first step already is, to distinguish between framework principles and implementing measures. For being framework directives, the draft prospectus and market abuse directives went already into much detail, and this will be even more so after the amendments of the European Parliament have been incorporated. As the European Parliament will have no more direct say in decisions by the Securities Committee, it has proposed many amendments, over 100 in the case of the draft market abuse directive. Moreover, the EP may have a different view on what is framework and what is detail than the European Commission, as there is certainly no basic theory on this. Framework directives under the Lamfalussy approach could thus be considered as a contradiction in terms. They were designed to ease regulation and enforcement, but may end up in rendering it just heavier.

An issue, that is often overlooked is the role self-regulation and disclosure can play in enforcement. The European Commission is now trying to promote the use of ombudsmen at national level to ease the resolution of conflicts between providers and consumers of financial services. The role of self-regulation was almost absent in the Lamfalussy report, however, while it plays a very important role in securities markets. Intermediaries, such as investment banks, law firms, rating agents, compete on the basis of their reputation, which contributes importantly in improving the standards in securities markets regulation. The same applies for standards setters such as accounting standards boards and professional federations.

The problem of enforcement will not diminish in the years to come, as the EU intends soon to enlarge with 12 new member states, 10 of which may join in 2004. Each of the applicant states need to have transposed all applicable EU legislation in national law by the day of entry, or they need to negotiate transition periods to the full application of specific elements of legislation. The applicant states are well advanced in this process of approximation of laws, although problems with effective enforcement may only appear at a later stage, and will undoubtedly escalate in an EU of 27.

4.2 The Need to Open-Up Consumer Financial Markets

The lack of integration of consumer financial markets is an old problem, which does not seem to come much closer to a solution. The core of the problem is the difficult interaction of financial market legislation, which liberalises market access under the control of the home country and minimal harmonisation of rules, and the consumer protection legislation, which falls largely under the responsibility of the member states, and requires maximal harmonisation to allow market integration. Consumer protection legislation is however so vast that EU attempts to harmonise will always somewhere fall short, allowing member states to argue that a product sold on a cross-border basis by a firm from another member state is not in line with domestic rules. The way out of this eternal dilemma is to require member states to recognise each other's systems as equivalent, and set a sunset clause for the application of host country rules in harmonising measures.

Examples of this difficult interaction are the e-commerce directive and the draft distance selling of financial services directive. The former directive, adopted in 2000, enables on-line providers to supply services throughout the EU based on the rules of the country from which the provider effectively carries out his activities – also called the country of origin (not necessarily the home country).[5] However, the directive excludes amongst others financial services contracts and host country measures which are needed to protect consumers. The applicable rules for the latter should be defined in the distance selling of financial services directive, on which a political agreement was reached in September 2001. This directive defines in much detail the information to be supplied to consumers before the conclusion of a contract, the form of contract, the financial services covered, the right of withdrawal (with a cooling-off period of 14 to 30 days), and the settlement of disputes. Article 13 of the draft directive states that member states can impose additional rules on providers from countries where the distance marketing directive has not been properly implemented, which in practice overrules the country of origin rules of the e-commerce directive. Some member states have therefore called for a clause in the distance selling directive to ensure that in case of disagreement, the e-commerce directive rules will apply.

5 The country of origin rules have also been proposed for the application of conduct of business rules in a communication on the revision of the EU's investment services directive, see European Commission (2001a).

4.3 Systemic Risk and Crisis Management

The question of monitoring systemic risk and crisis management has been discussed frequently since the start of EMU. It is now accepted that there will be some role for the ECB and the EFC in crisis management, without it being openly formalised. Three problems stand out: 1) who monitors? 2) the interaction Euro zone – EU, or Europe; and 3) who is responsible and who will pay?

Monitoring financial stability is and remains a responsibility of the national central banks, not of the ECB, under the EU Treaty. Although there is some co-ordination of macro-prudential supervision by the ECB's Banking Supervisory Committee, which also includes non-Euro zone countries, our feeling is still that there is weak monitoring at the centre, and insufficient oversight of the cross-border dimension.

On the Euro zone-EU dimension, the ECB has been more pronounced. Its role is limited to the Euro zone, and the co-ordination at EU level is weaker than it is at Euro zone level. The question could be raised whether the risk is also lesser. On central counterparties in securities clearing, on the other hand, the ECB has clearly indicated that they should be located in the Euro zone, because of the systemic dimension (ECB, 2001b). However, the ECB's role is limited to payment systems, it has strictu sensu no responsibility for securities clearing.

Three years after the start of EMU, the ambiguity regarding crisis management remains. This point has been raised by many academic commentators, but also at official level, in the Brouwer reports. The ambiguity about procedures and responsibilities is not seen as constructive, as it reduces confidence, accountability, and possibly the effectiveness of crisis management. The current system is seen as one of 'improvised co-operation'. If ever a failure of a financial institution with European-wide dimension happens, it is likely that supervisors and national states will have rows over who is responsible and who pays. The second Brouwer Report has tried to meet these concerns by requesting national supervisory authorities to add procedures for crisis management to the bilateral Memoranda of Understanding. It also called for removing remaining legal impediments to the exchange of information among supervisors. But, for the remainder, the ambiguity remains.

4.4 The Emerging Post-Lamfalussy Committee Structure

The breakthrough on the Lamfalussy approach may have important implications for financial regulatory processes in the EU. The model could be followed for other sectors of financial regulation, for example for the implementation of Basle II, but this may require adaptation to the existing Banking Advisory Committee (BAC).

The Securities Committee could in some way be considered as an embryonic Securities and Exchange Commission (SEC). The Committee will have broad decision making powers, and will decide by qualified majority. Decisions in the Committee could thus go against the interests of certain member states.[6] The structure of the European SEC will, however, remain de-centralised for some time to come. The Securities Committee will be chaired by the European Commissioner in charge, but its decisions will be largely prepared by the Committee of European Securities Regulators (CESR), which will work independently from the European Commission. CESR will have its own secretariat in Paris, and is chaired by a member state representative. CESR and the European Commission will thus co-operate and compete at the same time, which should be beneficial for the quality of the regulation and its enforcement.

An important corollary of the breakthrough on the Lamfalussy approach is that a European FSA should be off the agenda. The Lamfalussy report stated that, in case of no progress on the proposed approach, a single European Financial Services Authority (FSA) should be considered. Functional co-operation among member states will most likely be more appropriate in a European context than a European FSA. An EU FSA would not be adequate for a host of reasons, most importantly from a financial regulatory perspective. It would also be difficult to reconcile with the basic single market principles of subsidiarity, minimal harmonisation and home country control, as discussed above.

4.5 The Implementation of the Basle Review

The Review of the Basle Capital Accord raises a host of issues. Within the context of this paper, the most important are the transposition of Basle II in EU law, the role of a the Banking Advisory Committee for technical adaptations to the directive, and the impact of the Supervisory Review on the (non-)convergence of supervisory practices in the EU.

Basle II will become a complex EU directive, this can already be said with certainty now. The level of technical detail in Basle II is high, which raises the question about the handling of the directive by the European Commission, the processing of the directive by the European Parliament and the EU Council, and its implementation into national law. The positions of different interest groups vis-à-vis Basle are high, which predicts a difficult decision process and an uncertain outcome.

---

6 The Stockholm European Council (March 2001), while endorsing the Lamfalussy report, stated explicitly that: "The European Council notes that within the framework of the comitology decision of 28 June 1999, the Commission has committed itself (...) to avoid going against predominant views which might emerge within the Council." The European Parliament on the other hand had to be satisfied with the promise that the Commission would take "utmost account" of its views.

As with the Lamfalussy Committee, it is likely that the Commission will choose for a framework directive with a high degree of powers for a Committee. This will most likely become the Banking Advisory Committee, although this is not sure. The BAC has got limited comitology powers so far, and is not comparable to the composition of the new Securities Committee. The latter is composed of high-level civil servants from the finance administrations of the member states, whereas the BAC works with the heads of the banking supervisory authorities. Would this mean that the Securities Committee will be transformed into a form of high-level finance committee? This is a move that the European Parliament will certainly not like to see.

The convergence of supervisory practices is another priority. However, it is the question whether pillar II of the Basle Review, whereby authorities can determine when to intervene with a bank in trouble, will be used as an excuse for national authorities to keep supervisory practices uncoordinated. Finally, regarding the proposal for increased disclosure under pillar III of the accord, this practice is still infrequent and underdeveloped in Europe. The number of listed banks issuing half-yearly accounts in the EU is less than half of that in the US. The production of quarterly accounts by EU banks is almost non-existent, whereas it is standard in the US (Enria and Vesala, 2001: 29). Disclosure furthermore raises the problem of differences in accounting conventions, but this should now be addressed as a result of the move towards International Accounting Standards (IAS).

4.6 Adequate Regulation and Supervision of Securities Markets

Most works remains to be done to improve the regulation and supervision of EU securities markets and to further harmonise rules. This is commonly accepted since the adoption of the Lamfalussy report. However, whether the outcome of this exercise will be a more harmonised and workable regulatory environment is another matter, as the reactions to the new draft directives have proven, and the number of amendments in the European Parliament.

On the supervisory side, a more homogeneous structure at national level may be emerging. The draft prospectus directive requires member states to de-couple listing from trading, and to transform the listing authority in an independent supervisory agency, away from for-profit exchanges. The market abuse directive requires member states to appoint one competent independent authority to track insider trading. Both measures should ease thus convergence among and co-operation between supervisory authorities, and facilitate market integration.

5 Conclusion: A Model for Europe?

Great progress has been realised in creating more co-operation between supervisory authorities on all levels. The matrix of the structure of European regulatory and supervisory co-operation has been (almost) completed with the creation of the Securities Committee and more cross-sector co-operation. The ensuing structure is however complex, which raises the question whether gradual change is sufficient, or whether a grand design will at some stage be needed.

A single European financial supervisory authority is, however, not the solution. Apart from the fundamental problems it raises from a financial supervisory perspective, it would also politically be very difficult to promote. A better structure for the future is to re-design the European financial system upon the basis of the objectives of supervision, and to examine where more centralisation is needed. Beyond any doubt, this is most needed for financial stability reasons. The ECB has tacitly stepped up its activity in this field, as recent developments indicate, but more may be needed, and some more profile may be desirable. It does, however, raise the problem of the desirability of a higher involvement of the ECB in supervisory matters, and the problem of Euro zone versus the broader EU framework.

At the level of prudential supervision, the structure of co-operation is in place, but much work remains to be done. There is the streamlining of the home country principle, upgrading of the Memoranda of Understanding and the improvement of the mechanisms and quality of information exchange. The biggest issue, however, is the standardisation of the supervisory practices in the EU, where work still has to begin. The outcome of the Basle Review, and in particular its pillar II should also indicate how this work will be taken forward.

At the level of conduct of business rules, there is probably the least need for harmonisation, but at the same time the greatest opportunity for member states to protect national markets on the basis of many pretexts. A commonly agreed solution for the interaction of market liberalisation and consumer/investor protection rules at a general level is urgently needed.

Appendix

EU and EEA Fora for Co-operation in Financial Regulation and Supervision

1 Banking

1) Banking Advisory Committee (BAC)

- Established in 1977 by the First Banking Co-ordination Directive.
- Threefold role: 1) assists the European Commission in drawing up new proposals for banking legislation, 2) helps to ensure adequate implementation, and 3) serves as the "regulatory committee" under the so-called "comitology" procedures for technical amendments to EC banking legislation. The latter are changes that can be made outside the normal legislative procedure.
- Consists of high-level officials from finance ministries, central banks and supervisory authorities of the member states and from the Commission, with a maximum of three representatives per national delegation; officials from other EEA countries and the ECB participate as observers; the chairman of the Groupe de Contact also attends.
- Chairman is chosen for a three-year period from representatives of member states, secretarial services are provided by the European Commission.
- Meets three to four times a year.
- Discussions are confidential, but a tri-annual report is published by the chairman.
- When committee acts as "regulatory committee", it is chaired by the European Commission.
- Does not consider specific problems related to individual credit institutions.

2) Groupe de Contact (established 1972)

- Set up by banking supervisors of EEA member states on a co-operative basis.
- Deals with micro-prudential co-operation, including information-sharing both in general and in particular cases, and carries out comparative studies on policies and techniques of supervision. It also assembles, as required under the banking directives, various EEA-wide statistical services including on solvency, profitability and liquidity.
- Consists of one official from each banking supervisory authority in the EEA; an official from the Commission also attends as adviser on legal issues but does not attend discussions dealing either with individual firms or sensitive supervisory assessments.

3) Banking Supervision Committee of the ECB (established 1998)

- Succeeded Subcommittee on Banking Supervision of the European Monetary Institute, which had originally been created in 1990 as the Banking Supervisory Subcommittee of the Committee of Governors of the EC Central Banks.
- Assists the ESCB with regard to policy issues in the area of macro-prudential supervision, i.e. the stability of financial institutions and markets, and in preparing ECB opinions on legislation as provided for under the Treaty.
- Consists of high-level officials from all central banks and non-central bank supervisory authorities in member states plus ECB officials; Commission officials participate as observers.

Duplication of work is avoided through regular informal co-ordination meetings between chairmen of each of the three committees dealing with banking supervisory matters.

2 Securities markets

1) Contact Committee (established 1979)

- Advisory committee, without comitology role (except for one issue, which was never touched).
- Facilitates harmonised implementation and advises the Commission on any supplements or amendments to the 1979 stock exchange admission, 1980 listing particulars, 1989 prospectus, 1989 insider dealing, 1988 major holdings and forthcoming take-over bids directives.
- Allows regular consultation between the member states on these matters.

2) UCITS Contact Committee (established 1985)

- Advisory committee, without comitology role.
- Facilitates harmonised implementation and advises the Commission on any amendments to the 1985 UCITS directive (unit trusts directive).

3) High-Level Committee of Securities Market Supervisors (established 1985)

- Strategic committee, meets 2 to 3 times a year at the initiative of the European Commission.
- No formal legal basis, functions as Commission working group until Securities Committee is formally established by an EU directive.

- Advises the European Commission on regulatory and supervisory matters.

4) *CESR, formerly FESCO (established December 1997)*

- Originates from Informal Group of Chairmen of EU Securities Commissions.
- Brings together securities commissions of the EU. Functioned originally on an intergovernmental basis and with delegates from the European Economic Area (the EU, Iceland and Norway, in the context of the Forum of European Securities Commissions, FESCO).
- Aims to enhance the exchange of information between national securities commissions, to provide the broadest possible mutual assistance to enhance market surveillance and effective enforcement, to enhance uniform implementation of EU directives and to develop common regulatory standards in areas that are not harmonised by European directives.
- Formally established as the Committee of European Securities Regulators (CESR) as further to the Lamfalussy report. The Charter was adopted on 11 September 2001. It will function as fully independent Committee with its own secretariat.

5) *Securities Committee (established September 2001)*

- High-level committee with implementing powers for directives to be adopted as further to the Lamfalussy report
- Was rejected twice before because of procedural problems and sensitivity of European Parliament to "comitology"
- Relaunched in the Commission's financial services action plan (May 1999), formal decision taken in June 2001
- First meeting under the chairmanship of Commissioner Bolkestein in September 2001
- Operational since the approval by the European Parliament of the von Wogau report on 5 February 2002

3 Insurance

1) Insurance Committee (established 1992)

- Assists the European Commission with regard to policy issues in the formulation and implementation of EC legislation for the insurance sector, consultative role for new Commission proposals.
- Consists of high-level officials from finance ministries and supervisory authorities of the member states plus Commission officials; officials from other EEA countries participate as observers.
- Serves as "regulatory committee" under the so-called "comitology" procedures for technical amendments to EC insurance legislation (life and non-life insurance).
- Does not consider specific problems related to individual insurance undertakings

2) Conference of Insurance Supervisory Authorities of the EU (established 1958)

- Forum for debate among EU supervisors on micro-prudential issues relating to individual insurance undertakings
- Agreed on 'protocols', a form of multilateral memorandum of understanding between insurance supervisors, to deal with supervisory problems
- Composed of 15 EU states and 3 EEA countries, with European Commission as observer (no formal link with EU)
- Meets twice a year

4 Cross-sector fora

1) Commission Mixed Technical Group on Financial Conglomerates

- Established in 1999, involving representatives of the sectoral regulatory committees
- Considers proposals for improving the framework of information sharing between supervisors and co-ordination of prudential supervision on a cross-sectoral and cross-border basis.

2) Cross-Sectoral Roundtable of Regulators

- Established in 2001 to discuss cross-sectoral supervisory problems.

References

Austrian National Bank (2001), *Reform of Financial Market Supervision in Austria*, Financial Stability Report, October.

Deutsche Bank (2000), Regulation and Banking Supervision: Caught Between the Nation State and Global Financial Markets, *EMU Watch*, June.

Diez Guardia, N. (2001), *Regulating E-Commerce in Financial Services*, CEPS working party report, October.

Enria, A. and J. Vesala (2001), Externalities in Supervision: the European Case, forthcoming in: Kremers, J. et al. (Eds.), *Financial Supervision in Europe*.

European Central Bank (2001a), *The Role of Central Banks in Prudential Supervision*, April.

European Central Bank (2001b), *The Eurosystem's Policy Line with Regard to Consolidation in Central Counterparty Clearing*, September.

European Central Bank (2001c), *Memorandum of Understanding on Co-Operation Between Payments Systems Overseers and Banking Supervisors in Stage III of EMU*, April.

European Commission (2001a), *Overview of the Proposed Adjustments to the Investment Services Directive*, July.

European Commission (2001b), *Report on Financial Crisis Management*, July.

European Commission (2000), *Report on Financial Stability*, Economic Papers No. 143, May.

European Commission (1999), *A Review of Regulatory Capital Requirements for EU Credit Institutions and Investment Firms*, Consultation document, November.

European Shadow Financial Regulatory Committee (1998), *EMU, the ECB and Financial Supervision*, Statement No. 2, October.

Jonk, A., J. Kremers and D. Schoenmaker (2001), A Cross-Sector Model for Financial Supervision, *Financial Regulator*, December.

Kremers, J., D. Schoenmaker and P. Wierts (2001), *Financial Supervision in Europe*, forthcoming with Dutch ministry of finance.

Lamfalussy Group (2001), *Final Report of the Committee of Wise Men on the Regulation of European Securities Markets*, February 15.

Lannoo, K. (1999), *Does Europe Need an SEC?* Capital Markets Institute Occasional Paper No.1.

Lannoo, K. (2000), *Challenges to the Structure of Financial Supervision in the EU*, CEPS working party report (Chairman: David Green), July.

Lannoo, K. (2001), *EU Securities Market Regulation, Adapting to the Needs of an Integrated Capital Market*, CEPS working party report, March.

Meister, E. (2000), *Challenges for Regulators in Europe*, Unpublished conference speech, October.

Padoa-Schioppa, T. (1999), EMU and Banking Supervision, *International Finance* 2 (2), 295-308.

Schoenmaker, D. (1995), Banking Supervision in Stage Three of EMU, in: Lannoo, K., D. Schoenmaker and S. Van Tilborg (Eds.), *The Single Market in Banking: From 1992 to EMU*, CEPS research report No.17.F

Druck: betz-druck GmbH, D-64291 Darmstadt
Verarbeitung: Buchbinderei Schäffer, D-67269 Grünstadt